PACIFIC BASIN DEVELOPING COUNTRIES:
PROSPECTS FOR THE FUTURE

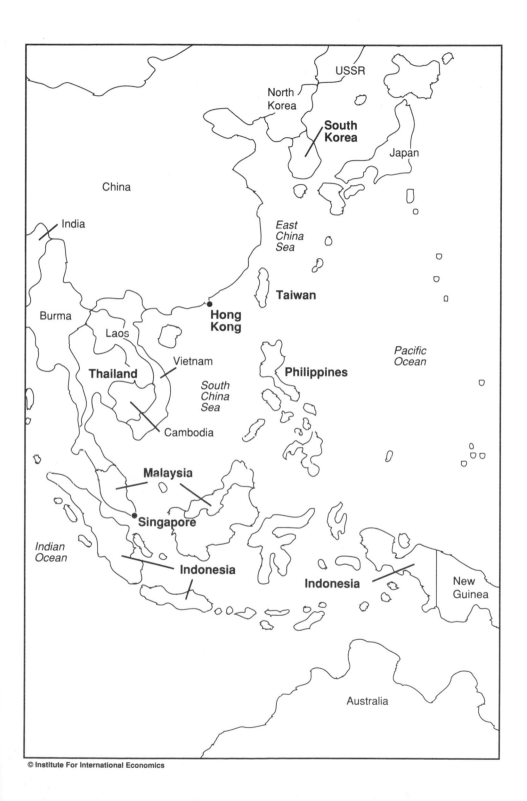

China

India

Burma

Laos

Vietnam

Thailand

Cambodia

USSR

North
Korea

**South
Korea**

Japan

East
China
Sea

Taiwan

**Hong
Kong**

South
China
Sea

Philippines

Pacific
Ocean

Malaysia

Singapore

Indian
Ocean

Indonesia

Indonesia

New
Guinea

Australia

MARCUS NOLAND

Pacific Basin Developing Countries: Prospects for The Future

INSTITUTE FOR INTERNATIONAL ECONOMICS
WASHINGTON, DC 1990

Marcus Noland is an Assistant Professor of Economics at the University of Southern California and a Research Associate at the Institute for International Economics. He was formerly Visiting Professor at the Graduate School of Policy Science, Saitama University, Japan, and is coauthor with Bela Balassa of *Japan in the World Economy* (1988), as well as numerous articles on international economics and the economies of East Asia.

INSTITUTE FOR INTERNATIONAL
ECONOMICS
11 Dupont Circle, NW
Washington, DC 20036
(202) 328-9000
Telex: 261271 IIE UR
FAX: (202) 328-5432

C. Fred Bergsten, *Director*
Linda Griffin Kean, *Director of Publications*

The Institute for International Economics was created by, and receives substantial support from, the German Marshall Fund of the United States.

Printed in the United States of America
94 93 92 91 90   5 4 3 2 1

Library of Congress Cataloging-in-Publication Data

Noland, Marcus, 1959–
    Pacific Basin Developing Countries:
    Prospects for the Future/
    Marcus Noland
    p.   cm.
    "December 1990"
    Includes index
    1. Pacific Area—Foreign economic relations. 2. Pacific Area—Commerce. I. Title
HF1642.55.N65   1990
382'.099—dc20
                                90-25083
                                   CIP

ISBN 0-88132-141-9 (cloth)
ISBN 0-88132-081-1 (paper)

Contents

Figures

Acknowledgments

I would like to thank the participants at the study group meeting in Washington, as well as participants at several conferences in the United States and Asia for comments on preliminary versions of this research, in particular C. Fred Bergsten, Kimberly Ann Elliott, Hugh Patrick, Charles Pearson, Jane Rossetti, Jeffrey J. Schott, and Philip K. Verleger, Jr. Michael Treadway, Linda Griffin Kean, and Tracey Smith through their editorial efforts greatly improved the expository quality of this book. Lastly, my greatest thanks go to Bela Balassa, who was a collaborator during the earliest stages of this project and made useful contributions to the original drafts of what are now chapters 5 and 6, and to Peter Uimonen, who provided herculean research assistance for the duration of the project.

Preface

The developing countries of East Asia have led the world in economic growth for the past two decades and have become major factors in the world economy. They are virtually certain to become even more important in the years ahead. This volume traces their record to date, projects their trade and growth patterns into the future, and draws lessons for the world economy.

In *Adjusting to Success: Balance of Payments Policy in the East Asia NICs*, by Bela Balassa and John Williamson, the Institute has previously analyzed the external financial picture of "the four little tigers." This study extends the assessment to include the ASEAN nations and to focus on the sectoral changes that are likely to ensue as specialization in manufactures moves southward from Japan through the NICs to the ASEAN nations.

This project was originally undertaken as a collaborative effort between Bela Balassa and Marcus Noland, but we decided to separate Balassa's studies of the individual countries from Noland's focus on future trade patterns. Balassa's work will be published separately as *Economic Policies in the Pacific Area Countries*. This volume owes a great deal to Balassa's contributions during the early stages of its preparation, as much of the data was assembled under his supervision and some of his revisions to early chapter drafts have been incorporated.

The Institute for International Economics is a private nonprofit research institution for the study and discussion of international economic policy. Its purpose is to analyze important issues in that area, and to develop and communicate practical new approaches for dealing with them. The Institute is completely nonpartisan.

The Institute was created by a generous commitment of funds from the German Marshall Fund of the United States in 1981, and now receives about 15 percent of its support from that source. Major institutional grants are also being received from the Ford Foundation, the William and Flora Hewlett Foundation, the Alfred P. Sloan Foundation, and the C. V. Starr Foundation.

A number of other foundations and private corporations are contributing to the increasing diversification of the Institute's financial resources. About 15 percent of the Institute's resources in our latest fiscal year came from outside the United States, including about 4 percent from Japan. A generous grant from The J. Howard Pew Freedom Trust supported this project.

The Board of Directors bears overall responsibility for the Institute and gives general guidance and approval to its research program, including identification of topics that are likely to become important to policymakers over the medium run (generally one to three years) and which thus should be addressed by the Institute. The Director, working closely with the staff and outside Advisory Committee, is responsible for the development of particular projects and makes the final decision to publish an individual study.

The Institute hopes that its studies and other activities will contribute to building a stronger foundation for international economic policy around the world. We invite readers to let us know how they think we can best accomplish this objective.

C. FRED BERGSTEN
Director
December 1990

Introduction and Overview

One of the most positive international economic trends of the past quarter century has been the rapid emergence of the developing countries of the Pacific Basin.[1] The eight economies considered in this book—Hong Kong, Singapore, Taiwan, Korea, Malaysia, Thailand, the Philippines, and Indonesia—are a diverse group of small, open economies. They range in size from the city-states of Hong Kong and Singapore to sprawling Indonesia with a population of more than 185 million. Some have considerable mineral resources (Indonesia, Malaysia) or are rich in agricultural land (Thailand, the Philippines), whereas others have virtually no natural resources (Hong Kong, Singapore, Korea). Governmental policies have ranged from laissez-faire (Hong Kong) to interventionist (Indonesia). Ethnically, culturally, and even geographically these countries are diverse: it is nearly as far from Seoul to Jakarta as it is from Washington to Madrid.

Economic Profile

In the past 25 years these eight economies have more than doubled their share of world production, and their share of world trade has more than tripled (table 1.1). Together they account for a greater share of world trade than Japan, and nearly as much as Japan and China combined. On current trends, by the year 2000 their collective share of world production will exceed that of Japan in the 1960s when it became a developed country.

International trade has come to play an increasingly important role in all

---

1. Throughout this study the term "country" will be used for expositional convenience, although legally not all of the Pacific Basin economies are countries. Similarly, the Republic of Korea will be referred to as "Korea."

of these countries. The share of exports and imports in gross domestic product (GDP) ranges from more than 100 percent in Hong Kong and Singapore (where entrepôt trade has long been an important activity) to more than 25 percent in Indonesia, making these economies among the most open in the world. This expansion of trade activity has benefited these economies in a variety of ways. Specialization according to comparative advantage has increased the efficient use of factors of production and encouraged the exploitation of scale economies and the maintenance of high capacity utilization. The generation of export revenues has reduced the likelihood of growth-constraining foreign-exchange shortages. Indeed, a virtuous circle has emerged, with exports financing the imported intermediate inputs and capital equipment needed for additional growth. In a dynamic sense, exposure in world markets to new products and techniques has spurred even greater growth (Balassa and Williamson 1990).

The expansion of trading activity by the Pacific Basin developing countries has been accompanied by dramatic changes in the commodity structure of their trade (tables 1.2 and 1.3). In particular, there has been a pronounced shift in their exports toward manufactured goods and other high-value-added activities. The city-states of Hong Kong and Singapore specialized in labor-intensive manufactures at an early stage in their postwar economic development. They were followed by natural resource–poor Korea and Taiwan. Between 1963 and 1988 the share of manufactures in total exports increased from 46.6 percent to 91.9 percent in Korea, and from 18.1 percent to 91.9 percent in Taiwan. The more natural resource–abundant ASEAN–4 (Malaysia, Thailand, the Philippines, and Indonesia—all members of the Association of Southeast Asian Nations[2]) began specializing in manufactures at a later stage in their development, and have done so to a lesser extent: between 1963 and 1988 the share of manufactures in total exports rose from 4.0 percent to 35.8 percent in the Philippines; from 1.8 percent to 51.3 percent in Thailand; from 2.9 percent to 41.4 percent in Malaysia; and from 0.3 percent to 25.1 percent in Indonesia.

Exploiting the gains from trade, the Pacific Basin developing countries have experienced impressive increases in per capita income (table 1.4). With the exception of the Philippines, growth rates of per capita income in all of these countries have been among the highest in the world. Starting from a much lower base, the richer Pacific Basin developing countries have already achieved income levels comparable to the poorer countries of the European Community, with per capita incomes in Hong Kong and Singapore already

---

2. Singapore is also a member of ASEAN but is included with the NICs (newly industrializing countries) for analytical purposes. The small, oil-producing sultanate of Brunei is the sixth member of ASEAN.

exceeding those of the United Kingdom, Italy, and Spain. Per capita income in Taiwan is now roughly equal to that in Greece, and per capita incomes in Korea and Malaysia surpass that of Turkey.

The rapid growth of income through specialization in the production of labor-intensive manufactures has tended to reduce income inequalities in the so-called newly industrializing countries (Hong Kong, Singapore, Taiwan, and Korea), which were relatively low to begin with. In Korea and Taiwan this income-equalizing trend was aided by comprehensive land reform programs that reduced inequalities in the rural sector. The subsequent expansion of labor-intensive production in the manufacturing sector raised real wages and contributed to further reductions in inequality. As a consequence, Taiwan currently has one of the most (if not the most) egalitarian income distributions in the world. Rapid increases in asset prices (especially land) threaten to reverse the tendency toward greater equality in both Korea and Taiwan, however.

In comparison with the NICs, income growth rates have been slower, and the distribution of income has been more unequal, in the ASEAN–4. The ASEAN–4 have larger agricultural sectors, and slower productivity gains in agriculture have retarded income growth relative to that in the NICs. At the same time, the greater prevalence of large, estate-style farming has contributed to income inequality in rural areas. In the industrial sector, the ASEAN–4 have been slower to move into income-equalizing, labor-intensive manufacturing activities than the NICs.

Underlying these transformations has been a rapid accumulation of human and physical capital (table 1.5). Between 1968 and 1988 the average annual growth rate of the physical capital stock was 10.8 percent in Hong Kong, 8.3 percent in Singapore, 9.8 percent in Taiwan, 12.7 percent in Korea, 10.0 percent in Malaysia, 7.0 percent in Thailand, 5.2 percent in the Philippines, and 11.3 percent in Indonesia (see appendix A for details of the calculations). By way of comparison, capital stock growth rates for Japan and the United States were 9.0 percent and 4.6 percent, respectively.

Complementing the rapid growth of the physical capital stock have been generally high rates of human capital accumulation. The NICs have all achieved high rates of adult literacy and rapid increases in the overall level of educational attainment embodied in the labor force. The NICs also have trained and retained considerable numbers of scientists and engineers, thus ensuring an indigenous capacity for technological adaptation, an important contributor to successful industrialization.

The situation among the ASEAN–4 is more varied. The Philippines has a strong educational tradition and has maintained both high rates of adult literacy and formal education through the university level. Yet the share of science and engineering graduates among its university graduates is the lowest

Table 1.1 Basic economic data for the Pacific Basin developing countries

Country	Land area (1000s of km²)	Population (millions)		Per capita income (1980 PPP US dollars)		World income share (percentages)	
		1963-65	1987-88	1963	1988	1965	1987
All Pacific Basin developing countries	3,185	211.4	376.0	683	2,221	1.5	3.2
NICs	136	44.2	70.2	974	5,162	0.5	1.9
Hong Kong	1	3.6	5.7	2,247	11,952	0.1	0.3
Singapore	1	1.8	2.7	1,777	11,693	0.1	0.1
Taiwan	36	19.9	19.9	980	4,607	0.2	0.6
Korea	98	26.9	42.0	747	4,094	0.2	0.8
ASEAN-4	3,049	167.2	305.8	606	1,546	1.0	1.3
Malaysia	330	8.8	16.9	1,233	3,643	0.2	0.2
Thailand	514	28.5	54.5	537	1,627	0.3	0.3
Philippines	300	29.9	58.7	965	1,460	0.4	0.2
Indonesia	1,905	99.9	175.6	463	1,348	0.2	0.5
Memoranda:							
Japan[b]	378	96.8	122.6	2,931	10,568	5.4	16.5

Country	World trade share (percentages)		Trade balances (millions of current US dollars)		Exports[a]		Imports[a]	
	1963	1988	1963	1988	1963	1988	1963	1988
All Pacific Basin developing countries	3.0	9.8	-1,187	23,889	n.a.	58.7	n.a.	54.2
NICs	1.9	7.7	-1,190	15,372	n.a.	71.5	n.a.	63.7
Hong Kong	0.7	2.3	-424	-734	78.6	136.0	89.7	130.8
Singapore	0.8	1.5	-263	-4,547	151.4	210.5	166.7	202.6
Taiwan	0.2	2.0	-29	10,908	17.8	57.0	18.9	47.4
Korea	0.2	2.0	-474	9,745	4.8	42.0	15.9	34.4
ASEAN-4	1.1	2.1	3	8,517	n.a.	36.3	n.a.	37.8
Malaysia	n.a.	0.7	n.a.	4,558	43.2	70.3	41.5	65.6
Thailand	0.3	0.6	-133	-300	14.8	37.5	18.0	40.8
Philippines	0.4	0.3	47	-1,628	16.5	27.2	15.4	30.2
Indonesia	0.4	0.6	89	5,887	9.2	25.7	8.9	27.6
Memoranda: Japan[b]	3.8	8.0	-1,290	77,478	10.9	13.2	9.8	10.2

PPP = purchasing power parity; n.a. = not available.

a. As a percentage of GDP.

b. The trade figures as a proportion of income for the earlier year are for 1965.

Sources: Land area: Food and Agriculture Organization, Production Yearbook, various issues. Population and per capita income: Kravis et al. (1988) and International Monetary Fund, International Financial Statistics, various issues. World income shares. World Bank, World Development Report, various issues. World trade shares and trade balances: International Monetary Fund, Direction of Trade Statistics, various issues. Exports and imports of goods and nonfinancial services: World Bank. Data on population, income, trade shares, and trade balances for Taiwan are from Republic of China, Taiwan Statistical Data Book, various issues.

Table 1.2 Product composition of Pacific Basin developing-country exports, 1963 and 1988 (percentages)

	1963				1988			
Country	Fuel	Nonfuel primary	Manufacturing	Other	Fuel	Nonfuel primary	Manufacturing	Other
Hong Kong	0.0	7.8	72.5	19.7	0.2	3.2	95.0	1.5
Singapore	16.7	52.0	26.7	4.6	12.5	13.2	70.2	4.1
Taiwan	0.9	61.1	18.1	19.9	0.6	7.4	91.9	0.1
Korea[a]	3.4	50.0	46.6	0.0	1.5	6.1	91.9	0.4
Malaysia[a]	4.1	90.3	2.9	2.7	19.2	39.1	41.4	0.3
Thailand[a]	0.0	96.5	1.8	1.7	0.7	46.8	51.3	1.2
Philippines	0.4	94.7	4.0	0.9	2.1	36.1	35.8	26.0
Indonesia[a]	38.5	61.2	0.3	0.0	48.9	26.0	25.1	0.0

a. Latest data refer to 1987.

Source: General Agreement on Tariffs and Trade.

Table 1.3 Product composition of Pacific Basin developing-country imports, 1963 and 1988 (percentages)

Country	1963				1988			
	Fuel	Nonfuel primary	Manufacturing	Other	Fuel	Nonfuel primary	Manufacturing	Other
Hong Kong	3.5	40.6	45.5	10.4	1.9	13.4	83.1	1.6
Singapore	13.7	45.5	37.9	2.9	14.1	13.3	71.1	1.5
Taiwan	7.2	45.6	14.4	32.8	8.6	20.3	69.4	1.7
Korea[a]	6.1	42.9	49.8	1.2	14.3	20.8	64.7	0.2
Malaysia[a]	11.1	38.8	31.2	18.9	7.1	16.3	74.2	2.4
Thailand[a]	9.6	10.7	73.0	6.7	13.3	14.1	66.7	5.9
Philippines	11.4	23.4	50.8	14.4	13.2	17.1	48.7	21.0
Indonesia[a]	n.a.	n.a.	n.a.	n.a.	9.0	15.5	74.9	0.6

n.a. = not available.

a. Latest data refer to 1987.

Source: General Agreement on Tariffs and Trade.

Table 1.4 GDP per capita in the Pacific Basin developing countries, 1963 and 1988[a] (US dollars except where noted)

Country	At purchasing power parities in 1980 prices				At 1988 market exchange rates
	1963	1988	Average growth rate (percentages)	Atkinson inequality index[a]	
Hong Kong	2,247	11,952	6.9	0.392	8,249
Singapore	1,777	11,693	7.8	n.a.	7,623
Taiwan	980	4,607	6.4	0.201	4,804
Korea	747	4,094	7.0	0.369	2,849
Malaysia	1,233	3,643	4.4	0.556	1,886
Thailand	537	1,627	4.5	0.408	887
Philippines	965	1,460	1.7	0.442	603
Indonesia	463	1,348	4.4	0.407	409
Memoranda:					
United Kingdom	5,277	9,582	2.4	0.294	8,909
Italy	3,817	8,106	3.1	0.341	6,156
Spain	3,130	7,260	3.4	0.287	4,095
Ireland	2,857	5,657	2.8	0.271	4,382
Greece	1,807	4,636	3.8	n.a.	1,348
Turkey	1,378	2,822	3.0	0.553	447

n.a. = not available.

a. The Atkinson inequality index is defined as $1-[\sum_i (y_i^{-1}/n)]^{-1}/y$ where y_i = income of group i and n is the number of income groups. The index varies from 0 to 1, with higher values indicating greater income inequality.

Sources: 1963–81 figures from Kravis et al. (1988). 1988 estimates were updated from 1985 figures by utilizing national data on economic growth rates from International Monetary Fund, *International Financial Statistics*, various issues. The household income distribution data for Atkinson index calculations were for the following years: Hong Kong and Taiwan, 1980; Korea and Indonesia, 1976; Malaysia and Turkey, 1973; Thailand, 1975–76; Philippines, 1985; Italy, 1977; Spain, 1980–81; Ireland, 1973; and United Kingdom, 1979. These data are from World Bank (1989).

among the eight countries. Thailand also has a broad-based educational system and has made impressive strides in raising the human capital embodied in the labor force. In Malaysia, levels of educational attainment vary widely throughout the labor force, so that although there are considerable numbers of college graduates, 30 percent of the adult population remains illiterate.

Educational attainment rates in Indonesia are the lowest among this group of countries.

What is probably most striking about the ASEAN-4 in comparison with the NICs is the far lower numbers of scientists and engineers in their populations. The relatively low number of technically trained people in these countries may slow the efficient adaptation of technology from abroad.

Trade Policies

In conjunction with their rapid accumulation of human and physical capital, the Pacific Basin developing countries have created a set of institutions and policies that have facilitated their successful entry into world manufactures markets. In a 1987 World Bank study of 41 developing countries, Hong Kong, Singapore, and Korea comprised (in its entirety) the group classified as "strongly outward oriented." Malaysia and Thailand fell into the "moderately outward oriented" group, while Indonesia and Philippines were classified as "moderately inward oriented." Taiwan was not included in the study because of its peculiar political status, but had it been, it certainly would have joined the "strongly outward oriented" group. None of the Pacific Basin developing countries were classified as "strongly inward oriented." Hong Kong and Singapore are effectively free traders, and planned trade liberalizations will reduce protection in Taiwan and Korea to levels comparable to those of the industrialized countries by the early 1990s (table 1.6). Reforms in the Philippines and Indonesia are opening previously highly protected markets.

Although the specifics differ from country to country, certain common themes emerge from the success stories. First, the successful exporters have surmounted their lack of technical, managerial, and marketing know-how and, more broadly, their lack of knowledge of world markets. This has been accomplished by finding ways of combining local productive capacity with foreign expertise. Second, the successful exporters have provided a policy environment that ensures that domestic firms compete with foreign firms on an equal footing. In particular this means ensuring adequate short-term trade financing at world market interest rates, unrestricted access to imported intermediate goods at world market prices, the avoidance of currency overvaluation, and adequate access to the capital goods and investment finance necessary for efficient production and expansion (Rhee 1989).

Historically there has been little economic interaction among the developing countries of the Pacific Basin. Certain data problems make the comparison hazardous, but if anything the share of intraregional trade in the total trade of these countries has declined slightly, from 18.8 percent in 1963 to 18.7

Table 1.5 Human capital indicators in the Pacific Basin developing countries

Country	Adult literacy rate (percentages)		Psacharopoulos index[a]		Scientists and engineers (per million population)
	1970	1980	1968	1986	
Hong Kong[b]	77.3	n.a.	1,172	2,010	n.a.
Singapore	68.9	82.9	1,024	2,179	1,939 (1984)
Taiwan	85.3	89.7	1,097	1,966	1,426 (1986)
Korea	87.6	n.a.	1,013	2,261	2,123 (1986)
Malaysia	58.0	69.6	563	1,210	182 (1983)
Thailand	78.6	88.0	213	930	150 (1975)
Philippines	82.6	83.3	1,030	1,921	213 (1982)
Indonesia	56.6	67.3	296	842	228 (1984)

n.a. = not available.

a. The Psacharopoulos index measures the per capita educational capital embodied in the labor force.

b. The earlier figure for Hong Kong is for 1971.

Sources: UNESCO (1988); Alavi (1988).

percent in 1988.[3] Yet the emergence of sizable trade surpluses in Taiwan and Korea (see table 1.1), combined with exchange rate realignment and relaxation of capital controls, has led to an enormous growth in intraregional investment. Starting in 1987 (and continuing in succeeding years, although complete data are unavailable), there has been an explosion of foreign direct investment (FDI) into the ASEAN–4, most of it from Japan and the NICs, especially Hong Kong and Taiwan (table 1.7). This investment is spreading the technology, subcontracting networks, and global marketing experience that in part will be the vehicle by which the ASEAN–4 expand their presence in the global trading system. Similarly, the NICs are hosts to increasingly large amounts of FDI from Japan. From the standpoint of US trade politics this threatens to turn the "Japan problem" into an "Asia problem." Yet it is through this process of investment and corporate penetration that a regionally integrated economy is emerging, and this is what justifies the analysis of these apparently dissimilar economies as a group.

---

3. As calculated from data in International Monetary Fund, *Direction of Trade Statistics.* Of course, intraregional trade in absolute terms has grown dramatically. If Japan is included in the calculation the share of intraregional trade in total trade has grown as well, from 23.7 percent in 1963 to 31.5 percent in 1988.

Table 1.6 Comparative trends in trade liberalization (percentages)

Country	Year and sector	Average nominal tariff	Liberalization ratio
Taiwan	1986	28.6	n.a.
	1989		
	Agriculture	24.2	n.a.
	Manufactures	8.0	n.a.
	1992 (planned)	10.3	98.3
	Agriculture	19.8	n.a.
	Manufactures	5.0	n.a.
Korea	1983	23.7	80.4[a]
	1989	12.7	94.7[b]
	Agriculture	n.a.	72.0
	Manufactures	n.a.	99.4
	1994 (planned)[c]	7.9	n.a.
	Agriculture	n.a.	85.0
	Manufactures	6.2	n.a.
Malaysia	1980	11.6	<5
	1985	13.5	<5
Thailand	1981	31.0	<5
	1985	34.0	<5
Philippines	1984	43.1	63.0
	1988	27.9	90.0[d]
	Agriculture	27.1	n.a.
	Manufactures	28.3	n.a.
	Mining	13.1	n.a.
Indonesia	1980	28.0	n.a.
	1989	26.0	84.4

n.a. = not available.

a. Excludes 26 percent due to health, safety, and security.

b. Excludes 19 percent due to health, safety, and security.

c. Originally scheduled for 1993.

d. Excludes 4.7 percent due to health, safety, and security.

Sources: National and international sources.

Financial Policies

Because of their histories as trading centers, Hong Kong, Singapore, and Malaysia traditionally have had relatively well developed financial sectors. All accepted Article VIII of the International Monetary Fund (IMF) Articles of Agreement in the 1960s and had fully convertible currencies by the 1970s.

Table 1.7 Foreign direct investment in the ASEAN–4 economies, 1984–87 (millions of US dollars)

| | | | | Direct investment from: | | | |
Year	Total from all sources	Japan	Total NICs	Hong Kong	Singapore	Taiwan	Korea
1984	1,865	284	155	77	69	6	3
1985	1,283	242	127	84	−20	7	56
1986	1,369	490	271	129	51	77	14
1987	2,589	935	554	160	59	302	33

Source: Chen (1989), table 5.

There are no significant capital or investment controls in Hong Kong or Singapore; direct investment in Malaysia is subject to prior approval and local-participation requirements.

In comparison, Taiwan and Korea traditionally have had more highly regulated and less developed capital markets. Domestic financial institutions were generally under considerable direct or indirect government control, and the role of foreign financial institutions was circumscribed. External transactions were similarly regulated. In recent years both countries have undertaken gradual reforms to improve financial intermediation and promote greater integration into world capital markets. As part of the liberalization effort, Korea, which is a member of the IMF, accepted Article VIII in 1988, and has announced plans to fully open its financial services sector to foreign participation by 1992.

Reform efforts are also under way in Indonesia and Thailand. Indonesia accepted Article VIII in 1988 and has deregulated its financial services sector. Direct investment is still subject to local-participation rules and requires the approval of the president upon the recommendation of the Investment Coordination Board. There are also some remaining restrictions on the repatriation of funds. Similarly, Thailand announced its acceptance of Article VIII in May 1990 and is in the process of dismantling existing capital controls.

The Philippines alone maintains transitional arrangements under IMF Article XIV, which permits a country to impose restrictions on current payments and transfers until it is satisfied that its balance of payments is strong enough to remove the restrictions. Under these provisions, the Philippines continues to maintain extensive controls on portfolio and direct investment as well as the repatriation of invested funds.

A key to strong trade performance has been the maintenance of a competitive real exchange rate. The East Asian NICs have generally avoided the currency overvaluation that has plagued many other developing countries. If anything, the NICs have tended to maintain undervalued currencies, which by the mid-1980s were the source of international economic frictions.

The situation with the ASEAN–4 is somewhat more complicated. Both the Philippines and Thailand have had episodes of overvaluation, as policymakers did not respond adequately to negative terms-of-trade shocks. In the 1980s, however, both countries have experienced corrective devaluations, and through their links to the US dollar they have benefited further from dollar depreciation in the late 1980s.

Malaysia and Indonesia have had in some ways the opposite experience. The oil booms of the 1970s and early 1980s led to symptoms of the "Dutch disease," as the temporary positive terms-of-trade shock caused a real over-valuation of the currency, threatening the international competitiveness of the nascent manufacturing sector. In the 1980s, the weakening of commodity prices (and in the case of Indonesia two large devaluations) have contributed to real currency depreciation and a restoration of competitiveness in both economies.

Plan of the Book

It is likely that the Pacific Basin developing countries will continue to play a role of growing importance in the global trade system. Moreover, an explosion of intraregional investment is strengthening the bonds among these apparently dissimilar economies.

This study will analyze the impact of these prospective changes on the world economy. To this end we begin with a review of the Pacific Basin developing countries, their current trade regimes, and the historical evolution of their economic policies (chapters 2 and 3). Trade composition projections for each country, derived from an econometric model, are presented for the year 2000 in chapter 4. This analysis indicates that the Pacific Basin developing countries are likely to successfully penetrate world markets in a growing range of manufactured goods.

The implications for the role of the Pacific Basin developing countries in the world trade system, and how future developments in the world economy might affect these outcomes, are discussed in chapter 5. Finally, the implications of these developments for the United States, from both an economic adjustment and a policy perspective, are outlined in chapter 6.

For labor-intensive, import-competing manufacturing industries in the rest of the world, the developing countries of the Pacific Basin will remain strong competitors for the foreseeable future. Indeed, the gradual shift of these economies into manufacturing sectors of greater capital intensity and sophistication will mean increasing competitive pressure in a variety of industries. At the same time, however, the prospect of continued rapid growth in these economies presents a significant opportunity for foreign investors and US export industries. Indeed, the Pacific Basin developing countries are likely to emerge as a major growth area for US exports, with their share of total US exports rising steadily over the next decade.

2

The Newly Industrializing Countries

The four newly industrializing countries—Hong Kong, Singapore, Taiwan, and Korea—have been among the most spectacular performers in the world economy over the past 25 years, quadrupling their shares of world production and trade. The four have shared a commitment to outward-oriented growth strategies, although the policy specifics have differed considerably from country to country. Today each of these countries faces the common problem of managing the transition from a low-wage economy exporting labor-intensive manufactures, to a high-wage economy competing increasingly on the basis of product design and innovation.

At the same time, each of the NICs is becoming an increasingly important investment and technology source for the less developed countries of the region. In this regard there is an important difference between the city-states on the one hand and Taiwan and Korea on the other. Because of their history as entrepôt trade centers, Hong Kong and Singapore have developed sophisticated financial sectors and have permitted free international capital flows. Government control has retarded the development of efficient financial intermediation in Taiwan and Korea, however, and these countries' high rates of growth, combined with a relative paucity of investment instruments, has contributed to a rapid runup in the price of land and (until recently) stocks. This asset price explosion has led to growing wealth inequality and social tensions even as both countries make the transition to more democratic rule. Moreover, the relative backwardness of the financial sectors of these countries compounds the problem of responding to mounting external pressure to liberalize international capital flows. If not handled carefully, these could lead to massive net capital inflows and exchange rate overshooting, with deleterious implications for the nonfinancial sector.

The ongoing transitions in each of the NICs raise issues for their domestic policies and for the international economic policies of their trading partners. This chapter examines the historical development of the NICs' economies and the challenges that they are likely to face.

Hong Kong
Historical and Policy Background

With a population of more than 5 million confined to an area of just over 1,000 square kilometers (about 400 square miles), Hong Kong has one of the highest population densities of any country on earth. Since the end of World War II Hong Kong has experienced extraordinary economic growth, emerging first as a manufacturer and more recently as an international financial center. Hong Kong has accomplished all of this while absorbing millions of immigrants, mostly from the People's Republic of China. However, the prospects for continued growth and prosperity are less certain now than at any time since entrepôt trade with China was suspended during the Korean War. Recent developments have called into question the government's traditional hands-off approach to the economy, and above all else looms the issue of China's resumption of sovereignty over Hong Kong in 1997.

Government policy in Hong Kong is undoubtedly the closest approximation to laissez-faire in the world economy. The government owns no manufacturing establishments, there are few business regulations, and there are no restrictions on international trade. Taxes are low and uniform across activities (the personal income tax is 15 percent, and the business profit tax is 15.5 percent). The government has largely limited its role to the provision of physical, social, and legal infrastructure. The government maintains the airport, port facilities, some transportation systems, extensive low-rent housing facilities, and the water supply. Health care for young women and children is subsidized. Schooling is compulsory to age 15. Primary education is free, and secondary education heavily subsidized. The government has also supported some higher education and training programs.

Hong Kong's only natural resource is its harbor. The initial industrialization of Hong Kong was spurred by the immigration of Chinese capitalists and skilled workers from Shanghai in the late 1940s. They brought with them the technical and managerial know-how (as well as some textile machinery) necessary to establish production. As a result of Hong Kong's long history as an entrepôt trade center, there were already a large number of banks and merchant trading houses which were able to provide financial and international marketing support to the nascent textile industry. A host of small trading companies provided international trade intermediation. The colony's free-trade status helped ensure that Hong Kong's producers were able to compete against foreign firms on a relatively equal footing (Rhee 1989). Subsequent growth has been achieved through the rapid accumulation of human and physical capital. This has been accompanied by changes in the composition of output, especially the upgrading of the industrial structure and the emergence of the financial services sector.

Exchange Rates

Hong Kong's exchange rate is set by a currency board and is currently fixed at HK$7.80 to US$1.00. The money supply adjusts automatically to accommodate free capital flows.

Wages and prices move flexibly to maintain the full employment of productive factors.[1] Hong Kong's real effective exchange rate (REER) can be calculated in two ways: using a consumer price index (CPI) or an export price index.[2] The CPI has the advantage of indicating overall movements in costs and prices (and thereby the competitiveness) of an economy. Its disadvantage is that it includes those goods and services (such as housing) that do not enter into international trade, and thus can give misleading indications of a country's international trade competitiveness.[3] On the other hand, REERs derived from export price indices concentrate more narrowly on the export sector and indicate the competitiveness of exporters, but do not indicate changes in the competitiveness of the domestic import-competing sector.

REERs derived from both CPI and export price series have been calculated in two ways: using the shares of each of Hong Kong's principal trading partners in Hong Kong's total trade as weights (trading-partner weights), and using the other seven Pacific Basin developing countries' shares of the group's total exports in computing the weights (competitor weights).[4] The trading-partner-weighted REERs indicate changes in Hong Kong's competitiveness with respect to its trading partners. The competitor-weighted REERs show how Hong Kong's competitiveness vis-à-vis the other Pacific Basin countries has changed in third-country markets. The four series of REERs thus calculated are shown in figure 2.1.

---

1. For a detailed analysis of Hong Kong's recent macroeconomic performance see Balassa and Williamson (1990).

2. "Effective" exchange rates are calculated by averaging a country's bilateral exchange rates to create an index using the rates observed during a particular time period as the base. The calculation of "real" (i.e., differential inflation–adjusted) effective exchange rates is motivated by the idea that a country's competitive position is affected by cost-price relationships as well as changes in nominal exchange rates. In this study REERs are expressed as the ratio of foreign-currency to domestic-currency prices, so that an increase (decrease) in the REER denotes a real currency depreciation (appreciation) and an increase (decrease) in the country's international competitiveness.

3. Wholesale price indexes, which more closely capture movements in the prices of goods traded internationally, are unavailable for Hong Kong.

4. For the competitor weights, these country shares are then multiplied by the shares of each major industry in the index country's exports.

Figure 2.1 Hong Kong: real effective exchange rates, 1970–88

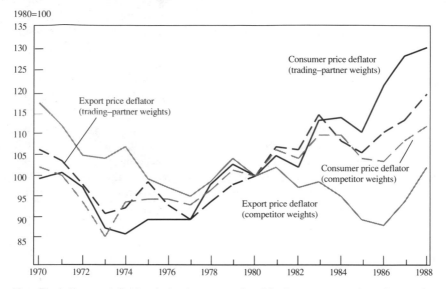

Note: The indices are defined as the local-currency price of foreign currency, so that a rise in the index signifies a depreciation.

According to the CPI-based REERs, the Hong Kong dollar depreciated in real terms between 1985 and 1988. Against its trading partners the depreciation was significant—nearly 17 percent—but against the other Pacific Basin developing countries it was only about half as much. Similarly, the trading-partner-weighted export price REER exhibits a general tendency toward depreciation starting in the mid-1970s, and in 1988 it was 20.0 percent higher than it was at the start of the decade. The competitor-weighted export price REER shows a different pattern, however. There was considerable appreciation by this measure in the mid-1970s, and in 1988 the competitor-weighted export price REER stood at 102.3—only slightly higher than its value at the beginning of the decade. Thus, despite considerable real depreciation, Hong Kong's gain in export competitiveness against the other Pacific Basin developing countries was minimal. This underscores the need for Hong Kong to achieve future competitiveness gains through product and quality upgrading.

Table 2.1 Hong Kong: composition of trade by major product group, 1963 and 1988 (percentages)

Industry	Exports		Imports	
	1963	1988	1963	1988
Fuels (SITC 3)	0.0	0.2	3.5	1.9
Nonfuel primary products	7.8	3.2	40.6	13.4
Food and live animals (SITC 0)	3.6	0.7	9.9	6.5
Beverages and tobacco (SITC 1)	1.5	1.0	16.7	1.5
Industrial raw materials (SITC 2, 4, 68)	2.7	1.5	14.0	5.3
Manufactures (industrial classification)	72.5	95.0	45.5	83.1
Textiles, apparel, and leather (ISIC 32)	47.8	39.6	16.4	22.9
Wood products and furniture (ISIC 33)	0.7	0.4	0.3	1.1
Paper and paper products (ISIC 34)	0.7	2.7	0.8	2.1
Chemicals (ISIC 35)	3.7	5.9	7.1	11.3
Nonmetallic mineral products (ISIC 36)	0.3	0.7	1.9	1.5
Iron and steel (ISIC 37)	0.7	0.1	2.8	2.5
Engineering products (ISIC 38)	8.8	34.5	12.7	36.8
Miscellaneous (ISIC 39)	9.7	6.1	3.5	4.9
Other products	19.7	1.5	10.4	1.6
Memorandum: trade in goods and nonfactor services as a share of GDP	78.6	136.0	89.7	130.8

SITC = Standard International Trade Classification.

ISIC = International Standard Industrial Classification.

Source: General Agreement on Tariffs and Trade. Memorandum data are from the World Bank.

Trade and Investment Patterns

The challenge facing Hong Kong is reflected in the commodity composition of exports (table 2.1; manufacturing trade shares by individual industry are presented in appendix B, table B.1). Most notable are the declines in export share of the labor-intensive textile and "other products" categories and the dramatic rise in importance of engineering products. At the same time there has been an continual upgrading of goods within these product categories. In the clothing industry there have been shifts away from undergarments and products made from man-made fibers to higher-value-added goods such as natural-fiber outerwear garments, especially those made of cotton and silk

(Chen and Li 1989, tables 4 and 5). This shift in composition within the clothing industry has been at least in part a response to the Multi-Fiber Arrangement (MFA), a system of bilateral quotas covering textile and apparel trade. Trela and Whalley (1988) have estimated that if these quotas were abolished, Hong Kong's textile and apparel exports would rise by approximately 25 percent. If all tariffs on textiles and apparel were removed as well, Hong Kong's textile and apparel exports could rise by nearly 46 percent.

Within electronics, there have been shifts away from production of transistor radios and toward more sophisticated products such as televisions and computing equipment (Chen and Li 1989, table 8). Hong Kong has also emerged as a major supplier of watches, clocks, and watch parts, even though it did not produce these articles as recently as 1970 (Chen and Li 1989, table 2). Manufactured imports have also grown, with import share increases particularly noticeable in the engineering products and textile industries, reflecting horizontal specialization and the expansion of intraindustry trade.

China is today Hong Kong's largest trading partner, having supplanted Western Europe, which has steadily declined in importance both as an export market and as a source of imports (table 2.2). The United States is Hong Kong's second-largest export market, and Japan its second-largest supplier of imports. The other Pacific Basin developing countries as a group have increased in importance as both an export and an import market, with their share in Hong Kong's exports growing from 6.6 percent in 1963 to 12.3 percent in 1988, while their share in Hong Kong's imports grew from 7.6 percent to 21.5 percent over the same period.

With the emergence of trade surpluses in the 1980s, rising labor costs, and uncertainties about the economic environment after 1997, Hong Kong has become a major investor in the surrounding economies. This new role has further strengthened Hong Kong's economic ties with its neighbors. In 1987, Hong Kong was the largest foreign investor in China, the second-largest in Indonesia, the third-largest in the Philippines, Thailand, Singapore, and Taiwan, and the fifth-largest in Malaysia (Chen and Li 1989). Most of this investment is in labor-intensive industries such as footwear and toys, where Hong Kong has a declining comparative advantage.

Issues for the 1990s

This flow of capital out of Hong Kong could turn into a flood unless three issues are resolved. The first concerns the adequacy of regulation of the Hong Kong financial markets. During the worldwide stock market crash of October 1987, the Hong Kong stock and futures exchanges closed for four days, locking outside investors into growing losses while permitting some influential

Table 2.2 Hong Kong: geographical composition of trade, 1963 and 1988[a] (percentages)

Country	Exports		Imports	
	1963	1988	1963	1988
Developed countries	61.2	52.6	55.3	41.7
United States	20.3	24.8	10.6	8.3
Western Europe	29.1	18.0	23.9	12.9
Japan	6.1	5.9	16.7	18.6
Canada, Australia, New Zealand	5.7	4.0	4.1	1.9
Developing countries	38.6	46.9	44.0	57.8
Pacific countries (other than China)	6.6	12.3	7.6	21.5
Other East Asian NICs	1.6	9.0	3.0	17.9
Singapore	n.a.	2.8	n.a.	3.7
Taiwan	1.2	3.6	2.3	8.9
Korea	0.4	2.6	0.7	5.3
ASEAN–4	5.1	3.2	4.6	3.7
Malaysia	n.a.	0.7	n.a.	1.2
Thailand	2.2	0.9	3.6	1.2
Philippines	1.1	0.9	0.2	0.5
Indonesia	1.7	0.8	0.8	0.8
China	1.4	27.0	20.1	31.2
Other developing countries	30.6	7.6	16.4	5.0
Other Asia	19.3	2.6	9.7	2.0
Africa	6.1	1.7	2.9	0.8
Europe[b]	n.a.	0.3	n.a.	0.1
Middle East	2.8	1.8	2.2	1.0
Latin America	2.4	1.2	1.6	1.1
European socialist countries	0.0	0.5	0.7	0.5

n.a. = not available.

a. Regional aggregates may not sum to 100 percent because of inclusion in the world total of special categories and other countries not specified.

b. Principally Portugal, Greece, and Turkey.

Source: International Monetary Fund, *Direction of Trade Statistics,* various issues.

insiders to escape them. The government then organized a HK$4 billion (US$500 million) rescue of large futures brokers and traders, the costs of which were borne by taxpayers and investors. In the aftermath of the crisis, the chairman of the stock exchange and several of his associates were tried and convicted on corruption charges, and an outside committee was appointed to review the functioning of the markets and recommend possible reforms. In its May 1988 report, the Securities Review Committee described the ruling council of the stock exchange as "an inside group which treated the exchange as a private club, rather than a public utility" (*The Economist,* 21 January 1989, 80). The committee recommended the creation of a new regulatory agency, the Securities and Futures Commission (SFC). The question now is whether the SFC, established in April 1989, will have the capacity to supervise and enforce a stricter regulatory environment.

A second issue facing the Hong Kong economy is the role of the government in encouraging industrial upgrading. Rising labor costs in Hong Kong relative to surrounding areas, especially China, necessitate expansion into higher-value-added activities. It has been argued, most notably in a report commissioned by a group of Hong Kong's top firms, that the government's traditional hands-off approach cannot meet this challenge. The consultancy report recommended large increases in expenditures on education and retraining. Others have called for a more prominent government role in supporting research and development (Chen and Li 1989).

Lastly, overhanging all of these concerns is the transfer of sovereignty from the United Kingdom to China scheduled for 1997. The draft of the Basic Law, which is intended to set out the rules governing Hong Kong's affairs for at least 50 years after 1997, appears to give sweeping powers to the central government in Beijing. The resulting unease has led to increased emigration, which in the late 1980s was more than 55,000 a year, or five times the 1985 level. A survey found that 46 percent of professional households polled had plans to move to a country with a clearer political future (*South China Morning Post,* 1 February 1988). The June 1989 repression of political demonstrations in China has given further impetus to emigration. The beginnings of capital flight can also be seen. Major firms have begun increasing their stakes in companies based in the United States and Europe; the outflow of capital has swollen from HK$2 billion in 1988 to HK$23 billion in 1989, with an even greater outflow expected for 1990.

Singapore

Historical and Policy Background

Like Hong Kong, Singapore has no natural resources apart from its harbor. It too is a city-state that has developed from an entrepôt trade center into a manufacturer, and increasingly into a provider of services. Singapore was a

British crown colony until it was granted independence in 1959. It briefly entered into a federation with Malaysia in the 1960s, and has operated since 1965 as an independent country under the leadership of Prime Minister Lee Kuan Yew. The constant in Singapore's economic development, and what distinguishes it from the other NICs, has been the major role of foreign firms in the economy.

The industrialization process began with independence. The government encouraged the development of manufacturing through a strategy of import-substituting industrialization. This effort was intensified during the two-year federation with Malaysia, but by the late 1960s it was apparent that the import substitution strategy, greatly limited by the small size of the domestic market, had reached a dead end. Trade liberalization was undertaken, and export subsidies were introduced to equalize incentives across different activities and ensure that domestic producers competed on equal terms with foreign firms (Tan and Ow 1982). Additional export promotion measures, such as the development of overseas marketing services, were also undertaken (Tay 1986). Most import duties have been set at 5 percent since 1981, and in 1988 the last quota (on air conditioners) was removed, making Singapore practically a free-trade economy (Kng et al. 1988).

The shift in trade policy toward greater export orientation was accompanied by labor law revisions introduced with the explicit intent of enhancing the attractiveness of Singapore to foreign investors. Legislation enacted in 1969 lengthened the standard work week; reduced the number of holidays; placed various restrictions on the payment of retirement benefits, paid leave, overtime, and bonuses; limited unions' ability to represent managerial or executive employees; exempted promotions, transfers, firings, and work assignments from collective bargaining; and lengthened the minimum and maximum duration of labor contracts (Haggard 1990).

Other policy measures were similarly designed to promote inward foreign direct investment (FDI): restrictions on establishment, equity participation, and the repatriation of profits were avoided, as were local-content requirements and requirements to employ nationals. Tax incentives to encourage inward FDI were introduced in 1967 and later extended. This encouragement of foreign investment, particularly from multinational corporations, was the primary way in which Singapore solved the problems of combining local productive factors with foreign technical and managerial know-how, overcoming local producers' lack of knowledge or information about world markets, and dealing with the need to ensure trade finance.

As a result, the foreign presence in the Singapore economy has steadily grown, especially in manufacturing, where foreign firms regularly account for more than 80 percent of net investment. Foreign companies (defined as firms with more than 50 percent foreign equity) produced 71 percent of Singapore's total output and accounted for 63 percent of value added and 82 percent of manufactures exports in 1984 (Koh 1987, table 2.3). The banking sector is similarly dominated by foreign firms.

The next major policy change came in 1978 when the government launched its "Second Industrial Revolution," intended to promote the development of high-technology industries by expanding education and training programs, encouraging research and development (R&D), and, most controversially, forcing industrial upgrading by raising wages. These measures have included fiscal incentives for plant expansion, automation, computerization, and R&D.[5] The Economic Development Board also has provided capital to firms in priority sectors, mainly human capital–intensive engineering products. Parallel to this effort, the government has sought to upgrade labor force skills by establishing technical institutes, industrial training centers (operated jointly with foreign firms and governments), and a system of employer-funded retraining grants. The government's education policies have been criticized as inadequate and overly elitist in orientation, however (Krause et al. 1987). Lastly, the authorities have actively encouraged the relocation of low-wage activities to neighboring countries, to support their development and to assure Singapore's manufacturers of access to low-cost intermediate inputs (Lim and Pang 1986).

The capital needed to finance these schemes is generated by public saving. Singapore maintains one of the highest savings rates in the world, around 40 percent, with the public sector accounting for most of national saving. Much of the public-sector savings come from the Central Provident Fund (CPF), a kind of social security fund to which employers and employees are obliged to contribute 10 percent and 25 percent of wage payments, respectively. This policy has been criticized by Krause et al. (1987), who argue that channeling savings through the CPF gives the government too much influence on the allocation of capital. In particular, employee contributions to the CPF can be withdrawn to purchase housing, but not for business investment. As a consequence, there has been overinvestment in housing relative to other assets.

The policy of enhancing labor force skills and promoting R&D has arguably facilitated Singapore's later development of higher-value-added activities, but the wage increase policy simply priced existing industries out of world mar-

---

5. Capital equipment can be completely written off in five to ten years, plant and machinery for R&D in three years, and computers in one year. Additional R&D tax credits are also available (Lim and Pang 1986).

kets and was eventually reversed. Nevertheless, it is clear that the Singapore government has attempted to use a variety of industrial policies to affect the composition of output.

Exchange Rates

Exchange rate policy in Singapore is reportedly a basket peg within a band (Balassa and Williamson 1990). Real exchange rate indices (calculated as described above for Hong Kong) are shown in figure 2.2. The different REERs show widely divergent patterns. The export price REERs exhibit considerable secular appreciation over the sample period, perhaps reflecting an upgrading of exports. The broader REERs based on the wholesale price index (WPI) do not exhibit this trend, however, and in fact the trading-partner-weighted REER shows a rise in the price of foreign currency of more than 40 percent between 1980 and 1988. This implies that the Singapore dollar rode the US dollar down in the mid-1980s, so that Singapore gained competitiveness against the Japanese in particular, while upgrading its export structure in response to increasing competitive pressures from the other Pacific Basin developing countries.

Trade Patterns

The changes in the composition of Singapore's output are reflected in the export shares shown in table 2.3, which reveal a dramatic shift into manufactures, especially engineering products (manufacturing trade shares by industry are presented in appendix B, table B.2). Much of this shift was due to growth in the foreign-dominated electronics industry, including radio, television, and telecommunications equipment (which had a 20.2 percent share of exports in 1988) and office and computer equipment (with a 13.8 percent share). These changes were nearly matched on the import side, reflecting the importance of assembly activities and the horizontal international division of labor to Singapore's economy.

The geographical composition of trade is shown in table 2.4. Singapore has stopped reporting trade with Indonesia, and as a consequence the figures for 1963 and 1988 are not directly comparable. Nevertheless, they show the dramatic rise of the United States as an export market and a decline in the importance of Western Europe. On the import side, the United States and Japan have both become more important sources of imports. The other East Asian NICs have increased in importance as both export markets and import suppliers; the role of the ASEAN-4 is clouded by the data problem with regard to Indonesia.

Figure 2.2   Singapore: real effective exchange rates, 1970–88

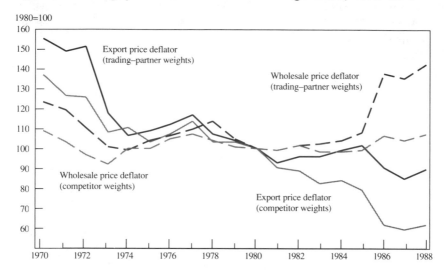

Note: The indices are defined as the local-currency price of foreign currency, so that a rise in the index signifies a depreciation.

Issues for the 1990s

Singapore must confront a challenge similar to that facing Hong Kong, namely, to upgrade its industrial structure in the face of rising relative labor costs. It already has made some headway in the electronics and chemicals industries, and it is trying to attract inward FDI in other sophisticated manufacturing activities. It also hopes to benefit from uncertainty regarding the future of Hong Kong. In July 1989 the government announced sweeping changes in its emigration laws to attract labor and capital from Hong Kong, and it is encouraging Singapore's development as the international financial center of Southeast Asia, as an alternative to Hong Kong.

Singapore's future as an international financial center depends on the further development of its financial markets and institutions. Its banking sector is not as highly developed as Hong Kong's. The domestic stock market is relatively small, and its growth has been retarded by the government's large shareholdings in major firms and by the practice of taxing brokers' profits. The market has also been dealt a recent blow by Malaysia's decision to eliminate the dual listing of Malaysian firms on the Singapore exchange; this move is expected to halve the exchange's capitalization. In contrast, the futures exchange, SIMEX, has been very successful. SIMEX recently launched the first oil futures contract trading in Asia, and its trading volume exceeds that of the London futures exchange.

Table 2.3 Singapore: composition of trade by major product group, 1963 and 1988 (percentages)

Industry	Exports 1963	Exports 1988	Imports 1963	Imports 1988
Fuels (SITC 3)	16.7	12.5	13.7	14.1
Nonfuel primary products	52.0	13.2	45.5	13.3
Food and live animals (SITC 0)	15.9	4.6	18.5	5.7
Beverages and tobacco (SITC 1)	1.5	0.7	1.8	0.8
Industrial raw materials (SITC 2, 4, 68)	34.5	7.9	25.3	6.8
Manufactures (industrial classification)	26.7	70.2	37.9	71.1
Textiles, apparel, and leather (ISIC 32)	5.9	5.2	9.4	5.4
Wood products and furniture (ISIC 33)	0.3	1.9	0.4	1.0
Paper and paper products (ISIC 34)	1.2	1.4	1.8	1.6
Chemicals (ISIC 35)	3.9	7.6	5.7	8.2
Nonmetallic mineral products (ISIC 36)	1.1	0.4	1.2	1.4
Iron and steel (ISIC 37)	1.6	0.9	2.5	3.1
Engineering products (ISIC 38)	11.9	51.7	15.7	49.3
Miscellaneous (ISIC 39)	0.8	1.0	1.3	1.0
Other products	4.6	4.1	2.9	1.5
Memorandum: trade in goods and nonfactor services as a share of GDP	151.4	210.5	166.7	202.6

SITC = Standard International Trade Classification.

ISIC = International Standard Industrial Classification.

Source: General Agreement on Tariffs and Trade. Memorandum data are from the World Bank.

Compared with those in Hong Kong, Singapore's financial markets (with the exception of the foreign-exchange and commodity futures markets) are small and not as well integrated into world capital markets. The US$114 billion of funds under management in Hong Kong is nearly 10 times the US$15 billion under management in Singapore, and the regulatory environment is considerably more lenient in Hong Kong than in Singapore (Overholt 1990). Nonetheless, it is difficult to predict the development of these markets in light of Hong Kong's return to China in 1997.

Ultimately, the success of Singapore's financial sector development strategy may hinge on political developments. In the past several years, Prime Minister Lee has been involved in a series of squabbles with *Time*, the *Far Eastern Economic Review*, the *Asian Wall Street Journal*, and *Asiaweek* over their report-

Table 2.4 Singapore: geographical composition of trade, 1963 and 1988[a] (percentages)

Country	Exports		Imports	
	1963	1988	1963	1988
Developed countries	31.4	50.6	38.1	54.4
United States	6.7	23.8	5.3	15.6
Western Europe	16.3	14.2	19.0	14.0
Japan	3.9	8.6	9.5	22.0
Canada, Australia, New Zealand	4.5	4.0	4.3	2.9
Developing countries	62.1	48.7	61.1	45.0
Pacific countries (other than China)	49.0	31.4	42.2	28.1
Other East Asian NICs	3.1	11.0	4.0	10.2
Hong Kong	2.6	6.2	2.9	2.8
Taiwan	0.2	2.8	1.1	4.5
Korea	0.2	2.0	0.1	2.9
ASEAN–4	45.9	20.3	38.2	18.0
Malaysia	35.3	13.6	20.6	14.7
Thailand	2.8	5.5	2.9	2.7
Philippines	0.4	1.3	0.2	0.6
Indonesia	7.5	n.a.	14.5	n.a.
China	0.5	3.0	4.9	3.8
Other developing countries	12.7	14.3	14.0	13.0
Other Asia	6.1	7.2	5.7	1.8
Africa	2.0	2.0	1.0	0.6
Europe[b]	0.7	0.8	0.0	0.3
Middle East	1.9	2.8	6.5	9.3
Latin America	2.1	1.5	0.8	1.1
European socialist countries	6.6	0.7	0.8	0.6

n.a. = not available.

a. Regional aggregates may not sum to 100 percent because of inclusion in the world total of special categories and other countries not specified.

b. Principally Portugal, Greece, and Turkey.

Source: International Monetary Fund, *Direction of Trade Statistics,* various issues.

ing of Singaporean political affairs, and each has had its circulation in Singapore restricted as a consequence.[6] To the extent that the free flow of information (particularly business information) is necessary for an international financial center to flourish, these restrictions can be expected to hamper Singapore's aspirations in that regard. Moreover, emigration from Singapore (reportedly concentrated among educated people) actually exceeds that from Hong Kong on a per capita basis.

Singapore's future development as an international financial center may depend at least in part on the character of the post-Lee political regime. Lee is expected to resign the prime minister's post by the end of 1990, and will be succeeded by Deputy Prime Minister Goh Chok Tong. Lee will remain in the cabinet as a "senior minister without portfolio." An expansion of the powers of the now largely ceremonial presidency is under discussion, and some observers expect that Lee will eventually seek this office.

Taiwan

Historical and Policy Background

Taiwan is a tropical island with fertile agricultural land and some mineral resources. However, the high population density of the island has encouraged specialization in manufacturing activities, initially in highly labor-intensive activities, and more recently in industries characterized by higher physical and human capital intensity. Taiwan is regarded as a province of China both by the Republic of China (ROC) government in Taipei, which maintains a claim on mainland China, and by the People's Republic of China, which maintains a counterclaim on Taiwan. Taiwan and mainland China have been politically separate since the conclusion of the Chinese revolution in December 1948.

The end of the revolution was accompanied in Taiwan by hyperinflation and a currency collapse. Beginning in 1949, the ROC government undertook a broad economic reform plan, which included a currency reform, large-scale land redistribution and reform, and a program of import-substituting indus-

---

6. A new press law passed in August 1990 requires that foreign publications with circulations of more than 300 copies that contain "news, intelligence, reports of occurrences, or any remarks, observations or comments pertaining to the politics or current affairs of any country in South-East Asia" obtain government permission to circulate in Singapore (*The Economist*, 20 October 1990, 40). The minister granting this approval may attach any condition desired (including the posting of a bond). Dow Jones & Company, owner of the *Asian Wall Street Journal* and the *Far Eastern Economic Review*, has withdrawn these publications from circulation in Singapore in protest.

trialization. The land reform was important in that it did much to equalize the distribution of income and facilitate backward and forward linkages with the manufacturing sector (Lee and Liang 1982). The entire policy package was supported by massive infusions of US aid, which during the 1950s accounted for 5 percent to 7 percent of GNP and financed nearly 40 percent of investment.

The import substitution program combined considerable trade protection for domestic manufacturers with an overvalued currency (and until 1958 a multiple exchange rate system) that discriminated against exports, which were overwhelmingly agricultural. This strategy initially promoted industrialization, but the allocative efficiency of the economy declined, as the resource allocation system discriminated among different manufacturing activities without any economic rationale, while encouraging corruption and rent-seeking behavior. By the late 1950s the import substitution program had exhausted the possibilities of the domestic market, and the growth of national income slowed. From 1958 to 1961 a reform program was introduced that included a currency devaluation and unification of the exchange rate regime, trade liberalization, and the introduction of export promotion measures, including tax incentives, preferential loans, and rebates on duties of imported intermediates (Lee and Liang 1982). Free-trade zones and bonded manufacturing warehouses were established beginning in 1965. These now account for approximately 6 percent and 14 percent of Taiwan's exports, respectively. Access to international markets was accomplished through historical ties to large Japanese trading companies, through subcontracting with foreign multinationals, and through smaller, local trading houses (Rhee 1989).

The government strategy was far from laissez-faire. It sought to roughly equalize the rates of return on sales to the domestic and foreign markets by limiting import protection while actively promoting exports (Liang 1987). Nonetheless, aspects of the import substitution approach have been maintained on a limited scale throughout the period (Hou 1987). Strategic industries have been promoted through preferential loans, tax exemptions, and special tax holidays (Balassa 1990). The establishment of high-technology firms has received additional encouragement through government-supported venture capital firms, the creation of a science park whose member firms receive additional tax and financial benefits, and programs offering economic inducements to Taiwanese abroad to return to Taiwan and establish high-technology firms. Plans for a second science park have been announced.

In this vein, foreign producers have also complained of inadequate protection of intellectual property in the form of patents, copyrights, and trademarks. The pirating of books, software, and videotapes and the infringement of pharmaceutical patents remain a problem, in the view of the Office of the US Trade Representative, because of the "ambiguous" nature of the relevant laws and lax enforcement. However, progress has been sufficient to warrant Taiwan's removal from the "priority watch list" under the Special 301 provision of the 1988 US trade act (US Trade Representative 1990).

Explicit protection has been considerably greater in agriculture. The nominal rate of protection rose steadily from 2 percent in 1970 to a peak of 52 percent in 1980, falling to 24 percent in 1989. In 1984, the most recent year for which data are available, the producer subsidy equivalents (the ratio of the domestic producer price inclusive of subsidies to the border price expressed in domestic currency units) were 1.70 for rice, 3.00 for wheat, 1.60 for coarse grains, 3.45 for sugar, 1.50 for dairy products, 1.55 for ruminant meat (beef and lamb), and 1.10 for nonruminant meat (pork and poultry; Vincent 1988, table 2).

Taiwan also maintains trade barriers in some service areas. A limited number of foreign insurance firms are allowed to enter the market each year. More generally, foreign investment outside the free-trade zones and the science park must be approved by a government commission. Restrictions on FDI are being liberalized, however. All industries except agriculture, power generation, petroleum refining, railroads, trucking, telecommunications, and those related to national defense are open to foreign investment, although in some cases (leasing companies, securities firms) limits on foreign ownership are still applied (US Trade Representative 1990).

Trade and industrial policies have been implemented in a generally stable macroeconomic environment. In the aftermath of the hyperinflation and currency collapse of 1949, economic policymakers pursued a conservative fiscal policy and an equally conservative monetary policy, with high interest rates, in contradistinction to the policies of many other developing countries at the time. The high-interest-rate policy had a number of beneficial impacts on the economy. First, the combination of low inflation and high real interest rates encouraged savers to shift their portfolios away from real assets and into financial assets, promoting the financial deepening of the economy. Second, the maintenance of equilibrium real interest rates probably raised the efficiency of investment by encouraging the allocation of capital along the lines of its economically most productive uses, and discouraging the practice of credit rationing, which tends to favor large, and politically influential, borrowers.[7] Lastly, the high-interest-rate policy encouraged the adoption of labor-intensive production methods, thus raising employment and reducing income inequality (Scitovsky 1986). In the mid-1980s, however, the emergence of a large cur-

---

7. This is not to say that credit rationing did not occur. Large firms did have preferential access to credit through the government financial institutions, but the degree of capital market distortion was probably not as great as that observed in many other developing countries.

rent account surplus and the associated sterilization of foreign-exchange inflows led to a ballooning of the money supply, an acceleration of inflation, and a runup in asset prices. In response to deteriorating domestic conditions and pressure from the United States, the monetary authorities initiated a policy of revaluing the currency.

Trade and Investment Patterns

Evidence of the remarkable changes in the Taiwanese economy can be gleaned from data on the commodity composition of output. Between 1953 and 1987, agriculture's share of GDP fell from 38.3 percent to 6.1 percent, while manufacturing's share rose from 17.7 percent to 47.5 percent, the highest in the world. Parallel to this was an extraordinary rise in the international trade share of national income. By 1987, exports accounted for 60.7 percent of GDP, with exports to the United States alone accounting for more than one quarter of domestic output. Following the appreciation of the New Taiwan (NT) dollar after 1986, growth in the traded-goods sector slowed, and manufacturing's share of output fell to 35.7 percent in 1989, while the services share rose to 17.2 percent. More detail on the changing composition of Taiwanese trade is revealed in table 2.5 (manufacturing trade shares by industry are presented in appendix B, table B.3).

The textiles, apparel, and footwear industries, traditionally important in Taiwan, increased their combined share of exports from 9.3 percent in 1963 to 22.9 percent in 1988. Export growth rates were even greater in the chemicals (mostly plastics) and engineering products industries, whose shares of total exports rose from 2.1 percent to 10.3 percent, and from 0.6 percent to 43.7 percent, respectively. Within the engineering products category, in 1988 the largest shares were accounted for by radio, television, and telecommunications equipment (10.9 percent), office and computing equipment (8.9 percent), fabricated metal products (5.5 percent), and other electrical appliances (5.1 percent). On the import side, the share of manufactured imports in total imports rose from 14.4 percent to 69.4 percent between 1963 and 1988.

Data on the geographical composition of Taiwan's trade are presented in table 2.6. What is perhaps most striking is the reversal of roles between the United States and Japan. In 1963 Japan was Taiwan's largest export market, accounting for 32.1 percent of Taiwanese exports. By 1987 this figure had fallen to 13.0 percent, while the United States had emerged as Taiwan's most important export market, absorbing 44.2 percent of Taiwanese exports, down from its peak of 48.8 percent in 1984. Over the same period, Japan supplanted the United States as the principal supplier of imports to Taiwan, with its share of Taiwan's imports rising from 30.5 percent to 34.3 percent, while the US share fell from 42.9 percent to 22.1 percent.

Table 2.5 Taiwan: composition of trade by major product group, 1963 and 1988 (percentages)

Industry	Exports		Imports	
	1963	1988	1963	1988
Fuels (SITC 3)	0.9	0.6	7.2	8.6
Nonfuel primary products	61.1	7.4	45.6	20.3
Food and live animals (SITC 0)	54.5	4.9	11.3	4.9
Beverages and tobacco (SITC 1)	0.3	0.1	1.1	0.6
Industrial raw materials (SITC 2, 4, 68)	6.3	2.4	33.1	14.8
Manufactures (industrial classification)	18.1	91.9	14.4	69.4
Textiles, apparel, and leather (ISIC 32)	9.3	22.7	0.6	3.1
Wood products and furniture (ISIC 33)	0.0	3.9	0.0	1.4
Paper and paper products (ISIC 34)	0.0	1.1	0.0	2.1
Chemicals (ISIC 35)	2.1	10.3	3.9	15.0
Nonmetallic mineral products (ISIC 36)	4.2	2.4	0.0	0.9
Iron and steel (ISIC 37)	1.8	1.6	5.5	6.3
Engineering products (ISIC 38)	0.6	43.7	4.4	39.9
Miscellaneous (ISIC 39)	0.0	6.2	0.0	0.6
Other products	19.9	0.1	32.8	1.7
Memorandum: trade in goods and nonfactor services as a share of GDP	17.8	57.0	18.9	47.4

SITC = Standard International Trade Classification.

ISIC = International Standard Industrial Classification.

Source: General Agreement on Tariffs and Trade. Memorandum data are from the World Bank.

Less dramatic shifts have been observed with respect to other countries. The importance of the other Pacific Basin developing countries as an import market has grown; their combined share of Taiwanese imports rose from 6.8 percent in 1963 to 10.0 percent in 1987. Their importance as an export market has declined, however; their combined share of Taiwan's exports fell during the period from 24.7 percent to 14.4 percent.

Meanwhile the importance of the other Pacific Basin developing countries as hosts of Taiwanese FDI has grown dramatically. The magnitude of FDI is difficult to ascertain precisely. Official statistics show that the annual FDI flow from Taiwan to the ASEAN–4 grew from $364 million in 1987 to $2.3 billion in 1988. The largest single recipient was Thailand, followed by Indonesia, Malaysia, and the Philippines. This investment is concentrated in manufacturing, mainly in textiles, footwear, electronics, and sporting goods. The official

Table 2.6 Taiwan: geographical composition of trade, 1963 and 1987[a]
(percentages)

Country	Exports		Imports	
	1963	1987	1963	1987
Developed countries	59.7	77.3	83.3	76.7
United States	16.5	44.2	42.9	22.1
Western Europe[b]	8.3	14.7	6.8	15.1
Japan	32.1	13.0	30.5	34.3
Canada, Australia, New Zealand[c]	2.8	5.4	3.0	5.2
Developing countries	40.0	21.9	16.7	22.8
Pacific countries (other than China)	24.7	14.4	6.8	10.0
Other East Asian NICs	17.0	11.4	1.4	5.1
Hong Kong	8.9	7.7	1.0	2.0
Singapore	3.3	2.5	0.2	1.5
Korea	4.8	1.2	0.2	1.5
ASEAN–4	7.7	3.0	5.4	4.9
Malaysia	2.3	0.5	1.6	2.1
Thailand	3.4	0.8	0.6	0.6
Philippines	2.0	0.9	3.2	0.6
Indonesia	0.0	0.8	0.0	1.6
China	0.0	0.0	0.0	0.0
Other developing countries	15.2	7.6	9.9	12.8
Other Asia	11.3	0.8	0.7	1.1
Africa	1.1	2.0	1.2	2.1
Europe[d]	0.0	n.a.	0.0	n.a.
Middle East	2.1	2.7	6.8	7.4
Latin America	0.7	2.0	1.3	2.2
European socialist countries	0.0	0.0	0.0	0.0

n.a. = not available.

a. Regional aggregates may not sum to 100 percent because of inclusion of a residual category in the world total.

b. All trade with Europe for 1987 is classified under Western Europe.

c. Data for 1987 are for Canada and Oceania.

d. Principally Portugal, Greece, and Turkey.

Sources: International Monetary Fund, *Direction of Trade Statistics,* various issues. Figures for 1987 are from Board of Foreign Trade, Ministry of Economic Affairs, Foreign Trade and Development of the Republic of China, 1988.

statistics probably greatly understate the actual investment flows, however, because of widespread evasion of Taiwanese regulations restricting FDI. Thailand alone, for example, approved Taiwanese investments of $2.1 billion in 1988. Unofficial estimates put Taiwanese FDI into the ASEAN–4 at well above $3 billion in 1988 (*The Economist*, 25 March 1989, 79). The partial figures available for 1989 are running even higher. In addition to these private flows, the ROC government has established a $1.2 billion development aid fund targeted at the surrounding Asian nations.

These investment outflows represent the movement offshore of labor-intensive manufacturing activities in which Taiwan is becoming internationally uncompetitive as a result of rising wage rates and currency appreciation in the wake of Taiwan's massive current account surpluses. The surpluses represent excess domestic saving, which emerged in the 1980s as investment fell while saving remained roughly constant. Investment declined from 34.3 percent of GDP in 1980 to 16.2 percent in 1986, by which time the current account surplus had grown to nearly 20 percent of GDP—probably the largest current account share of GDP ever recorded, with the possible exception of some oil producers during the heyday of OPEC. Common explanations for the fall in investment are political uncertainties caused by the US rapprochement with mainland China, and the reduction in public-sector investments (including utilities), which historically constituted a considerable share of national investment.

Current Trade and Exchange Rate Policy

Initially, in light of Taiwan's export-oriented strategy, policymakers were unwilling to revalue the currency in response to the mounting trade surpluses for fear of "dulling exports' competitive edge." Sterilization of the foreign-exchange inflow caused the money supply to grow by more than 50 percent in 1986, threatening an outbreak of inflation. The government, under pressure from both domestic critics and the United States, subsequently introduced a package of adjustment measures including import liberalization, currency appreciation, fiscal expansion, expansion of credit, and a partial relaxation of foreign-exchange controls.[8]

These policy measures have had some limited success in bringing down the current account surplus, which fell to 11.2 percent of GDP in 1989, still a very large number. There have been calls for additional measures including

---

8. For more detail on this policy package and recommendations for further adjustment measures, see Balassa and Williamson (1990).

further import liberalization, elimination of export incentives, further currency appreciation, a more expansionary fiscal policy including increased public investment, and further easing of domestic credit.

In August 1989, the ROC government reduced tariffs on 4,738 items (covering 61 percent of imports) by an average of 23 percent. This was followed by an announcement of a four-year timetable to cut tariffs further. In 1989, tariffs averaged 24.2 percent on agricultural goods and 8.0 percent on nonagricultural goods. The planned cuts would lower these to 19.8 percent for agricultural and 5.0 percent for nonagricultural goods. Cuts in later years would further lower average tariff rates on nonagricultural goods to 3.5 percent (Balassa and Williamson 1990). In addition to the scheduled tariff cuts, the number of items requiring import licenses has been cut so that 98 percent of all products can now be imported freely.

The Ministry of Economics announced in September 1990 that it was considering an acceleration of the previously announced timetable for tariff reductions. At the same time it was announced that taxes and quota restrictions on the importation of automobiles would be lifted. The single exception would be cars from Japan, which will still face import quotas and levies, as well as the requirement that Japanese exporters purchase a specified amount of Taiwanese auto parts.

Taiwan has also applied to join the General Agreement on Tariffs and Trade (GATT) under the name of "Taiwan, Penghu, Kinmen, and Matsu Customs Territory." Accession to the GATT would mean that Taiwan would automatically enjoy trade partners' tariff concessions under the most-favored-nation (MFN) rule; all such concessions at present have to be negotiated bilaterally. Conversely, Taiwan would be obliged by GATT membership to bring its tariffs that discriminate by origin, such as the discriminatory treatment of Japanese autos just noted, into line with the MFN practice. China, which is also trying to rejoin the GATT, opposes the Taiwanese bid.

In the meantime, the NT dollar has been allowed to appreciate. Since a number of Taiwan's competitors were simultaneously devaluing their currencies, in terms of the competitor-weighted index the Taiwanese REER has steadily declined, by 13.0 percent since 1980 according to the WPI-based REER, and by nearly 17 percent in export price terms (figure 2.3). However, when trading-partner weights are used the picture is less clear. The NT dollar rode the US dollar down in the middle 1980s, gaining competitiveness against the Japanese yen and other currencies. As a consequence, the trading-partner weighted REERs actually rose in 1985–86. The WPI-based REER is still above its 1980 level, and recent appreciation has only begun to depress the more narrow export price REER below its level at the start of the decade.

Figure 2.3 Taiwan: real effective exchange rates, 1970–88

1980=100

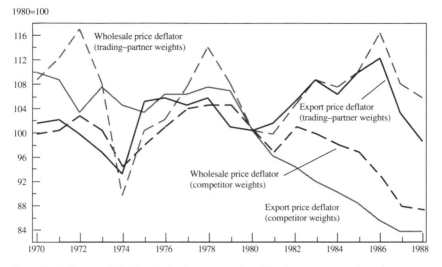

Note: The indices are defined as the local-currency price of foreign currency, so that a rise in the index signifies a depreciation.

Issues for the 1990s

Taiwan's trade liberalizations and the appreciation of the NT dollar have generated concerns that Taiwanese firms are being priced out of world markets, with potentially catastrophic effects on the national economy. In particular, some have argued that Taiwan's relatively small firms are unable to engage in the sort of investment and R&D needed to upgrade production to higher-value-added activities.

Here a comparison with Korea is instructive. Taiwanese firms are indeed small when compared to those of Korea. As Scitovsky notes:

> . . . the average Taiwanese firm in 1976 was only half as big as the Korean, with 34.6 employees compared to 68.8 in Korea. . . . The disparity in firm size between the two countries seems even greater when one looks at their largest firms. In 1981, the $10 billion gross receipts of Hyundai, Korea's largest conglomerate, were three times as big as the $3.5 billion gross receipts of Taiwan's ten largest private firms *combined*. (Scitovsky 1986, 146; italics in original)

It is less clear, however, that small size has handicapped Taiwanese firms' ability to adapt to a changing economic environment. The share of chemicals and engineering products in exports is actually slightly higher for Taiwan than for Korea. Within industries, the smaller Taiwanese firms have tended to specialize in more human capital–intensive and less physical capital–intensive activities (such as computer manufacturing and software design), whereas Korean firms have tended to specialize in more physical capital–intensive activities (such as semiconductor manufacturing). In Taiwan the development of large, physical capital–intensive projects has been accomplished largely in conjunction with foreign multinationals. Nonetheless, certain prominent economists in Taiwan have called for the government to more aggressively support R&D activities, technological upgrading, and the protection of intellectual property rights (Chen and Schive 1990), and to undertake a program to assist Taiwanese manufacturers in establishing original brand identity.

A second and related issue confronting Taiwan is the need to modernize its financial system. One of the distinguishing characteristics of corporate finance in Taiwan has been the absence of bond financing and the corresponding reliance on bank finance. The banking sector, in turn, has been dominated by large public institutions, which have been criticized for their bureaucratic and inefficient lending practices. The bureaucratic nature of the state-owned banks encourages the funneling of capital to very low risk projects and politically influential borrowers. One measure of capital market distortion is the interest rate differential between regulated and unregulated markets. Pyo (1989) presents data indicating that for the period 1974–86 the interest rate in the curb market was nearly three times that on one-year savings deposits; in 1986, the last year in his sample, the curb market rate was nearly five times the one-year deposit rate. This failure of the financial system to effectively channel capital and to intermediate between borrowers and lenders has contributed to the huge outflow of savings abroad.

In contrast to the highly regulated banking sector, the stock market is an exciting affair, characterized by lax regulatory and accounting standards, the participation of underground financial firms, insider trading, and extreme volatility. The Taipei market has also grown rapidly—in part because of the lack of alternative investment vehicles for savers—and now has a capitalization of $250 billion, making it the world's eighth largest (behind Paris and Sydney), with the third-largest daily volume (behind New York and Tokyo).

There is a compelling need to strengthen the whole financial system. Advisable reforms include expansion of the private commercial banking sector, deregulation of interest rates, a broadening of the instruments available in the money and bond markets, improvements in accounting and financial disclosure practices, and development of a reliable credit rating system. It would also be desirable to strengthen the Securities and Exchange Commission and the rules on broking practices and insider trading.

Reforms are progressing slowly. In July 1989 a new banking law was introduced which expands the role of private commercial banks by granting the first new banking licenses in 20 years. Interest rates are to be deregulated. Controls on foreign banks are to be relaxed. They will be permitted to take long-term deposits and long-term loans, thus facilitating their entry into the consumer credit market, and they will be allowed to apply for licenses to underwrite securities. Foreign banks that have been in Taiwan for more than five years will be allowed to open additional branches; at present most are limited to one. Additional reforms under consideration would allow foreign firms to own stakes in domestic banks, by participating in the development of new banks. This is viewed as a way of importing foreign management skill and experience without surrendering local control.

Other reforms under consideration would liberalize restrictions on foreign participation in the other domestic financial markets. A report by the Securities and Exchange Commission submitted to the Ministry of Economics and the Central Bank of China has recommended a phased opening of the stock market, which would eventually permit direct investment by foreign individuals, investment firms, and corporations; such investment is now restricted to closed-end mutual funds.

These changes have the potential to affect Taiwan's foreign-exchange regime. Since April 1989 the NT dollar has been floating. The market, however, is effectively limited to Taipei; existing capital controls prevent participation by offshore banks in a major way. As a consequence, trading is dominated by the four state-owned commercial banks. The major role of these public institutions, it has been argued, explains why the NT dollar's float thus far has been "the most orderly since that of the Canadian dollar in the 1950s" (Balassa and Williamson 1990, 87).

In the long run, the rapid productivity increases being achieved in the traded-goods sector imply a need for a secular real appreciation of the currency. This would be consistent with shifting the composition of output toward higher-value-added activities and reducing the external surplus, which remains large. From this standpoint, there is a need to promote net capital inflows. The relaxation of capital controls and a growing presence of private domestic and foreign banks in Taipei would promote a more genuine market determination of the exchange rate. This underlines the importance of proceeding with the modernization of the domestic financial sector; otherwise Taiwan runs the risk that, upon the relaxation of capital controls, large capital inflows would not be adequately offset by capital outflows, thus contributing to an exchange rate overshoot.

Korea

Historical and Policy Background

Like Taiwan, Korea is a densely populated country with few natural resources and subject to an abiding external security threat. The Korean peninsula was part of the Japanese empire from 1910 to 1945. At the end of World War II the peninsula was partitioned into zones of US and Soviet occupation, and in 1948 the Republic of Korea (ROK, or South Korea) was established in the US zone in the southern part of the peninsula, while the Democratic People's Republic of Korea (DPRK, or North Korea) was established under Soviet tutelage in the north. In 1950 North Korea invaded South Korea. The conflict ended in 1953 and the original borders were more or less reestablished, but the peninsula had been devastated by the fighting, and the ROK was left dependent on the United States economically and militarily.

Economic policy in the south after the war lacked any overarching rationale or coherence. A major land reform was carried on in 1954. As in Taiwan, this led to an increase in agricultural productivity as well as a broadening of economic and social opportunities in the rural areas. However, after accomplishing this reform the government undermined it by pursuing a policy of "three lows": low grain prices, a low exchange rate (i.e., an overvalued won), and low interest rates (Cho 1989). The results were recurrent balance of payments problems and misallocation of capital. The trade regime was characterized by considerable trade barriers, including an import licensing system, and multiple exchange rates for different activities; this, combined with an export-import-link system of allocating foreign exchange, encouraged rent-seeking behavior and the early growth of the giant conglomerates, or *chaebol*. The maintenance of negative real interest rates inhibited the development of the banking sector, which was permitted little freedom from government control, and encouraged the channeling of capital to large, politically influential borrowers. As one observer put it, "the basic goal of Korean economic policy was to maximize the amount of U.S. aid" (Cho 1989, chapter 2, 13), which by the end of the 1950s was financing 80 percent of Korean imports.

Economic Policy in the 1960s and 1970s

A military government under General Park Chung Hee took control in 1961. After two years of poor economic performance the military government reversed policy in 1963 and introduced its revised version of the First Five-Year Plan. The basic philosophy underlying this plan reflected a strong commitment to industrialization and an important role for the state in this process. The government would set the basic economic development goals and would selectively intervene to ensure their attainment. Although most economic activity would still be carried out by private firms, the state would complement or replace them as needed. Export targets were formulated in considerable detail by product, market, and exporting firm.

The single most important reform was the unification of the exchange rate and the devaluation of the currency in 1964. At the same time the government began to introduce a wide range of export promotion measures. A government-subsidized organization, the Korea Trade Promotion Corporation (KOTRA), patterned after the Japan Export Trade Organization (JETRO), was established to promote exports and perform market research. Exporters were provided exemptions from duties on imported intermediates, tax incentives, preferential access to capital, special depreciation allowances on imported capital equipment, and a variety of nonpecuniary awards. These, it should be noted, were calculated on the basis of gross, not net, export volumes, and thus encouraged the importation of semifinished products for assembly and reexportation.

This policy regime remained largely in place through the late 1960s and the Second Five-Year Plan. There was an expansion of export promotion measures, including generous wastage allowances on duty-free imports and reduced prices for electricity and railroad transport. The export-import-link system allowed exporters to earn rents through the importation of some restricted items. Overall, the trade regime could be characterized as modestly pro-export biased, with established industries receiving roughly neutral effective incentives while a few infant industries were actively promoted (Pack and Westphal 1986).

In 1972 General Park, who had been reelected for a third term, pushed through the "Yushin" (Revitalization) Constitution, which essentially made him president for life. To strengthen the regime's political legitimacy, economic development efforts were redoubled, and the Third Five-Year Plan was introduced. Although some of the more excessive incentive schemes were scaled down, export promotion remained the prime policy goal. Export targets were reemphasized. These targets were merely indicative, and firms failing to meet them were not subject to penalty; however, the targets were sometimes negotiated jointly with the wastage allowances, and there is some evidence that firms achieving their targeted goals could expect more favorable tax treatment (Westphal and Kim 1982).

The government also encouraged the establishment of general trading companies along Japanese lines, granting them special administrative and financial benefits and special allowances for foreign exchange. The idea was that these firms could capture scale economies in international information gathering and marketing and thus promote exports. In fact, the share of general trading company exports in total exports rose steadily, from 13.6 percent in 1975 to 51.3 percent in 1985. It is interesting to note, however, that in contrast to their Japanese counterparts, the Korean general trading companies are almost exclusively export-oriented: the proportion of trading company imports in total imports is less than 10 percent, compared with the 55 percent to 65 percent share observed in Japan (Cho 1989, chapter 3).

At the same time that trade policy was being reformed toward a more export-oriented regime, reforms were also being carried out in other areas. In 1963, the military government revised the labor laws to discourage the establishment of independent unions, instead encouraging the organization of unions within a centralized system, established so as to facilitate government control. This system was tightened further in 1971 by the introduction of legislation banning strikes and making virtually any form of collective bargaining or action illegal (Cho 1989, chapter 5; Haggard 1990).

Financial reform was begun in 1965, when interest rates were raised, encouraging saving and financial deepening as well as more efficient use of capital. The national saving rate rose from 7.4 percent of GNP in 1965 to 15.7 percent in 1970, and the ratio of M2 (a broad definition of the money supply) to GNP increased from 12.1 percent in 1965 to 35.0 percent in 1979 (Cho 1989, table 6.2). This policy was reversed in 1972, when interest rates were lowered and direct government control over the banking system was increased in order to channel capital into preferred sectors or projects. The government had earlier implemented industrial promotion policies for selected industries, but in the 1970s these efforts were intensified. In order to finance large-scale projects, special public financial institutions were established, and private commercial banks were instructed to make loans to strategic projects on a preferential basis. By the late 1970s the share of these "policy loans" in private domestic credit had risen to 60 percent (Yoo 1989). These loans carried, on average, negative real interest rates, and the annual interest subsidy grew from about 3 percent of GNP in 1962–71 to approximately 10 percent of GNP on average between 1972 and 1979 (Pyo 1989). The credit policies were augmented by extensive tax incentives for the priority industries, and it is estimated that the effect of the special tax measures was to reduce the marginal corporate tax rate from 50 percent to 20 percent for the targeted industries (Yoo 1989). These industries also received trade protection.

As a consequence of these credit, tax, and trade policies, Yoo estimates that during the late 1970s around 80 percent of fixed investment in the manufacturing sector went to the favored heavy and chemical industries (Yoo 1989). During the first three years of the Fourth Five-Year Plan (1977–81), investment in basic metals and chemicals was 130 percent and 121 percent, respectively, of the targets for the entire period, while textiles and other light industries received only 50 percent and 42 percent, respectively, of their planned investment (Balassa 1990). The detrimental impact of credit rationing was moderated by short-term foreign capital inflows and the existence of a large curb market, which provided nonpreferred customers with capital, albeit at high interest rates. Pyo (1989) reports that, between 1974 and 1986, nominal interest rates on one-year saving deposits averaged 14.4 percent, while the curb market rate averaged 35.0 percent.

These policies gave rise to serious moral hazard problems, as the large *chaebol* could undertake ever-larger investments, confident that the government would not permit large projects in priority sectors to fail. As a consequence, between 1978 and 1985 the share of the five largest firms in manufacturing shipments rose from 15.7 percent to 23.0 percent (Cho 1989, chapter 4). The system encouraged the *chaebol* to diversify by offsetting possible losses in some ventures with secure profits from others. As might be expected, allocative efficiency declined, and the marginal product of capital was lower in the favored sectors throughout the 1970s (Yoo 1989).[9]

Policy Reforms in the 1980s

It is difficult to assess the welfare implications of the industrial promotion policies of the late 1970s in the absence of evidence on what would have occurred in the absence of the interventions. Nonetheless, the fall in allocative efficiency and the relatively weak export performance of Korea relative to similarly endowed economies have led even ardent proponents of the interventionist strategy (e.g., Pack and Westphal 1986) to conclude that the policy of promoting heavy industry and chemicals was a failure. There were also undesirable macroeconomic effects: the expansionary credit policy aggravated inflation, while low real interest rates encouraged disintermediation and stagnation of the financial sector. By 1978 the economy was overheating, and in the following year the policy began to be scaled back; this process received further impetus with the 1979 oil price shock and the assassination of President Park. Yoo (1989) goes so far as to argue that the reversal of the heavy and chemical industries policy was the greatest policy achievement of the period.

This policy shift was ratified in the Fifth Five-Year Plan (1982–86), which marked a movement away from the interventionist strategy. The increases in

---

9. Leipziger (1988, 124) argues that these policies have left Korea in a difficult position: government policy has encouraged entry into selected sectors and the growth of the *chaebol*, but "Korea has no satisfactory 'exit policy' and no institutions capable of managing it." In the absence of a strong financial sector capable of managing restructurings, the government has been forced into playing this role itself, in effect socializing risk and validating the very moral hazards it has sought to discourage. Indeed, for this reason Leipziger identifies strengthening the banking sector as the foremost item on Korea's policy agenda.

trade protection that had accompanied the industrial promotion policies of the late 1970s were reversed. The government undertook a liberalization of the financial sector. Commercial banks were denationalized, but the state retained the right to appoint boards of directors and senior officers. There was, however, an easing of direct government control of banks and nonbank financial institutions. The share of "policy loans" in domestic credit was reduced from approximately 45 percent in the period 1974–82 to 35 percent in 1983–88, and commercial banks were required to extend at least 35 percent of their loans to small and medium-sized firms, to compensate for the effects of the earlier policy. Interest rates were deregulated, and the economy experienced considerable financial deepening, as the ratio of M2 to GNP increased from an average of 30.6 percent in 1979–82 to 39.6 percent in 1988 (Nam 1989).

By 1986 the negative shocks of the early 1980s had been reversed, and Korea was experiencing the "three blessings": the fall in oil prices, the fall in world interest rates, and the appreciation of the Japanese yen. The Sixth Five-Year Plan (1987–91) reinforced the trend toward liberalization, which was accelerated further under pressure from the United States. Average tariff rates were reduced from 23.7 percent in 1983 to 12.7 percent in 1989; additional cuts to 7.9 percent were originally planned for 1993 but have been postponed for a year. This would reduce the average tariff on manufactures to 6.2 percent, a level comparable to those observed in the United States (6.1 percent) and the European Community (6.7 percent; Balassa and Williamson 1990). Korea has also lowered, by as much as 30 percent, special luxury taxes that had the effect of repressing imports.

Accompanying the tariff cuts have been reductions in quantitative barriers. The percentage of product categories not covered by any quantitative import restrictions (the liberalization ratio) has risen from 80.4 percent in 1983 to 94.7 percent in 1989. These figures mask, however, considerable differences in the distribution of restrictions between manufactured and agricultural products. For 1989 the liberalization ratio for manufactures was 99.4 percent, while the figure for agriculture was 72 percent (Young 1989). These agricultural barriers appear to have had a significant impact on trade flows. In 1984, the most recent year for which data are available, the producer subsidy equivalents (calculated as for Taiwan above) were 3.05 for rice, 1.10 for wheat, 2.35 for coarse grains, 4.20 for sugar, 2.00 for dairy products, 3.25 for ruminant meat, and 1.30 for nonruminant meat (Vincent 1988, table 2). Elimination of this protection would be expected to more than double agricultural imports, with cereals (mainly rice) accounting for most of the increase (Vincent 1988, table 4). The Korean government has committed itself to raising the agricultural liberalization ratio to 85 percent by the end of 1991.

The Korean government is also in the process of reviewing a variety of laws and regulations—such as the administration of import licenses; standards, testing, and certification requirements; and quarantine inspections—which although not designed to restrict imports may have that practical effect. In 1986, when the government began its review, these special laws covered 26 percent of import categories; by the end of 1988, coverage had been reduced to 19 percent (Young 1989).

Trade reform has also been pursued in other areas. New patent and copyright laws have been enacted and resources devoted to enforcement have been increased, and Korea was removed from the "priority watch list" under the Special 301 provision of the 1988 US trade act. Restrictive policies toward inward FDI have been significantly liberalized. In the services sector, the life insurance market has been open to foreign investors since 1986, advertising and motion picture distribution since 1987, and shipping since 1988. Restrictions on wholesaling and retailing remain in a number of sectors, but the government is committed to a liberalization schedule. Restrictions on telecommunications services are under negotiation. Although there has been a substantial move toward nominal liberalization in these sectors, genuine liberalization has been considerably impeded by government regulation and imperfectly competitive markets.

In this regard, trade liberalization not only plays its conventional role of improving the efficiency of resource allocation, but importantly may serve as a check on the exercise of market power by the giant *chaebol*, which have disproportionately received trade protection in the past.

Parallel with deprotection have been reductions in export incentives.[10] The tariff drawback system on imported inputs and the exemption of exports from the value-added tax, which allow exporters to operate under internationally competitive conditions, remain. The government continues to offer long-term credit at international interest rates (which are significantly below domestic interest rates) to finance the exportation of ships, industrial plants, and other large projects with long lead times, again presumably to allow domestic firms to compete on equal terms with their foreign competitors. Two other provisions, namely, automatic preferential credit allocations for export production and special export-related tax provisions, contain elements of export subsidy. The government has begun to phase out the preferential credit scheme, and it has excluded large firms as beneficiaries since 1988. Reduc-

---

10. However, following the cabinet reshuffle of 1990 and the first-quarter decline in the trade surplus, the press began reporting the increasing use of government administrative guidance to discourage imports, and the reintroduction of export incentive measures (*Washington Post*, 6 June 1990; *Wall Street Journal*, 12 June 1990; *The Economist*, 18 August 1990; *Los Angeles Times*, 11 September 1990). President Roh Tae Woo denied any such policy change during his June 1990 meeting with the EC ambassadors to Korea and on his visit to Washington, however.

tions in tax preferences are under discussion (Young 1989).

At the same time, Korea faces significant barriers to its exports. The most important of these is the Multi-Fiber Arrangement. According to Trela and Whalley (1988), elimination of the bilateral quotas alone would lead to a 185 percent increase in Korea's textile and apparel exports. Elimination of all tariffs and quotas would lead to a 241 percent increase. Like the MFA, most other significant trade restraints take the form of so-called voluntary export restraints (VERs). At present Korea faces bilateral VERs in eight product categories.[11] These, together with other nontariff barriers, affect more than 20 percent of exports (Young 1989).

The trend of continued liberalization was also apparent in the financial sector. The deregulation of banks and nonbank financial institutions, together with the growth of the stock and bond markets, has led to the withering of the curb market, which now accounts for less than 10 percent of domestic credit. The stock and bond markets have grown despite tax laws that encourage debt over equity finance. The stock market, after languishing for many years, took off in 1986, and capitalization increased 10-fold between 1986 and 1989. With a capitalization of approximately $100 billion, the Korean stock market is now the 10th largest in the world, although it is less than half the size of the market in Taiwan (the eighth largest).

Foreign participation in Korean financial markets is limited. Foreign banks' activities are restricted, although they are now allowed to open multiple branches. Investment by foreigners is limited to indirect investment in two mutual funds, seven unit trusts, and convertible bonds issued by seven Korean firms. Foreign securities firms have been permitted to own up to 10 percent of the paid-in capital of Korean securities firms, and in 1991 they will be allowed to establish branch offices or joint ventures. A timetable has been announced that would permit foreigners to purchase Korean stocks, and domestic residents to own foreign stocks, by 1992.

Output, Investment, and Trade Patterns

The transformation wrought by Korea's economic policies over the postwar decades can be seen in the data on industrial composition. The most obvious change is the enormous fall in agriculture's share of output, from 43.4 percent in 1963 to 11.4 percent in 1987. Conversely, manufacturing's share has risen from 14.7 percent to 30.3 percent over the period. The share of exports in

---

11. These are cutlery (Germany, United Kingdom, and the Benelux countries), silk products (Japan), tuna (Japan), footwear (Ireland, United Kingdom, Italy), steel (European Community, United States), color televisions (United Kingdom), stoneware (United Kingdom), and knitwear (Japan).

GDP has increased from 4.8 percent in 1963 to a peak of 42.0 percent in 1987, falling to 35.4 percent in 1988, while the import share has doubled from 15.9 percent in 1963 to 34.4 percent in 1987, dropping to 28.7 percent in 1988. These data indicate the dramatic opening of the Korean economy during this period.

The question naturally arises as to what explains the explosive growth of exports. Some industrialization occurred during the Japanese colonial period, and the Koreans were able to maintain some production in all sectors after the Japanese withdrawal, indicating that Korea had acquired a substantial base of relevant skills during the colonial period (Westphal et al. 1981). The Koreans were able to further expand their skill base through cooperation with the United States. American aid directly contributed to the rapid expansion of education within Korea and made overseas education and training possible for thousands of Koreans (Westphal et al. 1981). Some transfer of technical skills and management techniques through close contact with US military forces undoubtedly occurred, but its significance is difficult to assess. Likewise, local firms certainly benefited from participation in local military procurement programs and, later, from offshore procurement programs during the Vietnam War (Rhee 1989).

Foreign direct investment, however, does not appear to have been an important contributor to Korea's export success. Most foreign investment in Korea took the form of commercial loans, not direct investment, and even if it were assumed that all FDI went into the manufacturing sector, it would have accounted for less than 5 percent of the manufacturing capital stock in 1970 (Westphal and Kim 1982). Indeed, FDI flows into Korea were small relative to those experienced by other developing countries such as Brazil, Mexico, and Taiwan, and there does not appear to be any strong correlation between the sectors that attracted FDI and those that enjoyed subsequent export success. Similarly, the evidence on the importance of technological licensing in spurring exports is mixed (Westphal et al. 1981).

Subcontracting not related to FDI and contact with foreign trading companies may have been of greater importance. Westphal et al. (1981) give several examples of foreign buyers assisting Korean exporters with product design and process technology.

What is apparent, however, is the fact that, through whatever channels, the Koreans attained a certain level of technological and managerial competence, providing a basis for the exploitation of international trade opportunities.[12] Government policy attempted to develop this base through a vari-

---

12. Kwon (1986) reports that total factor productivity growth in manufacturing averaged 3 percent a year between 1961 and 1980. According to his model, 45 percent of this can be attributed to technical change, 38 percent to scale economies, and 17 percent

ety of supportive measures. Starting in the mid-1960s, potential exporters were granted access to inputs at world market prices, and to trade finance through the mechanisms previously described, which were administered in a relatively nondiscretionary and automatic way. Free-trade zones, introduced in the 1970s, appear to have been of little importance, generating only 2.8 percent of total exports. Bonded warehouses appear to have been somewhat more important, accounting for 12 percent of exports and 6 percent of imports (Rhee 1989). The exchange rate was kept competitive, if not artificially high. Korea also benefited from the rapid growth of world markets during the postwar decades. Changes in the composition of trade have been astounding (table 2.7; manufacturing trade shares by industry are presented in appendix B, table B.4). In 1963, nonfuel primary products accounted for 50.0 percent of Korean exports; by 1987 this figure had fallen to 6.1 percent. At the same time the share of manufactures nearly doubled, from 46.6 percent to 91.9 percent. Within manufactures, textiles, apparel, and leather had the largest share (14.8 percent) in 1963. This share peaked at 40.0 percent in the early 1970s before declining to 31.7 percent in 1987. Engineering products, which generated only 5.7 percent of exports in 1963, increased their share to 41.9 percent in 1987, with radio and television equipment (16.3 percent of total exports) and motor vehicles (6.9 percent) making up the greater part of this category. Manufactures have accounted for an increasing share of imports as well, growing from 49.8 percent in 1963 to 64.7 percent in 1987. This growth is due in large part to Korea's dependence on imported capital equipment, as well as to the export incentive policies, which have encouraged the importation of semifinished products for assembly and reexportation.

In 1963 Japan was Korea's largest export market, accounting for 28.6 percent of Korean exports, with the United States a close second at 28.1 percent (table 2.8). By 1988 the United States was by far the most important export market, absorbing 35.4 percent of Korean exports, far greater than the share of Japan, which has become Korea's second-largest market. The other Pacific Basin countries have declined in importance as export markets, falling from a 17.3 percent collective share in 1963 to a 12.5 percent share in 1988 (although in absolute terms exports to these countries have risen considerably).

On the import side, the United States supplied more than half of Korean imports in 1963. This share has fallen steadily: in 1988 the United States was Korea's second-largest supplier of imports, accounting for 24.8 percent. Japan is now the largest source of imports, providing nearly a third of the total. As a consequence of these trade patterns, Korea maintains a large trade surplus

---

to the growth of capital utilization.

with the United States while running a large deficit with Japan. This has become a policy concern in Korea, and the government has undertaken a number of policies to reduce its bilateral imbalances.

Korea's overall current account balance registered a $4.6 billion surplus in 1986, its first since 1978. The surplus grew to $9.9 billion in 1987, and $14.1 billion in 1988, before declining to $4.7 billion in 1989. The emergence of these surpluses was initially ascribed to the declines in oil prices and world interest rates, but it soon became apparent that the predominant cause was a rise in exports associated with a real depreciation of the won. Balassa and Williamson (1987) called for a revaluation of the won on the grounds that sustained capital outflows from a capital-scarce country violate basic precepts of neoclassical welfare economics; they recommended that Korea target a current account deficit of around $2 billion. This view was rejected by others, including Dornbusch and Park (1987), who argued that for reasons of risk aversion, and given the prospect of a reduction in the demand for Korean exports associated with changes in US fiscal policy, a small surplus was desirable. The possible negative impact on the Korean trade balance due to a $100 billion reduction in the US trade deficit would be on the order of $4.5 billion (Balassa and Williamson 1990); this suggests that maintenance of a surplus of this magnitude in excess of the target could be defensible.

Exchange Rates

The emergence of current account surpluses and the pronounced bilateral imbalances with the United States and Japan have focused attention on the Korean exchange rate regime. The US Treasury in its first three semiannual reports to the Congress on international economic and exchange rate policy (1988–89) accused Korea of "exchange rate manipulation" for the purpose of preventing balance of payments adjustment or gaining unfair advantage in international trade (see, e.g., US Treasury 1989). Korea was belatedly removed from the list of "exchange rate manipulators" in the Treasury's fourth report in April 1990. In theory, the won is pegged to a basket of the currencies that constitute the special drawing right (i.e., the currencies of the Group of Five major industrialized nations; the weights of these currencies in the basket are undisclosed), plus a "policy adjustment" factor. In reality, the policy adjustment factor has been predominant, as the won depreciated against all five currencies in the basket between 1984 and April 1987 (Balassa and Williamson 1990). The Korean government has committed itself to opening capital markets and allowing the won to float by 1992; the US Treasury notwithstanding, the real issues are whether the currency is correctly valued and how to secure greater transparency in exchange rate management.

Table 2.7 Korea: composition of trade by major product group, 1963 and 1987 (percentages)

Industry	Exports		Imports	
	1963	1987	1963	1987
Fuels (SITC 3)	3.4	1.5	6.1	14.3
Nonfuel primary products	50.0	6.1	42.9	20.8
Food and live animals (SITC 0)	21.6	4.3	21.4	6.2
Beverages and tobacco (SITC 1)	0.0	0.2	0.0	0.0
Industrial raw materials (SITC 2, 4, 68)	28.4	1.6	21.4	14.6
Manufactures (industrial classification)	46.6	91.9	49.8	64.7
Textiles, apparel, and leather (ISIC 32)	14.8	31.7	5.3	5.3
Wood products and furniture (ISIC 33)	6.8	0.8	0.0	0.4
Paper and paper products (ISIC 34)	0.0	1.2	0.5	2.0
Chemicals (ISIC 35)	3.4	6.7	14.5	12.5
Nonmetallic mineral products (ISIC 36)	1.1	1.4	1.1	1.1
Iron and steel (ISIC 37)	13.6	5.1	5.9	4.6
Engineering products (ISIC 38)	5.7	41.9	22.3	38.4
Miscellaneous (ISIC 39)	1.1	3.1	0.2	0.5
Other products	0.0	0.4	1.2	0.2
Memorandum: trade in goods and nonfactor services as a share of GDP	4.8	42.0	15.9	34.4

SITC = Standard International Trade Classification.

ISIC = International Standard Industrial Classification.

Source: General Agreement on Tariffs and Trade. Memorandum data are from the World Bank.

As figure 2.4 shows, on a trading-partner basis the Korean REER increased by either 30 percent or 65 percent between 1980 and 1986, depending on the measure used. Subsequent nominal appreciation and the slowing of US dollar depreciation generated a significant real appreciation of the won in 1987 and 1988, partly reversing the earlier depreciation. A similar pattern is evident with respect to the competitor-weighted export price–based REER. Although this measure of the Korean REER declined rapidly in 1987 and 1988, this merely offset the earlier depreciation, and in export price terms the won was actually weaker in 1988 than it was at the beginning of the decade.

As in the case of Taiwan, rapid productivity growth in the traded-goods sector implies the need for secular real appreciation of the won in the long run. In the short run, however, the real exchange rate may fluctuate around this long-run path. As a consequence, the need for long-run appreciation does

Table 2.8   Korea: geographical composition of trade, 1963 and 1988[a]
(percentages)

Country	Exports 1963	Exports 1988	Imports 1963	Imports 1988
Developed countries	65.7	75.1	90.1	75.4
United States	28.1	35.4	51.0	24.8
Western Europe	8.7	15.5	7.3	13.6
Japan	28.6	19.8	29.2	30.8
Canada, Australia, New Zealand	0.3	4.4	2.6	6.2
Developing countries	33.9	23.1	9.7	18.8
Pacific countries (other than China)	17.3	12.5	7.5	8.6
Other East Asian NICs	12.4	9.7	4.3	3.5
Hong Kong	10.5	5.9	1.1	1.1
Singapore	0.8	2.2	0.5	0.8
Taiwan	1.1	1.6	2.7	1.5
ASEAN–4	4.8	2.8	3.2	5.2
Malaysia	n.a.	0.7	0.4	2.6
Thailand	1.8	0.9	0.3	0.5
Philippines	3.0	0.6	2.2	0.4
Indonesia	n.a.	0.7	0.3	1.8
China	n.a.	0.0	n.a.	0.0
Other developing countries	16.7	10.6	2.2	10.2
Other Asia	16.6	2.0	1.7	1.3
Africa	0.1	1.3	0.1	0.5
Europe[b]	n.a.	0.6	n.a.	0.2
Middle East	n.a.	4.2	n.a.	5.4
Latin America	n.a.	2.5	0.4	2.8
European socialist countries	n.a.	0.0	n.a.	0.0

n.a. = not available.

a. Regional aggregates may not sum to 100 percent because of inclusion in the world total of special categories and other countries not specified.

b. Principally Portugal, Greece, and Turkey.

Sources: International Monetary Fund. *Direction of Trade Statistics,* various issues.

not imply the desirability of real appreciation at any given time. Indeed, the recent experience of more rapid decline in the real, as opposed to the nominal, exchange rate highlights the inadequacy of current policy discussions: the US Treasury focuses solely on the nominal exchange rate and ignores the repercussions of labor market developments that affect the real exchange rate; meanwhile the Korean side focuses solely on the bilateral dollar rate.

Figure 2.4 Korea: real effective exchange rates, 1970–88

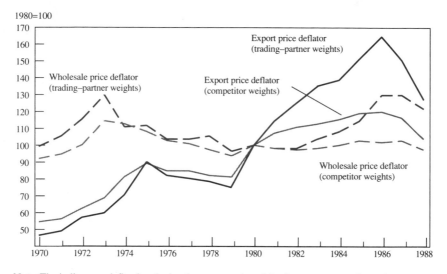

Note: The indices are defined as the local-currency price of foreign currency, so that a rise in the index signifies a depreciation.

Issues for the 1990s

As mentioned earlier, independent trade unions were effectively banned in 1971. The Korean labor movement subsequently developed a dualistic structure, with government-approved unions on the one hand and informal or underground unions on the other. The labor laws were revised in the early 1980s, but the reforms did not adequately address this situation. The official unionization rate fell from 20 percent of the force in 1980 to 15.7 percent in 1985, as workers became increasingly disaffected with the officially approved unions (Cho 1989). The labor laws underwent further revisions in 1986 and 1987, partially liberalizing unionization in the context of political democratization.

The result was an explosion of repressed discontent. The number of labor-management disputes surged from 276 in 1986 to 3,749 in 1987, 1,873 in 1988, and 1,166 in 1989. Resolution of these disputes was impeded by the coexistence of *de jure* and *de facto* unions, and by the desire of public officials to minimize the problems. Accordingly, various legal and extralegal means were used to settle the disputes, sometimes causing conflicts and distrust to spread (Cho 1989). The problems were exacerbated by the fact that many of the disputes involved the oligopolistic *chaebol*. As a consequence, the negotiations could be likened to those between bilateral monopolists, and thus involved the disposition of potentially enormous economic rents. The high stakes, the broad diversification of the *chaebol* (which obscures the relationship between the economic viability of an individual enterprise and that of the firm as a whole), and the inexperience of the negotiators on both sides are all factors that have contributed to difficulties in resolving these disputes. The creation and institutionalization of peaceful and equitable labor market dispute-resolution mechanisms is the single most important challenge on the Korean policy agenda.

Adding to these problems has been an explosion of asset, especially land, prices. This has led to growing wealth inequality, which, along with the labor market problems, threatens to undermine the social compact. Concern over income inequality and the conspicuous consumption of imports has also been cited as a motivation behind the government's recent anti-import campaign, and thus has direct relevance to the outside world. As in the case of Taiwan, the most appropriate policy response is to attack these domestic problems directly: by modernizing domestic financial markets to reduce asset price volatility, and by introducing domestic tax reforms to deal with income and wealth inequality.

3

The ASEAN–4

Compared with the NICs, the ASEAN–4 (Malaysia, Thailand, the Philippines, and Indonesia) have plentiful natural resources, whose exploitation has played an understandably larger role in their economic development. Today the ASEAN–4 are emerging as manufacturers in their own right, in part spurred by the relocation of labor-intensive manufacturing activities from the NICs and Japan. Each of the four must now manage the transition from a natural resource–based economy to an efficient manufacturer able to compete in the world economy. The success of this transition will in part be determined by the widely differing histories and endowments of each of the countries. Indeed, as much of Malaysia's and Indonesia's resource endowments are located in some of the world's largest remaining tropical rain forests, it is likely that the rest of the world will take an increasingly keen interest in their future development choices.

Malaysia

Historical and Policy Background

Malaysia is a federation of 13 states. Eleven are in the Malay Peninsula and collectively comprise West Malaysia, where roughly 85 percent of the population lives. The other two states, Sabah and Sarawak, are located on the northern part of the island of Borneo, more than 400 miles east across the South China Sea.

For centuries the Malay Peninsula was a transit zone for maritime commerce between China and India. Various groups successively ruled the peninsula, and in the late 1700s the British began establishing settlements there. The discovery of rich tin deposits around 1850 started an economic and social transformation of the peninsula. Large numbers of Chinese immigrants were brought in to work in the mines, and the British established a system of indirect rule through the local Malay sultans. A second wave of immigration, this time from India, began in the late 1800s with the successful introduction of the rubber tree and the establishment of rubber plantations.

Subsequent growth was concentrated in the mining and rubber-growing regions. Despite the intensification of economic activities in these areas, little internal migration occurred and there was scant intermingling of immigrant and indigenous groups. At the time of independence in 1957, the population distribution of West Malaysia was 50.8 percent Malay, 37.9 percent Chinese, and 11.3 percent Indian. The Malays were disproportionately concentrated in farming; the Chinese in mining, financial services, and manufacturing; and the Indians in rubber cultivation and public-sector activities. Chinese and Indian per capita incomes were considerably higher than that of the Malays (Spinanger 1986).

In the runup to independence, the United Malays National Organization (UMNO) opposed common citizenship for Malays and non-Malays. Eventually a social compact was reached in which Malays would maintain their political predominance while the other groups would be free to pursue their economic and religious activities without hindrance. The constitution gave common citizenship to all residents but made Islam the national religion, granted certain political powers to the Malay sultans, and gave Malays preferential access to the civil service. This modus vivendi worked for a time, but race relations eventually deteriorated, culminating in the 1969 race riots, which resulted in the suspension of the national parliament and state assemblies and the imposition of a state of emergency (Anand 1983).

Malaysia has the most unequal income distribution of the Pacific Basin developing countries (table 1.4), and as a consequence, distributional issues are central to Malaysian economic policy. Since 1971, policy has been explicitly oriented toward the improvement of the indigenous peoples, the *bumiputra*. Although there has been some improvement in the relative position of the *bumiputra* (see Balassa 1990), the gains have fallen short of expectations, and it is likely that distributional issues will remain central to the formation of policy in Malaysia.

Malaysia has abundant natural resources. In addition to its tin mines and rubber plantations, it has palm plantations producing palm oil, paddy land used for rice cultivation, and extensive tropical forests, plus oil and natural gas. Historically these natural resource industries have dominated the economy. At the time of independence, tin and rubber alone accounted for about 80 percent of exports and 30 percent of GDP. Less than 10 percent of GDP originated in the manufacturing sector (Spinanger 1986).

Industrialization received its first push in 1958, when the government enacted the Pioneer Industries Ordinance. This legislation granted a three- to five-year corporate income tax holiday, tax exemptions on dividends to shareholders, and accelerated capital depreciation to manufacturing firms qualifying as pioneer enterprises. The effect of these provisions was to promote manufacturing activities and the adoption of capital-intensive techniques of production. Ironically, the ordinance also had the effect of exacerbating regional and racial income disparities, because the new manufacturing establishments located primarily in urban areas where the necessary skilled labor and physical infrastructure already existed (Spinanger 1986).

The government's industrial estate policy reinforced this tendency toward the concentration of manufacturing activities. Beginning in 1958, the government began constructing industrial estates, providing developed sites with utilities and transportation links and offering long-term leases. All of these were located around urban areas with above-average income levels (Spinanger 1986). The government also created several development boards and financial institutions to promote industrialization.

Initially the growth of manufacturing output was quite rapid. However, the rate of real fixed-capital investment began falling in the early 1960s, and in 1968 the government enacted the Investment Incentives Act, which still serves as the basis for investment incentives. The legislation extended the previous pioneer manufacturing industries legislation to any commercial undertaking, and it established conditions under which firms could qualify for extended tax holidays. An "increased capital allowance" and additional accelerated depreciation provisions were introduced (Balassa 1990).

Having subsidized the use of capital, the authorities then set about offsetting this policy by subsidizing the use of labor. The 1971 Labor Utilization Relief Act stipulated that investment incentives would be granted according to the number of jobs created. Additional tax exemptions were tied to location in targeted regional development areas (Spinanger 1986).

Following the race riots and political crisis of 1969, the government announced a New Economic Policy (NEP), embodied in the Second Malaysia Plan put forth in 1971. This policy identified the goals of "eradicating poverty irrespective of race, and restructuring Malaysian society to reduce and eventually eliminate the identification of race with economic function" (quoted in Spinanger 1986, 62). The NEP established the target of 30 percent *bumiputra* ownership of all commercial enterprises by 1991. This was to be accomplished through an affirmative action program of subsidies, quotas, scholarships, investment licensing, and rural development. The government also began establishing what became a plethora of nonfinancial public enterprises (NFPEs), which were intended to "hold in trust" newly acquired economic wealth on behalf of the *bumiputra* until such time as they were in a position to control it themselves.

In the early 1980s the government shifted the emphasis of these parastatal enterprises to heavy industry, establishing two petroleum refineries, a petrochemical complex, a methanol plant, a urea-ammonia plant, two cement plants, two sponge iron plants, a cold rolling steel mill, a paper pulp plant, and an automobile factory to produce the Malaysian car, the Proton Saga (Balassa 1990). The government used the Employee Provident Fund (EPF) as a source of forced saving to fund these endeavors.

Established in 1951, the EPF is a retirement trust funded by contributions from both employers and employees. The rate of contribution has risen from 10 percent of wages (with the employer and employee each contributing half) during 1951–75 to 20 percent (11 percent from the employer and 9 percent from the employee) since then. By law the EPF must invest most (at present 70 percent) of its funds in government securities (Institute of International Finance 1990).

As the government's demand for capital increased, the financial system was forced to move toward forms of credit rationing. The financial sector at this time was relatively well developed by developing-country standards. At the time of independence the financial system consisted of a currency board, some trading banks, and a postal saving system. In 1959 Bank Negara was established as the central bank. The following year a local stock market was created in Singapore, and a development bank was established. Commercial banks and finance companies soon began operation. In 1960, the share of M2 in GDP was 24.2 percent, the highest among the Pacific Basin developing countries for which data from that period are available. The total assets of the financial system were equivalent to 53 percent of GDP (Institute of International Finance 1990). Consequently, in 1975 when Bank Negara was forced to begin channeling capital into the government's priority sectors, it did so by issuing guidelines to the private-sector financial institutions stipulating minimum portfolio allocations for the priority areas, thereby preserving market-based lending criteria.

Nonetheless, the government began encountering problems with the proliferating NFPEs. By 1988, the government held an interest in 745 NFPEs and 102 financial institutions and was the majority owner in 565 of these, with investments of 12,531 million ringgit (M$), or 15.4 percent of GNP. Nearly half (383) of the NFPEs had accumulated losses of M$5,610 million (6.9 percent of GNP; Institute of International Finance 1990). The reasons for this poor performance include weak management and overexposure to foreign-currency liabilities, especially yen-denominated loans. There have been some spectacular failures. The M$1,200 million steel plant is the biggest NFPE. Originally Heavy Industries Corp. of Malaysia, a government trustee agency, owned 51 percent of the operation; a Japanese consortium led by Nippon Steel Corp. owned 30 percent, and the remaining 19 percent was held by the Terenggamu state government. The plant was to use a new steelmaking technology developed by Nippon Steel, but the plant was never able to produce output according to specifications. Eventually the Japanese consortium sold its share of the operation to the Malaysian government for a nominal 1 ringgit and paid M$56 million (the cost of the plant) in compensation. Annual debt-servicing costs on the largely idle plant are M$100 million. Another money loser has been the urea-ammonia plant, which has generated M$100 million in foreign-exchange losses alone.

In response to these disasters, in the Industrial Master Plan (IMP) for 1985–95 the government reoriented its industrial policy away from heavy-industry, import-substitution projects and toward building on the natural resource base. Products such as cocoa butter, frozen prawns and shrimps, and wood panel products have been identified as priority products expected to make significant contributions to employment, value added, and exports. The plan envisages exploiting foreign capital, technology, and marketing networks extensively in developing these industries. These goals and some of the distributional targets of the NEP may conflict, however.

The NEP equity participation guidelines limit foreign ownership in the corporate sector to 30 percent in 1991, although this and other investment restrictions are regularly waived in return for investor acceptance of performance requirements. A study found that 90 percent of surveyed investors supported the basic goals of the NEP, but nearly all of them "voiced reservations on the inconsistencies, deviations and timing of implementation, administrative pressures and vagueness of guidelines in discussion with various officials and the frequent piecemeal imposition of changes" (Kamal et al. 1988, 110). For example, under current policies certain performance requirements may be waived for new but not for existing investors, and for foreign but not for domestic investors.

Historically, foreign investors have been attracted to Malaysia's natural resource sectors. More recently, Malaysia has had to compete with the other Pacific Basin developing countries for foreign direct investment in the manufacturing sector. After exceeding $1 billion annually in 1981–83, FDI inflows fell steadily, reaching a trough of $423 million in 1987. In 1988 inflows of FDI rebounded to $649 million.[1] Malaysia has done a reasonably good job of attracting FDI from the United States and Japan: it attracted the most US FDI of the ASEAN–4 economies in 1988, and among the ASEAN–4 it was behind only Indonesia in attracting Japanese FDI.

In total, the government's investment incentives have encouraged large-scale, capital-intensive, domestically oriented investment and implicitly

---

1. International Monetary Fund, *International Financial Statistics*, various issues.

discouraged the development of labor-intensive export industries. When confronted with evidence of the inadequate performance of these firms, the authorities' response has been to try and steer investment in the desired direction by enacting additional incentive and performance schemes, rather than by liberalizing the existing structure.

Trade Policies

Although they have had an impact on Malaysia's trade structure, for the most part these industrial policies have not discriminated between foreign and domestic sales. Prior to independence in 1957, tariffs, the sole explicit trade policy tool, were used primarily for revenue purposes. The adoption of more-protectionist policies was opposed on the grounds that nonindigenous groups would be the chief beneficiaries (Ariff and Hill 1985). After independence there was some support for using tariff protection to support industrialization, and a Tariff Advisory Committee was formed in 1959. The government was relatively cautious in extending protection, however, and in 1963–65 nominal tariffs averaged between 10 percent and 12 percent, corresponding to average effective rates of protection (ERPs) of 22 percent to 25 percent (Lee 1986). Except for tobacco products, which were assessed high tariffs for revenue purposes, tariffs on manufactured goods were somewhat lower, with nominal tariffs averaging 7 percent and effective rates averaging 12 percent in 1965 (Power 1971a).

In the first Malaysia Plan (1966–70), the government made its first commitment to use tariff protection to promote infant manufacturing industries. This was followed by a period of moderate import substituting trade policy. In 1967 a 2 percent surtax was levied on all imports, and the duty on imported automobiles was raised from 5 percent to 35 percent (Balassa 1990). Quantitative import restrictions were used for the first time as well.

In a partial reversal of this policy, the government began enacting export promotion measures in the early 1970s. These included the establishment of a duty drawback system, licensed manufacturing warehouses, and free-trade zones, to assure exporters of access to inputs at world prices. Use of the duty drawback system has been hampered, however, by long bureaucratic delays.

Probably the most important of these initiatives was the establishment of the free-trade zones, which by the late 1980s accounted for more than half of Malaysia's manufactured exports. Benefits to firms locating in the zones have included the duty-free importation of inputs, streamlined customs procedures, fully developed infrastructure, and long-term site leases at below-market rates (Balassa 1990). The zones have been used mainly by foreign multinationals for electronics assembly operations. Consequently, backward and forward linkages with the rest of the economy have been minimal: for example, only about 3 percent of the material inputs used in the Penang free-trade zone were procured domestically in the mid-1980s (Kamal et al. 1988). Moreover, since most of the zones are located in areas where industrial estates already existed, they have tended to reinforce regional disparities in income and opportunity. Nonetheless, cost-benefit analyses suggest that the free-trade zones have been qualified successes. Warr (1987) calculated that they and the licensed warehouses are a net benefit to the Malaysian economy, largely because of their substantial contributions to employment and foreign-exchange earnings; on the other hand, a World Bank–sponsored study concluded that "the net present value of the Malaysian [free-trade zone] investments may well be negligible, if not negative, over the lifetime of the investment" (Bhattacharya and Linn 1988, 95).

Thus, the structure of incentives in Malaysia could be characterized as an export promotion regime overlaid on (or coexisting with) an import-substitution regime. The average (unweighted) ad valorem tariff was 13.7 percent in 1986 (Kamal et al. 1988). ERPs have generally exceeded nominal rates, however. The average ERP increased from 25 percent in 1965 to 39 percent in 1978. The consumer durables sector received the highest levels of protection: its ERP increased sharply from –5 percent in 1965 to 173 percent in 1978. Although estimates of ERPs after 1978 are unavailable, Kamal et al. (1988) assert that the policies pursued in the 1980s have raised ERPs further.

Externally, Malaysia faces protection in a variety of important export sectors. In agriculture and tropical products, Malaysian exports of palm oil, cocoa products, canned pineapples, and fish encounter high tariff and nontariff barriers in many markets. Protection in these sectors tends to be particularly pernicious, since the tariffs escalate with the degree of processing and thus discourage the development of manufacturing in Malaysia. For example, the average tariffs faced by Malaysia on exports of cocoa beans, processed cocoa, and chocolate products exports are 2.6 percent, 4.3 percent, and 11.8 percent, respectively (Kamal et al. 1988). In addition to these border measures, Malaysian agricultural exports may be adversely affected by a recent US decision to label palm oil as a saturated fat. Malaysian palm oil exports to the United States are usually in the range of $200 million to $250 million per year. More generally, Malaysian agricultural exports are hurt by developed-country agricultural subsidies, which reduce world prices for these products.

Another area in which Malaysian exports are encumbered by developed-country trade policies is wood products. As in the case of agriculture, Malaysia faces escalating protection that discourages the development of processing activities. For example, the average tariff in developed-country markets for semimanufactured wood is 1.8 percent, compared with 9.2 percent for wood panels. In Japan, logs are imported duty free, whereas sawn timber and veneer are subject to 10 percent and 15 percent tariffs, respectively (after the quotas are fully utilized), and plywood is subject to a 20 percent tariff. Moreover, the allocation of quotas has favored developed countries in the past. In Australia, plywood is assessed a 34 percent duty (Kamal et al. 1988).

Lastly, Malaysia encounters external barriers in the form of textile and apparel trade restrictions under the Multi-Fiber Arrangement. Differences in the composition of textile and apparel exports to MFA and non–MFA markets suggest that the MFA has a disproportionate effect on Malaysia's textile exports. Although existing quotas have not been fully utilized in all cases, given the growth of the quotas over time and the high quota-utilization rate in some major markets (more than 97 percent in the United States), the MFA quotas will increasingly be a binding constraint on Malaysian exports in the future.

In contrast, Malaysia benefits from the Generalized System of Preferences (GSP). The magnitude of this benefit does not appear to be particularly large, however: throughout the 1980s exports under the GSP have been less than 10 percent of total exports. Although Malaysia may benefit from the implicit widening of preference margins associated with the 1 January 1989 graduation of the NICs from the US GSP program, in the long run most-favored-nation (MFN) tariff reductions would probably be a greater stimulus to export growth.

Exchange Rates

Malaysia accepted Article VIII of the International Monetary Fund's Articles of Agreement in 1968, and the ringgit was floated in 1973. Exchange rate policy is described by the Fund as a basket peg. The exchange value of the ringgit has been strongly influenced by the world prices of Malaysia's major commodity exports, particularly oil. Four real exchange rate indices are shown in figure 3.1. As measured using trading-partner weights, the Malaysian currency peaked in value in 1980, after the second oil shock. It then depreciated during the 1980s, especially after 1984. The REER based on the Malaysian consumer price index (CPI) stood at 137.6 in 1988, whereas the more narrow export price REER was 191.0.[2] Depreciation against the currencies of Malaysia's Pacific Basin competitors has been far less, however. The

---

2. The preferable WPI-based REER could not be calculated for Malaysia because of missing data.

Figure 3.1 Malaysia: real effective exchange rates, 1970–88

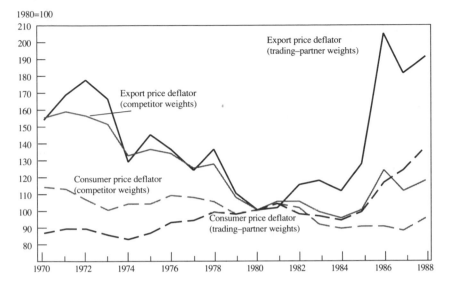

Note: The indices are defined as the local-currency price of foreign currency, so that a rise in the index signifies a depreciation.

export price REER was 117.2 in 1988, whereas the broader CPI-based REER actually fell for much of the 1980s and in 1988 was below its 1980 level. This points to a fundamental dilemma of exchange rate policy in Malaysia: the need to guard against the "Dutch disease," in which commodity price–driven currency appreciation prices the nascent manufacturing sector out of world markets.

Trade Patterns

The commodity composition of Malaysian trade is shown in table 3.1 (manufacturing trade shares by individual industry are presented in appendix B, table B.5). The commodity composition of exports changed dramatically between 1963 and 1987, with the share of fuels (oil and natural gas) rising from 4.1 percent to 19.2 percent, the share of nonfuel primary products falling from 90.3 percent to 39.1 percent, and the share of manufactures rising from 2.9 percent to 41.4 percent. The growth of manufactures exports has been narrowly concentrated in electronics (19.6 percent), with semiconductor assembly and packaging alone accounting for more than a third of

Table 3.1 Malaysia: composition of trade by major product group, 1963 and 1987 (percentages)

Industry	Exports 1963	Exports 1987	Imports 1963	Imports 1987
Fuels (SITC 3)	4.1	19.2	11.1	7.1
Nonfuel primary products	90.3	39.1	38.8	16.3
Food and live animals (SITC 0)	4.4	6.1	22.6	8.1
Beverages and tobacco (SITC 1)	1.3	0.1	4.0	0.6
Industrial raw materials (SITC 2, 4, 68)	84.5	32.9	12.1	7.6
Manufactures (industrial classification)	2.9	41.4	31.2	74.2
Textiles, apparel, and leather (ISIC 32)	0.3	4.9	4.1	4.3
Wood products and furniture (ISIC 33)	0.1	5.7	0.1	0.2
Paper and paper products (ISIC 34)	0.1	0.3	1.5	2.9
Chemicals (ISIC 35)	0.9	2.1	5.6	10.8
Nonmetallic mineral products (ISIC 36)	0.0	0.5	1.3	0.8
Iron and steel (ISIC 37)	0.1	0.8	3.4	4.2
Engineering products (ISIC 38)	1.2	26.3	14.6	49.9
Miscellaneous (ISIC 39)	0.2	0.8	0.5	1.0
Other products	2.7	0.3	18.9	2.4
Memorandum: trade in goods and nonfactor services as a share of GDP[a]	43.2	70.3	41.5	65.6

SITC = Standard International Trade Classification.

ISIC = International Standard Industrial Classification.

a. The later figures are for 1988.

Sources: General Agreement on Tariffs and Trade. Memorandum data are from the World Bank.

manufactured exports. The next most important manufacturing industry was wood products, with an export share of 5.6 percent.

Similarly, the composition of imports shifted toward manufactures and away from primary products between 1963 and 1987. The biggest increase was in engineering products, which accounted for just under half of all imports in 1987. The largest industries within this category were electronic equipment with 22.6 percent of total imports, and machinery with 9.2 percent. The other notable increase was in chemicals; this category nearly doubled its import share from 5.6 percent in 1963 to 10.8 percent in 1987.

The geographical composition of trade is reported in table 3.2. Comparison of the trade pattern in 1963 and 1988 is hindered by the fact that trade with

Table 3.2 Malaysia: geographical composition of trade, 1966 and 1988[a] (percentages)

Country	Exports		Imports	
	1966	1988	1966	1988
Developed countries	83.4	52.5	68.3	62.2
United States	18.2	17.3	6.2	17.7
Western Europe	29.5	14.9	39.3	15.3
Japan	27.9	16.9	12.8	23.0
Canada, Australia, New Zealand	7.8	3.3	10.1	6.2
Developing countries	16.4	46.4	31.8	37.0
Pacific countries (other than China)	5.7	35.2	13.9	28.2
East Asian NICs	3.5	30.4	5.6	22.7
Hong Kong	1.0	3.4	4.9	2.3
Singapore	n.a.	19.3	n.a.	13.2
Taiwan	1.2	2.9	0.6	4.6
Korea	1.3	4.8	0.1	2.6
Other ASEAN–4	2.2	4.8	8.3	5.6
Thailand	1.0	2.0	7.6	3.0
Philippines	1.2	1.5	0.7	0.8
Indonesia	n.a.	1.3	n.a	1.7
China	n.a.	2.0	n.a.	2.9
Other developing countries	10.7	9.2	18.0	5.8
Other Asia	4.9	4.7	15.9	1.6
Africa	1.0	0.6	0.5	0.7
Europe[b]	0.6	0.6	0.0	0.1
Middle East	1.6	2.5	1.3	1.7
Latin America	2.5	0.8	0.3	1.7
European socialist countries	n.a.	1.1	n.a.	0.7

n.a. = not available.

a. Regional aggregates may not sum to 100 percent because of inclusion in the world total of special categories and other countries not specified.

b. Principally Portugal, Greece, and Turkey.

Source: International Monetary Fund, *Direction of Trade Statistics*, various issues.

Singapore was not reported in 1963 because of the federation then in effect between the two countries. Current export trade shows an interesting pattern nonetheless: Singapore (19.3 percent), the United States (17.3 percent), Japan (16.9 percent), and Western Europe (14.9 percent) account for roughly equal shares of Malaysia's trade, although the Singapore share includes goods that are ultimately reexported to other destinations. On the import side, Malaysia's major suppliers are Japan (23.0 percent) followed by the United States (17.7 percent), Western Europe (15.3 percent), and Singapore (13.2 percent).

Issues for the 1990s

The outlook for the Malaysian economy depends on whether Malaysia can successfully make the transition to a manufacturing-led economy. Although Malaysia already successfully exports manufactures, this is primarily done through the free-trade zones, where domestic value added is slight and integration with the rest of the economy minimal. Failure to generate a successful manufactures export sector will encourage reliance on logging exports, which is likely to raise global concerns over the destruction of tropical rain forests. One could imagine under such circumstances a variety of global deals to discourage the destruction of these forests; in the worst case Malaysia could face punitive sanctions for continued logging.

The most pressing problem then is to reduce the large government budget deficit (approximately 8 percent of GDP), which has crowded out private investment. The most obvious way to reduce government expenditure is to reduce subsidies to loss-making NFPEs or privatize them entirely. At the same time, revenues could be increased through the enactment of a broad-based consumption or value-added tax.

With regard to the external sector, the strategy detailed in the Industrial Master Plan of developing manufacturing exports emphasizes the development of industries such as processed foods and wood products that build on the existing natural resource base. Although some have criticized this approach (e.g., Chan 1989), it appears to be a sensible one. Perhaps of greater concern are the underlying conditions for industrialization.

To begin with, there is a lack of infrastructural support to link the capacities of domestic producers with potential customers in world markets. There are no marketing organizations or quality control facilities to promote contact with foreign buyers and to ensure that products meet world market standards.

There is also concern about Malaysia's ability to absorb and adapt technology from abroad. The indigenous capacity for technological adaptation is well below that of the NICs. R&D expenditures account for a paltry 0.64 percent of GNP (Chan 1989). There are shortages of skilled and managerial labor. The technical training structure is inadequate. In the public sector there have been shortages of technical and specialized manpower in nearly all government departments and agencies, a situation exacerbated by the preferential hiring of the *bumiputra* over other ethnic groups (Anand 1983). The same problems are encountered in the financial sector, where regulations limiting compensation and mandating preferential hiring practices have contributed to skilled labor shortages (Institute of International Finance 1990).

Furthermore, existing investment incentives still favor import substituting over export-oriented projects. ERPs remain very high in consumer durables and other capital-intensive manufacturing sectors. Moreover, the emphasis on public investment through the NFPEs has crowded out private investment. Efforts to encourage export promotion have been tentative and ad hoc.

To strengthen its manufacturing competitiveness, Malaysia needs to reduce the variability of incentives across sectors and to shift incentives away from the promotion of capital-intensive activities toward more labor-intensive activities. This would require two reforms. The first would be to overhaul the existing investment incentive system, to simplify fiscal incentives and to reduce the bias toward the use of capital. Second, a reform of the structure of protection would be desirable. In particular it would be advisable to reduce the variability of protection and thus eliminate the very high ERPs accorded some sectors. A tariff ceiling of 25 percent should be considered. Export promotion measures should be strengthened. This would include simplifying the existing duty drawback system and extending it to indirect exporters.

These reforms would improve the efficiency of resource allocation. However, the underlying resource base needs to be developed as well. Here the imperative is to improve the indigenous capacity for technological adaptation. Formal education and training programs need to be expanded. Historically, considerable training has occurred within the firm. Although desirable on efficiency grounds, this practice has had the consequence of reinforcing the concentration of skills within the Chinese community. Hence the expansion of more broadly accessible training programs is desirable. At the same time, affirmative action programs that reduce the efficiency of job matching should be reconsidered. Greater government support of local R&D activities is also advisable.

Privatization of the NFPEs should also be considered. Many of the NFPEs are poorly run, and this is beginning to have ramifications for the financial sector, where the existence of nonperforming loans is the most immediate problem. Privatization of the NFPEs, together with the restructuring, merging, or liquidation of weak financial institutions, is recommended.

Other financial reforms should also be considered. Malaysia has a relatively well developed financial system. It would benefit, however, from relaxation of regulations that contribute to an excessive segmentation of financial services. Such deregulation would also be useful in facilitating the restructuring of ailing financial institutions. Another prospective area of deregulation is exchange controls. Current regulations limit the breadth and depth of the exchange market and restrict the ability of firms to manage exchange risk (Institute of International Finance 1990).

In the end, however, the prospects for successful economic reform depend crucially on the Malaysian political system's ability to find ways of reconciling the goals of wealth redistribution and economic efficiency. At least two of the problems confronting the Malaysian economy—the faltering NFPEs and the shortage of skilled labor—are due at least in part to redistributive policies. The policy choices the government makes are ultimately political ones, and these will have a considerable impact on the future of the Malaysian economy.

Thailand

Historical and Policy Background

The modern state of Thailand was forged by a succession of modernizing monarchs in the late 19th and early 20th centuries. Since the advent of the constitutional monarchy in 1932, Thailand has experienced frequent changes of government, often in the form of bloodless military coups. The military continues to take a strong interest in governance.

In part because it is one of the few non-European nations to have escaped colonization, Thailand has maintained a high degree of ethnic and cultural homogeneity. It has assimilated its Chinese minority, which now accounts for 7 percent to 8 percent of the population and is concentrated in the Bangkok area, more successfully than has its neighbor Malaysia.

Although Thailand has some coal, oil, natural gas, and tin, its main natural resource is its fertile agricultural land. Despite rapid productivity gains, however, agriculture's share of GDP has fallen steadily over the last 30 years, from 40.0 percent in 1960 to 27.0 percent in 1970, 20.6 percent in 1980, and 17.6 percent in 1987. A similar decline has occurred in the share of the labor force engaged in agriculture, from more than 80 percent in 1960 to around 60 percent in 1987. Rice has long been the staple crop of Thailand's agricultural economy, yet in recent years agricultural production had diversified to include cassava (tapioca), rubber, maize, and fruits and vegetables. And although the value share of rice in agricultural production has fallen from 37.7 percent in 1960 to 20.3 percent in 1987, Thailand remains one of the world's principal rice exporters (Tambunlertchai 1989).

The converse of agriculture's relative decline in importance has been the growth of manufacturing, from 11.7 percent of GDP in 1960 to 22.7 percent in 1987. Although some manufacturing operations had been established in Thailand prior to World War II, the growth of manufacturing received its first policy push in the decade following the war, when the nationalist government of Field Marshal Luang Pibulsonggram created state enterprises to produce cement, paper, sugar, tobacco, and a variety of other consumer products.

However, most of these were failures due to poor management and corruption, and the establishment of these state enterprises tended to crowd out private entrepreneurs, who were mostly confined to small-scale operations such as rice milling, sawmilling, and household handicrafts.

By the mid-1950s the emphasis had begun to shift toward the promotion of private manufacturing activities, which received further impetus with the ouster of Pibulsonggram by Field Marshal Sarit Thanarat in 1957. Although the first law (in 1954) promoting private industry was ineffectual, in 1959 the government established a Board of Investment (BOI) and the Industrial Finance Corporation of Thailand (IFCT), and in 1962 passed the Industrial Promotion Act. Under this regime, fiscal incentives were combined with trade protection to encourage manufacturing activities. At the time the government launched its import substitution program, the food, beverage, and tobacco processing industries accounted for 60 percent of manufacturing value added. The government's strategy was to promote capital-intensive manufacturing industries. Industries were classified into three groups. Group A, which consisted of heavy industries such as metal smelting, tires, and chemicals, received full exemption from tariffs and business taxes. Group B, consisting of assembly-oriented industries such as motor vehicles and electrical appliances, received a one-half exemption from tariffs and taxes. The lowest-priority industries, Group C, were natural resource– or labor-intensive activities such as agricultural processing and textiles, and these received a one-third exemption from tariffs and taxes (Akrasanee and Ajanant 1986; Tambunlertchai 1989). In exercising this authority the BOI was given broad discretionary power in selecting industries and projects for promotion and establishing criteria for receiving fiscal benefits.[3] These tax advantages could be complemented by financing through the IFCT, which although nominally a private corporation generally followed government priorities in its lending practices.

This policy was successful at raising the manufacturing share of output, but at considerable cost in terms of reduced allocative efficiency. The import substitution policy was sustainable in part because exports of primary products continued to supply foreign exchange, but by the 1970s policymakers were becoming increasingly skeptical about the policy in light of the superior performance of the more export-oriented NICs. Moreover, the program was encountering rapidly diminishing returns as the possibilities for import substitution within the small domestic market were exhausted.

The government decided to adjust its strategy and put greater emphasis on promoting manufactured exports. This policy was first outlined in the Third

---

3. For example, during the mid-1960s, most industries in Group A were reclassified into Groups B and C, and by 1967 only the Group C classification remained.

National Economic and Social Development Plan (1972–76) and its accompanying legislation, which provided full tax exemption on imported inputs and other promotional privileges on a discretionary basis for producers of manufactured exports. These included "rebates of all taxes in the production process . . . a discount facility on short term loans . . . and an exemption from business (sales) taxes on the products" (Akrasanee and Ajanant 1986, 87). An Export Promotion Committee was established to coordinate these measures.

The export promotion policy was extended in the Fourth National Economic and Social Development Plan (1977–81), under which the investment promotion law was revised to reduce the bias against exports. The BOI was authorized to grant exemptions or reductions of up to 50 percent of import duties and taxes on imported machinery, and of taxes on domestically produced machinery; reductions of up to 90 percent of import duties and taxes on imported materials and of taxes on domestic materials; exemptions on corporate income tax for three to eight years, with carry-forward losses for up to five years after the period of exemptions; exclusions from taxable income of dividends during the period of the tax holiday and exclusions from taxable income of fees for copyright and other rights for a period of five years (Balassa 1990). In some cases benefits were granted on the basis of export performance. Further emphasis on exporting was contained in the Fifth National Economic and Social Development Plan (1982–85), which outlined a package of policy reforms including a comprehensive rationalization of the tariff structure, an overhaul of the investment incentive system, and the development and improvement of export promotion measures. The growth rate of manufacturing output accelerated following the abandonment of the import substitution strategy.

Most manufacturing operations in Thailand are concentrated in the Bangkok area. The population of Bangkok is estimated to vary seasonally between 7 million and 10 million, out of a total national population of 53 million. (By comparison, Thailand's second largest city, Chiang Mai, has a population of only 250,000.) The port of Bangkok handles 90 percent of Thailand's foreign trade. The government and the best schools and universities are all located in Bangkok.

The rapid development of the Bangkok area has led to severe strains on the local infrastructure. Traffic congestion is endemic. Whereas in most cities worldwide approximately 10 percent of the land area is covered by roads, for Bangkok the figure is 4 percent (*The Economist*, 16 December 1989, 69). Moreover, the number of cars increased 40 percent between 1987 and 1989. Similarly, there are only 7 telephone lines per 100 residents, compared with 33 in Taiwan and 46 in Hong Kong.

The government has responded to the strain on Bangkok's resources by launching a regional development effort in an attempt to disperse economic activity away from the Bangkok area. This initiative has included public infrastructure investments in outlying areas, as well as tax and credit incentives for firms to locate in the hinterland. The government has also been using foreign aid money to finance the construction of industrial estates outside Bangkok. The centerpiece has been the Eastern Seaboard Development Program (ESDP) to develop the region from east of Bangkok toward the Cambodian border.[4]

The national government's participation in the economy also extends to 72 majority-state-owned enterprises. As in other Southeast Asian countries, these were originally established to counterbalance the economic power of immigrant Chinese and foreigners, as well as to provide a mechanism for political patronage (Akrasanee and Ajanant 1986). The largest are public utilities, transport, and communications companies, financial institutions, and the Thai Oil Company (Balassa 1990). There are also some public enterprises in directly productive industries. The government has attached a high priority to improving the financial health of these enterprises, and throughout the 1980s a variety of rules were introduced to circumscribe the availability of public subsidies. These actions appear to have been at least partly successful, as savings by the state enterprises have increased, and they have been able to finance larger shares of capital investments out of their own resources. Nonetheless, concerns about some loss-making enterprises remain, and the selective privatization of the more commercially oriented state enterprises is envisaged.

Financial liberalization was undertaken in the late 1950s. The financial system consists of domestic and foreign commercial banks, finance companies, life insurance companies, agricultural cooperatives, private moneylenders, and specialized development finance institutions, including the Government Savings Bank, the Bank of Agriculture and Agricultural Cooperatives, the Government Housing Bank, the IFCT, and the Small Industry Finance Corporation (Balassa 1990). Financial deepening has accompanied the process of development: the ratio of M2 to GDP has risen from 23 percent in 1960 to 28 percent in 1970, 38 percent in 1980, and 69 percent in 1988.

Money and capital markets are underdeveloped. The secondary government

---

4. The plan is to use the development of the deep-water port at Sattalip and associated transportation and communications networks to spur the development of energy, natural resource processing, and labor-intensive manufacturing industries. The planned heavy industrial estate would include offshore oil and natural gas production, a petrochemicals complex, a fertilizer plant, a number of chemical plants, and two steel mills. Firms producing light manufactures and processed foodstuffs for export through the deep-water port would be located in a planned light industrial estate. The development of two other ports has been on the drawing board, but these projects as well as some other aspects of the ESDP may be scaled back because of resource constraints.

bond and money markets are thin. The stock market, in contrast, has boomed. Its market capitalization was $14 billion in 1989. Foreigners own 13 percent of outstanding Thai stocks, but there are limits on the number of shares foreigners can own in individual companies.

Lastly, industrial competitiveness is affected by the development of human resources. Here, as with the provision of physical infrastructure, there is reason to believe that current efforts in Thailand are insufficient to sustain high rates of growth and development. Although primary education is practically universal, education beyond the primary level is concentrated in a relatively small elite. Secondary education participation rates are much lower in Thailand (29 percent) than in middle-income countries in general (54 percent) or in any of the other Pacific Basin developing countries (World Bank 1989, table 29). Higher education is tilted toward the social sciences and humanities and away from technical education. Only 15 percent of university graduates receive degrees in science or technology fields, compared with 40 percent in Korea (*The Economist*, 21 January 1989, 81). The 3,500 engineers graduated annually are fewer than half the number required according to labor surveys (*The Economist*, 16 December 1989). At the same time, the mismatch between the educational system's output and the needs of the labor force is creating a phenomenon of "educated unemployment."

Trade Policies

Whereas these policies and institutions affect competitiveness overall, other policies have had a specific impact on external trade. Prior to the first industrialization push in the late 1950s, tariffs were used mainly for revenue purposes and varied between 15 percent and 30 percent. Tariffs were raised on selected products in the early 1960s to afford protection for domestic manufactures. They were raised once again in 1971, with finished consumer-goods imports assessed rates of 30 percent to 55 percent. In 1974, tariffs were lowered across the board to fight inflation, but the pattern of the cuts actually increased tariff escalation, and in the late 1970s tariffs were again increased (Akrasanee and Ajanant 1986).

A major tariff reform was attempted in 1982. Although some progress was made in equalizing rates of protection within individual industries (such as textiles), the results for the industrial sector as a whole were modest. Some of these gains were reversed when tariff rates were raised once again in 1985, apparently because of concerns over the worsening budget situation and a desire to increase government revenues. This left Thailand with the highest average nominal rate of tariff protection (34 percent) of any of the Pacific Basin developing countries. The trade-weighted average tariff in 1989 was 23 percent (US Trade Representative 1990). Most food imports face duties of about 60 percent, whereas capital-goods duties are approximately 25 percent, and the average duty on other products is 16.5 percent. The dispersion of tariff rates is considerable, with some industries (including some finished consumer products, machinery and parts, and automobiles) receiving tariff protection of more than 60 percent, while others exhibit tariff rates of less than 10 percent. The escalation by degree of processing indicates that ERPs are even higher. Tariffs accounted for 22 percent of national government revenues from taxation in fiscal year 1989.[5]

Intellectual property protection is widely regarded as inadequate; the US government has held consultations with the Thai government on virtually all aspects of intellectual property protection including patents, copyrights, and trademarks. As a consequence, Thailand is on the "priority watch list" under the Special 301 provision of the 1988 trade act (US Trade Representative 1990).

Whereas trade policy has been unsteady, export promotion policy has been more consistent. As noted earlier, exporters are exempted from import duties, business taxes, and municipal taxes on imported inputs used directly or indirectly in export production, and they receive rebates on indirect taxes paid on domestic materials. Direct and indirect exporters are also eligible for preferential financing. Policy has also encouraged the establishment of trading companies to improve the linkage between domestic producers and world markets. Exporters receive a 20 percent rebate on electricity. In addition to these general promotion measures, an export processing zone has been established, but the share of exports it generates is relatively small.

Thailand's export prospects are also affected by the barriers maintained by its trade partners. In agriculture, Thai exports have been reduced by US rice subsidies under the US Farm Security Act and by the US sugar quota. Ajanant and Wiboonchutikula (1988) estimate the export revenue loss due to the US rice policy at $120 million, and that due to the sugar quota at $87 million at current prices. Thai exports have also been hurt by Japanese and European agricultural policies, most notably the Japanese ban on rice imports and EC restrictions on tapioca imports. Anderson and Tyers (1987) estimate the net foreign-exchange losses to Thailand resulting from Japanese agricultural protectionism to be $320 million, and that due to EC agricultural protectionism to be $580 million (both figures in 1985 dollars). Thai authorities have

---

5. In addition to tariff protection, quantitative restrictions apply to 65 products accounting for less than 5 percent of imports.

also complained of Japanese nontariff barriers on fish and seafood exports.[6]

In manufacturing, the principal export barrier Thailand faces is the MFA, which limits textile and apparel exports. Although the MFA restrictions initially benefited Thailand by encouraging the relocation of production there from quota-constrained economies such as Taiwan and Hong Kong, liberalization of MFA restrictions would now lead to a significant expansion of Thai exports. A similar pattern appears to be unfolding in the footwear industry, where quota-constrained Korean firms are relocating to Thailand.

Beyond these restrictions, Thai exports have been subject to countervailing duty actions in the United States on textiles and apparel, steel pipes and tubes, nails, and ball bearings. Thai manufactured exports may have also been disadvantaged in the European market because of trade diversion created by the Lomé Convention, which grants trade preferences to the products of a number of low-income African, Caribbean, and Pacific countries.

Thailand is itself a recipient of trade preferences under the GSP, but Thai participation has been rather low: only about 20 percent of Thai exports receive GSP preferences. Moreover, in 1989 Thailand lost some GSP privileges in the United States in a dispute over intellectual property protection.

The composition and pattern of trade are also affected by FDI links. FDI flows into Thailand exploded from $168 million in 1987 to $1,082 million in 1988; $746 million in inflows was recorded in the first half of 1989 alone. Japan was the biggest foreign investor, followed by Taiwan and Hong Kong. Semiconductors and canned pineapples are among the new export products generated by FDI. Other export items produced by foreign firms include toys, rubber gloves, ball bearings, automobile parts, and a number of processed food products.

Exchange Rates

The exchange rate in Thailand follows a basket peg. Export promotion was assisted by devaluations in 1981 and 1984 (figure 3.2). Following the 1984 devaluation, Thailand's currency, the baht, rode the US dollar down in

---

6. These include "quotas based on value, daily or monthly monitoring systems, and sanitation regulations and laws. The value quota is used to limit yen outflows and the size of the trade deficit of frozen marine products. It also tends to depress prices quoted by exporters. Even more complex are quotas regulating imports on a daily or monthly basis. Thai exports that cannot be shipped or imported in time are destroyed, adding to costs and reducing demand. Japan also introduces special tariffs once the value of an import item has reached a given level. Exporters dislike such arrangements because information is typically not received prior to shipment" (Ajanant and Wiboonchutikula 1988, 327–28).

Figure 3.2 Thailand: real effective exchange rates, 1970–88

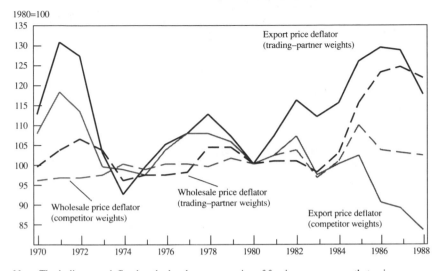

1980=100

Export price deflator
(trading–partner weights)

Wholesale price deflator
(trading–partner weights)

Wholesale price deflator
(competitor weights)

Export price deflator
(competitor weights)

Note: The indices are defined as the local-currency price of foreign currency, so that a rise in the index signifies a depreciation.

foreign-exchange markets, thereby gaining some competitiveness relative to its trade partners. This was sufficient to maintain a roughly stable real exchange rate against its competitors according to the WPI-based competitor-weighted REER. However, in terms of the more narrow export price REER, Thailand steadily lost competitiveness vis-à-vis the other Pacific Basin developing countries in the late 1980s, necessitating an upgrading of export composition. In May 1990 Thailand announced plans to dismantle its remaining capital controls and maintain a fully convertible currency under Article VIII of the IMF Articles of Agreement. In the short run, increased capital inflows could be expected to contribute to an appreciation of the currency.

Trade Patterns

The commodity composition of Thai trade, reported in table 3.3, changed dramatically between 1963 and 1987 (manufacturing trade shares by industry are reported in appendix B, table B.6). The share of nonfuel primary products fell from 96.5 percent to 46.8 percent, while the share of manufactured exports increased more than 25-fold from 1.8 percent to 51.3 percent. The

Table 3.3 Thailand: composition of trade by major product group, 1963 and 1987 (percentages)

Industry	Exports		Imports	
	1963	1987	1963	1987
Fuels (SITC 3)	0.0	0.7	9.6	13.3
Nonfuel primary products	96.5	46.8	10.7	14.1
Food and live animals (SITC 0)	56.2	35.4	5.8	4.2
Beverages and tobacco (SITC 1)	0.4	0.5	1.2	0.5
Industrial raw materials (SITC 2, 4, 68)	39.8	11.0	3.8	9.4
Manufactures (industrial classification)	1.8	51.3	73.0	66.7
Textiles, apparel, and leather (ISIC 32)	0.7	22.0	12.7	3.3
Wood products and furniture (ISIC 33)	0.0	2.3	0.2	0.8
Paper and paper products (ISIC 34)	0.0	0.7	2.5	2.1
Chemicals (ISIC 35)	0.0	3.4	12.7	14.9
Nonmetallic mineral products (ISIC 36)	0.7	0.9	1.3	0.9
Iron and steel (ISIC 37)	0.0	0.8	6.9	7.4
Engineering products (ISIC 38)	0.0	13.8	35.9	35.5
Miscellaneous (ISIC 39)	0.4	7.3	0.8	1.9
Other products	1.7	1.2	6.7	5.9
Memorandum: trade in goods and nonfactor services as a share of GDP	14.8	30.1	18.0	29.8

SITC = Standard International Trade Classification.

ISIC = International Standard Industrial Classification.

Source: General Agreement on Tariffs and Trade. Memorandum data are from the World Bank.

biggest drop, from 39.8 percent to 11.0 percent, was in industrial raw materials. Among these products, the export share of rubber fell from 20.1 percent of total exports to 6.9 percent, and the share of tin dropped from 7.9 percent to 0.8 percent.

In the agricultural sector, the share of rice exports in total exports fell from 36.3 percent to 7.6 percent from 1963 to 1987, and that of maize from 8.8 percent to 1.3 percent. These declines were partly offset by the export share increases exhibited by vegetables (mainly cassava), from 1.8 percent to 6.9 percent, and fish, from 0.8 percent to 5.3 percent.

In manufactures, the outstanding changes were in textiles, apparel, and leather goods, whose combined share rose from 0.7 percent to 22.0 percent, and engineering products, which rose from zero to 13.8 percent. More than half of the exports in the former category consisted of apparel, while the latter consisted primarily of electronic and electrical appliance assembly and packaging operations. The other significant manufacturing export category was the miscellaneous category (7.3 percent), which consisted mainly of gems and jewelry.

The import shares of fuels and industrial raw materials rose between 1963 and 1987, while the share of manufactures fell, reflecting Thailand's industrial development over this period. The biggest import categories in 1987 were petroleum and petroleum products (13.2 percent of total imports), machinery (10.2 percent), and iron and steel (7.4 percent).

The geographical pattern of trade is reported in table 3.4. Thailand's biggest export markets are Western Europe (22.7 percent of 1988 total exports), the United States (20.0 percent), Japan (15.9 percent), and the East Asian NICs collectively (15.5 percent). Europe and the United States increased their importance between 1963 and 1988, while the importance of Japan and the East Asian NICs declined somewhat. The share of Thai exports taken by the other ASEAN–4 countries declined dramatically, from 25.7 percent in 1963 to 3.9 percent in 1988. As a consequence the share of the Pacific Basin developing countries as a group in Thailand's exports fell from 45.1 percent in 1963 to 19.4 percent in 1988, less than the share of either Europe or the United States.

Western Europe replaced Japan as Thailand's biggest import supplier, with 22.9 percent of the total in 1988, but the import shares of Western Europe, Japan, and the United States all declined. The combined import share of the other ASEAN–4 countries also declined. The fall in ASEAN–4 import and export shares suggests that (with the exception of Singapore) there was a relative reduction in interdependence between Thailand and the rest of ASEAN, despite attempts to encourage integration. The big increase in import share was captured by the East Asian NICs, which more than tripled their share from 6.1 percent to 19.3 percent. The biggest single-country increase was that of Singapore (from 0.9 percent to 9.2 percent), in part reflecting Thailand's growing importation of petroleum and petroleum products.

Issues for the 1990s

Thailand is in a good position to continue along a successful development path. It appears to be developing new industries from its existing resource base. One major constraint on future growth and development is a lack of adequate investment. Infrastructure investment needs are enormous. Thailand has traditionally saved and invested somewhat less than some other East Asian developing countries, in part because of large government budget deficits, which at times during the 1980s surpassed 6 percent of GDP. Ex-

**Table 3.4   Thailand: geographical composition of trade,
1963 and 1988[a] (percentages)**

Country	Exports		Imports	
	1963	1988	1963	1988
Developed countries	43.5	62.4	83.5	55.5
United States	7.4	20.0	17.5	16.8
Western Europe	17.7	22.7	30.8	22.9
Japan	18.1	15.9	32.9	11.7
Canada, Australia, New Zealand	0.2	3.8	2.3	4.1
Developing countries	55.6	36.3	15.6	41.6
Pacific countries (other than China)	45.1	19.4	13.0	24.1
East Asian NICs	19.4	15.5	6.1	19.3
Hong Kong	9.8	4.4	2.6	1.5
Singapore	8.0	7.7	0.9	9.2
Taiwan	1.3	1.8	2.2	5.1
Korea	0.3	1.6	0.3	3.4
Other ASEAN–4	25.7	3.9	6.9	4.8
Malaysia	15.9	3.0	0.5	2.5
Philippines	1.7	0.4	0.0	1.2
Indonesia	8.2	0.5	6.4	1.1
China	n.a.	3.0	n.a.	4.1
Other developing countries	10.5	13.9	2.6	13.4
Other Asia	5.6	3.4	0.6	3.9
Africa	1.1	3.3	0.2	2.0
Europe[b]	0.3	0.4	0.1	0.2
Middle East	2.6	6.0	1.7	4.9
Latin America	0.9	0.7	0.1	2.4
European socialist countries	0.8	0.9	0.9	2.3

n.a. = not available.

a. Regional aggregates may not sum to 100 percent because of inclusion in the world
total of special categories and other countries not specified.

b. Principally Portugal, Greece, and Turkey.

Sources: International Monetary Fund, *Direction of Trade Statistics,* various issues.

penditure restraint and revenue growth have drastically cut public dissaving
in recent years, and the government ran a surplus in 1988 and 1989. The
share of investment in GDP has risen to 26 percent. Additional increases to
around 30 percent would be desirable for the long term. This could be financed through a combination of continued budget surpluses and capital
inflows from abroad.

Additional investment in human capital would also be desirable, including an expansion of secondary education in general, and of technical and vocational education in particular. There is also a need to strengthen science and engineering education at the university level and to encourage R&D activities domestically.

These physical infrastructure and educational investments would have the additional benefit of reducing urban-rural income inequality and discouraging further migration to the overcrowded Bangkok area. The dispersion of economic activity away from Bangkok would also ease the upward pressure on land prices, which have contributed to growing income inequality within the capital.

Thailand could attempt to increase both its human and physical capital by encouraging immigration from Hong Kong. Thailand offers much lower wages and greater investment opportunities than Singapore, and it has assimilated its Chinese minority more successfully than have Malaysia and Indonesia. Although wage rates are higher in Thailand than in China, investment in Thailand carries much less political risk.

Beyond increasing its accumulation of human and physical capital, Thailand needs to reform its incentive system, which still encourages import substitution. Thailand is in a good position to make these reforms. Although tariffs remain high, Thailand has avoided the introduction of extensive quantitative restrictions, which have bedeviled many other developing countries. And although tariffs are still a significant source of government revenue, the government budget is now in surplus, making it a propitious time to cut tariffs. This could be accompanied by long-overdue fiscal reform to reduce the role of indirect taxes. By reforming and strengthening the direct tax system, the government could ensure a stable revenue base, thereby eliminating the need to rely on import tariffs as a revenue source, and permitting permanent tariff cuts to improve the efficiency of the incentive system. In particular, the tariffication and phaseout of existing quantitative restrictions and the imposition of a 25 percent tariff ceiling would be desirable.

The Philippines

Historical and Policy Background

The Philippines consists of more than 7,100 tropical islands off the southeast coast of Asia. In 1521 Ferdinand Magellan claimed the Philippines for Spain, which ruled the islands until they were ceded to the United States in 1898. US suzerainty was interrupted by the three-year Japanese occupation during

World War II, but the postwar reestablishment of US rule was short-lived, and the country was granted independence on 4 July 1946. With its Spanish colonial heritage, abundant natural resources, and highly unequal income distribution, the Philippines is in many ways more akin to the developing countries of Latin America than to its geographical brethren in East Asia.

In 1963 agriculture contributed 26.1 percent of output. By 1989 this figure had fallen only slightly to 23.1 percent, and the sector still accounted for nearly half of employment in that year. Land is distributed highly unevenly. Plantations, making up only 3 percent of farms by number, cover 29 percent of the total agricultural land area. At the other extreme, 70 percent of all farms are smaller than 3 hectares (about 7.5 acres) and constitute less than 30 percent of the land area suitable for farming. As a consequence, there is extreme income inequality within the rural areas and between urban and rural areas. Rural incomes are, on average, less than half the average urban income, as they have been for the past 30 years.

Agriculture has essentially been neglected by Philippine economic policymakers. Import substitution policies in place since the late 1940s turned the terms of trade against agriculture. Monopolistic marketing boards established for the two major export crops, sugar and coconuts, further squeezed agriculture. Comprehensive land reforms have been enacted on several occasions (by President Ramón Magsaysay in 1955, by President Diosdado Macapagal in 1963, by President Ferdinand Marcos in 1972, and by President Corazon Aquino in 1987) but have never been widely implemented. Twelve years after the Marcos reform, only 11.5 percent of the land intended to be covered by the reform had actually been redistributed; only 10 percent of the beneficiaries had paid off their loans from the Land Bank; and only 13 percent of the dispossessed landowners had been compensated.

Sadly, this dismal performance has been replayed in the manufacturing sector. The import-substitution regime that has characterized much of the Philippines' postindependence economic development policy emerged as a byproduct of import and foreign-exchange controls imposed in the aftermath of World War II. The repression of imports promoted the local development of consumer-goods industries. Domestic consumer-goods manufacturers received further encouragement through exemptions from industrial taxes starting in 1946, and exemptions from custom duties on inputs starting in 1951. Tariff rates were raised significantly, reaching 100 percent on some finished goods. Lower rates were applied to capital goods and industrial materials, implying considerable effective protection for the consumer-goods sector (Balassa 1990).

The manufacturing sector expanded rapidly in the 1950s, but the Philippines continued to be plagued by chronic balance of payments problems, as the growth of manufactures production remained highly dependent on imported capital goods and industrial materials. Eventually the growth of the manufacturing sector began to slow as the opportunities for import substitution were exhausted. Exchange and import controls were removed in 1960–62, but the tariff system, which had been made redundant by these additional measures, preserved the protective character of the trade regime (Bautista 1989). By 1965, tariff rates were estimated to average 70 percent for consumer goods, 55 percent for inputs into construction, 27 percent for intermediate goods, and 16 percent for capital goods (Power 1971b). Tan concluded that "the structure of protection remained virtually unchanged between the 1950s and 1960s although the instruments of protection changed from import and exchange controls to tariffs" (Tan 1986, 53).

Beginning in the late 1960s, a variety of incentive policies were introduced to promote nontraditional exports. Fiscal incentives were instituted in 1967, followed in 1970 by the introduction of a direct subsidy to value added for firms exporting more than half of their output. A bonded warehouse system was created, and partial duty drawbacks were provided to exporters of selected products to assure them of access to duty-free imported inputs whenever domestic substitutes were unavailable. Export processing zones were established in 1972.

The trend toward greater outward orientation was reversed following the declaration of martial law in 1972, and the state once again began to increase its role in the economy. Philippines Airlines as well as several steel companies were nationalized, and the government encouraged multinational oil companies to sell their Philippine operations to the state-owned Philippines National Oil Company. Monopolistic marketing organizations were established for sugar and coconuts.

A major revision of the tariff code was implemented on 1 January 1973. It raised tariff rates, provided for retaliatory duties in response to dumping, subsidy, and discrimination against Philippine exports, and introduced an export tariff (Tan 1986). These measures encouraged the expansion of a number of capital-intensive industries including paper, industrial chemicals, rubber products, and metal products. Productivity declined. Total factor productivity growth in the manufacturing sector, which had increased at an average annual rate of 0.56 percent between 1956 and 1970, actually fell at an annual rate of 1.23 percent between 1971 and 1980 (Hooley 1985). The decline was entirely due to the shift in industrial composition toward increasingly inappropriate capital-intensive sectors, and to the development of inefficient intermediate-products industries.

This situation was exacerbated by the government's policy response to the oil shocks. In an attempt to maintain a high level of output, the government pursued expansionary monetary and fiscal policies, thereby allowing the peso to become overvalued. The resulting current account deficits were financed by heavy borrowing from abroad (Remolona et al. 1986). This capital inflow was largely invested in prestige projects, which did not generate sufficient earnings to repay the loans.[7] From 1981 on, the Philippines found it increasingly difficult to obtain long-term loans, and the current account deficit was increasingly financed through short-term borrowing. With the assassination of opposition leader Benigno Aquino in 1983, even short-term lending dried up, an estimated $200 million in private capital fled the country, the central bank's foreign-exchange reserves were exhausted, and the Philippines was plunged into an economic crisis, which culminated in a debt-repayment moratorium and the conclusion of a 1985 standby agreement with the IMF (Bautista 1989).

Deterioration in the real economy mirrored the deterioration in external finances. As the ratio of external debt to GNP increased substantially during the 1970s and early 1980s, the share of exports (less consignment imports) in GNP actually declined from approximately 15 percent in 1970 to 10 percent in 1983. Indeed, the inability of the Philippines to expand its export sector was an important contributing factor to the 1983 crisis.

Manufactured export growth has been heavily concentrated in three industries: garments, electronic components, and handicrafts. The garment and electronic industries remain largely export enclaves based on highly labor-intensive assembly and packaging activities, without strong linkages to the rest of the economy. Exports in these sectors have been concentrated in firms, mostly foreign, operating on a consignment basis. Spin-off benefits, in the form of backward linkages, entrepreneurial development, or technological advances, have been minimal. In the case of electronics, the cost of the imported components has remained roughly constant at 70 percent of the value of exports. In the case of garments, where the domestic textile industry could presumably supply inputs, garment exporters have sourced their entire input needs on a duty-free basis from abroad, so that virtually no integration of the textile and garment industries has occurred.

Beyond the enclave export sector, which competes on the basis of labor costs, concern exists about the international competitiveness of the rest of the manufacturing sector. This is particularly true for those industries that received excessive protection during the import substitution period. An unpublished World Bank study found that many Philippine firms producing behind high import barriers had negative value added at world prices in the

---

7. See Bautista (1989) for a detailed description of these projects.

early 1980s. Moreover, large variations in costs persist within individual sectors, and the domestic resource costs of a number of industries appear to be extremely high. Industrial efficiency issues are further complicated by the government's extensive ownership of productive assets. As noted earlier, the government nationalized a number of firms in 1972–73. More private enterprises were acquired during the financial crisis of 1983. By 1985, there were 96 government corporations with 149 subsidiaries (Balassa 1990). The takeover of financially distressed firms in 1983–84 swelled the number of publicly owned enterprises to more than 300, steadily increasing the share of publicly owned corporations in industrial output. The government now owns mines, textile factories, sugar mills, steel mills, chemical firms, construction companies, hotels, and shipping lines.

The indigenous capacity for technological adaptation is also of concern. In comparison with other developing countries, the Philippines' education system is relatively strong: adult literacy as of 1985 exceeded 85 percent, and the overall educational attainment embodied by the Philippine labor force is comparable to that of the NICs and exceeds that of the other ASEAN-4 economies (table 1.5). University educations, however, appear to involve significant consumption (as distinct from investment) aspects, and the university system produces more lawyers and fewer engineers than labor market conditions would seem to warrant. In fact, the share of scientists and engineers in the Philippine population is only about a tenth as high as in Korea. The apparent shortage of technically trained personnel and the associated lack of spending on R&D may be the major factor in the economy's limited assimilation of existing technology. Examples of this include the observed failure of firms to fully exploit the productivity of existing technology through modification, and the failure of firms to choose the most appropriate technology in terms of factor usage at the time of investment. This inability to adapt existing technologies to local conditions may be a significant factor in the failure of the economy either to sustain successful industrialization beyond the enclave export sector, or to generate backward and forward linkages from that sector to the rest of the economy.

The competitiveness of Philippine firms is further hindered by the relatively inefficient financial system. Like industry, the banking system is dominated by large government-owned firms: the Development Bank of the Philippines, the Philippines National Bank, and the Land Bank of the Philippines. These banks have proved to be poor financial intermediaries, rationing credit to large, politically influential borrowers. Moreover, as a consequence of their lending practices, the early-1980s fall in commodity prices, and the financial crises of 1983–85, they have accumulated considerable portfolios of nonperforming loans. Balassa (1990) reports that, at the end of 1985, nonperforming loans accounted for 87 percent of the assets of the Development Bank of the Philippines, and 58 percent of the assets of the Philippines National Bank. (Comparable figures for the Land Bank of the Philippines were not available.)[8]

Because of the inefficiency of the financial sector and the current macroeconomic policy mix, the cost of financial intermediation remains high relative to that in other East Asian developing countries. Many firms regard a lack of access to credit as a significant constraint on their operations. This constraint appears to be most important for domestic rather than multinational firms, and for small-scale industries and small and medium-sized enterprises. Similarly, nonbank sources of finance such as money markets, bond markets, and stock markets are relatively underdeveloped and do not adequately meet smaller domestic firms' capital needs.

Another factor reducing the competitiveness of the Philippines' manufacturing sector is the inadequacy of public investment and infrastructure. Examples include the communications, transportation, and electric power systems. The telephone system is inadequate, and (outside the main island of Luzon) the same could be said of the road network. There is a particular need to improve the rural road network in order to get agricultural exports to market. Similarly, almost all existing railway lines are concentrated on the islands of Luzon and Panay. The condition of the track has deteriorated in recent years, and a fifth of the Luzon track is not in operation. Shortcomings of the electrical power system include excessively high costs to industrial users and insufficient capacity. A recent survey found that industrial users in the Philippines pay on average 40.2 percent more per kilowatt-hour than their counterparts in the Pacific Basin. Moreover, since exporters in some of these competing countries are charged reduced rates, the Philippine producers' actual cost disadvantage is even greater. Meanwhile, the lack of capacity has forced the government to implement a power-saving plan, including four-day work weeks for some offices and factories.

Recent Reforms

The Philippines' manufacturing sector is thus really two sectors: the relatively efficient export enclave, dominated by foreign firms that have located in the Philippines primarily because of low labor costs, and the rest of the industrial

---

8. In addition to the large government banks, there are private commercial banks, offshore affiliates of foreign banks, saving and mortgage banks, private investment banks, savings and loan associations, rural banks, leasing companies, and finance companies.

sector, which is beset by the cumulative problems of four decades of economic mismanagement. In response to these problems the government has launched an ambitious program of economic reforms. It has begun to streamline and privatize the public corporate sector. Thus far, 58 corporations have been recommended for abolition, 121 for privatization, 18 for consolidation with other corporations, and 17 for regularization as part of existing government departments. Actual privatization has proceeded slowly. The government has offered for sale 37 corporations comprising more than a quarter of the book value of assets approved for privatization. As of late 1989, 29 of these had been sold (19 fully, 10 partially). What is important from the standpoint of industrial competitiveness is that the government force the remaining publicly owned enterprises to function without government support, thus halting the practice of taxing efficient firms, either explicitly or implicitly through higher interest rates, to subsidize inefficient ones.

Similar privatization efforts have been undertaken in the financial sector. So far, of the 399 nonperforming loans held by the public banks, 178, making up 13.5 percent of the total government exposure, have been fully or partially sold. The attempted rehabilitation of these banks appears to be reasonably successful thus far: the flotation in 1989 of 30 percent of the Philippines National Bank stock was a success, and the stock price has risen substantially (Intal and Pante 1989).

The government adopted a tax reform package in 1986 to increase the uniformity of tax rates across different activities, broaden the tax base, and improve the efficiency of collection. It is hoped that these actions will increase tax revenues, thereby lowering the fiscal deficit and reducing the upward pressure on interest rates and prices.

Investment incentives were overhauled in 1987. This reform appears to have reduced the importance of Board of Investments approval for project implementation, although the impact on sectoral incentives is unclear: Manasan (1990) claims that the reforms actually disadvantaged exporters and increased "capital cheapening" factor price distortions. Moreover, the investment code still limits foreign ownership of firms to 40 percent (except in "pioneer" and export sectors).[9]

Trade reform measures were initiated in 1980 to correct the adverse

---

9. The government has also recently revised its industrial policy guidelines regulating the development of the motor vehicles industry. Although the new policy guidelines represent a considerable improvement over the previous ones, the benefits of this policy are doubtful in light of the high domestic prices charged by the firms operating within these programs.

incentive effects accumulated during three decades of import-substituting industrialization by reducing the level and variability of protection in a comprehensive manner. This policy involved reform of all key areas of the trade regime: tariff protection, import restrictions, the tax system, and the export promotion system.

The tariff overhaul was the centerpiece of the trade reform. The principal objectives were to reduce the range of nominal tariffs, from zero to 100 percent in 1980 down to 10 percent to 50 percent in 1985; to reduce the average nominal tariff from 45 percent to 28 percent; and to reduce the degree of escalation and thus the extent of effective protection for final-goods production.

These goals were largely accomplished on schedule in 1985. The average nominal tariff rate was reduced to 27.9 percent. The standard deviation of tariff rates fell from 32.6 percent in 1980 to 15.1 percent in 1985, indicating the increased uniformity of rates. Moreover, because the largest declines occurred for consumer goods, as opposed to intermediate products and raw materials, the escalation of the tariff structure has been moderated.

Historically, the protective impact of import tariffs has been reinforced by tax practices that discriminate against imports and in favor of domestic substitutes. Tax reforms undertaken in 1983 and 1984 have redressed the major protective aspects of the indirect tax system. Sales taxes have been equalized on imported and domestic goods, except for automobiles, although importers still face the implicit costs associated with earlier payment of the advance sales tax. The extent of markup used in this calculation has been reduced to a flat 25 percent.

Quantitative import restrictions have a long history in the Philippines. They were the primary trade policy instrument in the 1950s, but were dismantled and replaced with tariffs in the 1960–62 liberalization. Quantitative restrictions on nonessential consumer-goods imports were reintroduced in the late 1960s, and coverage steadily widened during the 1970s. By 1980, quantitative controls covered 40 percent of the seven-digit classification level, and 27 percent of total imports. Two kinds of restrictions were applied: "banned" products were subject to a zero quota, and "regulated" products could only be imported with prior approval. In addition to encouraging the misallocation of resources into protected sectors, quantitative restrictions had the further detrimental effects of inducing rent-seeking behavior by firms and promoting the establishment of local oligopolies sheltered from external competition. Accordingly, the 1980 trade reform package included a plan to liberalize 960 out of a total of 1,301 items between 1981 and 1983. In addition, a liberalization schedule was set for 321 regulated items. Actual liberalization proceeded unevenly, with increases in the number of regulated items offsetting the reduction in the number of banned items. But by the end of 1986, trade in

936 products had been liberalized, or about 75 percent of the original program.[10] Data on ERPs indicate that the trade reforms led to a considerable decline in protection: the average ERP dropped from 24 percent in 1979 to 12 percent in 1985.[11] For manufacturing as a whole, the reduction was from 40 percent to 23 percent, while for import-competing manufactured products the decline was from 58 percent to 33 percent. Although the extent of deprotection revealed in these figures is substantial, some disturbing aspects of the trade regime have not been eliminated.

Three product categories exhibit negative value added at world prices: cooking oil, importable animal feed, and importable processed foods. Seven receive ERPs in excess of 100 percent: milk and other dairy products, animal feed, tobacco manufactures, importable textiles (excluding garments), paper and paper products, miscellaneous chemical products, and fabricated metal products. These extremely high ERPs, in combination with negative ERPs for both exports and primary products as a whole, indicate that even after the recent trade reforms the system still promotes import substitution. Considerable scope exists for further equalizing incentives across activities and encouraging greater outward orientation.

Even so, evidence suggests that the reforms carried out thus far have encouraged greater outward orientation and competitiveness. In 1985 the Department of Trade and Industry introduced an "advanced tax credit scheme," which allowed direct and indirect textile exporters quick recovery of taxes and duties paid on raw materials and intermediate inputs. Simultaneously the government began to convert quantitative restrictions on both textiles and inputs (such as polyester staple fiber, filament yarn, and spun yarn) to tariffs, with a limit set of 50 percent for textiles and 10 percent for inputs (20 percent for polyester fiber). Since then investment in both textiles and apparel has picked up. For certain types of export garments, producers have increased the share of domestic inputs to 30 percent. (However, while real value added grew 28 percent in apparel between 1987 and 1989, it actually fell slightly in textiles over the same period.) Other examples of

---

10. The remaining restrictions cover 600 items including cement, newsprint, consumer durables, motor vehicles, intermediate inputs, and spare parts. The restrictions on the importation on cement and intermediate goods are particularly onerous because they raise the costs and restrict the expansion of higher-value-added and more employment-oriented downstream industries.

11. These data are from the Philippines Institute of Development Studies–Tariff Commission study and take into account tariffs, taxes, and subsidies (but not quantitative import restrictions). The data for 1979 give an indication of the extent of protection prior to the policy reforms; since there have been no major changes in the tariff code since 1985, the 1985 figures approximate 1990 levels of protection. Data disaggregated at the industry level can be found in Alburo et al. (1988).

positive adjustment to liberalization include the once heavily protected tire industry: the Philippines became an exporter of tires in 1988. Canned tuna exports increased at a 47 percent annual rate between 1987 and 1989 in response to the liberalization of tin plate.

Unfortunately, another trade reform that would have further reduced the level and narrowed the range of nominal tariffs was postponed in September 1990. This setback has been accompanied by continuing problems in the area of intellectual property protection, where foreign firms regard both the laws in this area and their enforcement as inadequate. As a result, the Philippines has been placed on the "watch list" under the Special 301 provision of the 1988 US trade act.

In addition to attempts at trade liberalization, the Philippines has tried to strengthen its export promotion policies. The main goal of these policies is to provide direct and indirect exporters with unimpeded access to inputs at world market prices and to working capital for export production. To achieve these goals the Philippine government has introduced a duty exemption and drawback system, a bonded warehouse system, export processing zones, preshipment export finance, and international marketing support. Although these programs have a long history, their success has been mixed. The duty drawback system has been used by only some 20 percent of exporters, representing about 50 percent of nontraditional exporters. Its usefulness has been limited by the selectivity of products covered, the requirement that locally produced alternative inputs be unavailable, and the discretionary nature of its administration.

As noted earlier, the success of the export processing policy is debatable. Although these activities have generated considerable exports, employment, and foreign exchange, the costs have been high, largely because of enormous infrastructure costs and the policy of granting participating firms subsidized access to capital markets. Indeed, Warr (1986) found that both the infrastructure costs and the implicit capital subsidies outweighed the benefits to the economy, and that the net present value of the program was actually negative.

Preshipment export finance, available through the central bank, has also benefited only a limited number of exporters, mainly large firms. The problem is the general one of limited access to credit, the unavailability of domestic letters of credit for indirect exporters, and fluctuations in the provision of funds by the central bank.

International marketing support has been provided indirectly through the promotion of general trading companies and exporters' associations, and directly through myriad government agencies. The usefulness of the government agencies' activities has been limited by their fragmented, duplicative, and poorly coordinated implementation.

Finally, to evaluate the Philippines' competitiveness, foreign barriers to Philippine exports must also be taken into account. Although tariff rates have generally been reduced to low levels in most developed-country markets, tariff rates on raw materials exported by the Philippines are lower than on Philippine manufactured products, thus discouraging the development of processing activities in the Philippines. For example, tariff rates in Japan and the European Community on copra (dried coconut meat, from which coconut oil is expressed) are lower than on crude coconut oil. The same sort of escalation by degree of processing exists for wood veneer sheets and plywood.

Philippine exporters also encounter a variety of nontariff barriers in developed-country markets. The share of Philippine exports covered by nontariff barriers is 10.5 percent in the United States, 59.2 percent in the European Community, and 51.9 percent in Japan. These are most pervasive in the areas of agriculture and textiles and apparel. In a number of cases, nontariff barriers in the form of quotas, questionable health and sanitary regulations, and special taxes restrict the entry of imports that would otherwise enter duty-free. Examples include robusta coffee (duty-free on an MFN basis in the United States and Japan), copra (MFN duty-free in the European Community), and centrifugal sugar (duty-free under the GSP in the United States).

Among manufactures, garments and footwear, which enter developed-country markets on a preferential basis under the GSP, are subject to quotas, import licensing arrangements, and voluntary export restraints.[12] In some cases, quantitative restrictions on Philippine exports are nonbinding, however. Quotas on garment exports to the United States and other quota countries have not been filled in recent years. This suggests that the quotas themselves have not been binding constraints, although the domestic practice of allocating quota rights largely on a fixed basis to established firms retards competitiveness.

The Philippines benefits from some developed-country trade preference schemes, notably the GSP. Utilization of GSP preferences by the Philippines appears about average, with the Philippines' share of GSP exports roughly the same as its share of developing-country exports as a whole. The removal of

---

12. The absence of observable nontariff barriers in other markets does not necessarily indicate that the Philippines has had greater success in penetrating those markets, however. The bulk of Philippine electronic circuitry exports have gone to the European Community despite bilateral quotas and discretionary licensing, and not to the United States, which does not maintain nontariff barriers in this sector. Similarly, most garment exports have gone to the United States and the European Community despite their many nontariff barriers against those products, and not to Japan, which is without a known nontariff barrier against Philippine garment exports.

the NICs' GSP privileges by the United States at the beginning of 1989 effectively widened the preference margin the Philippines enjoys, and should act as a stimulus to further Philippine exports to the United States.[13]

Exchange Rates

The single most important aspect of the Philippines' export promotion policy is the maintenance of a competitive real exchange rate. Four REER indices are shown in figure 3.3. Those computed using trading-partner weights show a significant real depreciation of the Philippine peso between 1984 and 1986, mainly due to depreciation against the US dollar and the Japanese yen. Nonetheless, the WPI-based REER was still lower in 1988 than at the start of the decade. In contrast, the export price REER stood at 133.0, a considerable increase from its 1980 value.

This gain in competitiveness vanishes when changes in the real exchange rates of the Philippines' competitors are taken into account. Although the peso depreciated in nominal terms over the period, relatively rapid increases in domestic prices and contemporaneous devaluations by competitors offset the nominal depreciation. REERs calculated on the basis of competitor weights in world export markets were virtually unchanged between 1984 and 1988, indicating that no real depreciation occurred; indeed the broader WPI-based REER actually fell over this period. Although the Philippines did gain in competitiveness against some competitors (Hong Kong, Taiwan), it lost competitiveness against others, especially Indonesia. Overall, the competitor-weighted REERs were 10 percent to 15 percent lower in 1988 than at the beginning of the decade, and were 10 percent to 20 percent below their levels of 1982, suggesting that additional real depreciation may be necessary to maintain competitiveness in third-country markets.

---

13. When the United States applied voluntary export restraints to major footwear exporters in the early 1980s, production shifted quickly to the Philippines. Philippine footwear exports peaked at $73 million in 1981, but as the restraints were relaxed, production shifted back to the traditional suppliers, and Philippine footwear exports declined to $22 million in 1988. Although the removal of GSP privileges from the NICs will probably not have as dramatic an impact as the imposition of voluntary export restraints on footwear did, the footwear example nevertheless underscores the potential importance of trade preferences in promoting exports.

Figure 3.3   Philippines: real effective exchange rates, 1970–88

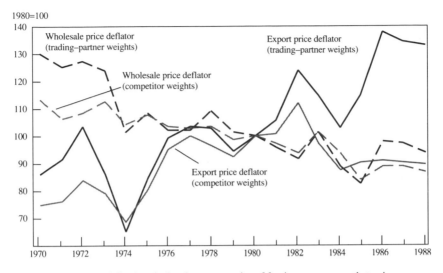

Note: The indices are defined as the local-currency price of foreign currency, so that a rise in the index signifies a depreciation.

Trade Patterns

The commodity composition of Philippine exports changed little between 1950 and 1970. The 10 principal exports remained unchanged and accounted for 75 percent to 85 percent of exports throughout the period. These were mainly tropical agricultural commodities such as coconuts and sugar, and basic minerals such as copper ore and gold. The income elasticity of demand for many of these products is low, and they are frequently subject to trade barriers in foreign markets. The principal destinations of the Philippines' exports during this period were the United States and Japan, which together typically absorbed approximately three-quarters of exports.

The composition of Philippine exports began to change significantly around 1970. If products that were only assembled or produced under consignment are counted as exports, the share of traditional export products in total exports fell from 78.5 percent in 1970 to 39.2 percent in 1988. Conversely, the importance of nontraditional manufactured exports (mostly garments and electronic components) grew, their share of total exports rising from 6.1 percent in 1970 to 56.1 percent in 1988.

The largest export category is garments, with a 19.7 percent share of total exports (again using the broader definition) for 1989, followed by electrical equipment (mostly electronic components) with a 16.7 percent share, and coconut products with a 6.3 percent share. No other category has more than a 5 percent share. The categories with the most rapid export growth in volume terms have been prepared tuna with a 34 percent annual increase between 1987 and 1989, shrimp and prawns with a 31 percent annual growth rate, gold (which in the Philippines is a byproduct of copper mining) at 24 percent, and semiconductors and garments, each with 19 percent annual volume growth rates between 1987 and 1989.[14]

Using more standard definitions of exports, which exclude products subject to minimal processing, the role of manufactures exports in the economy appears considerably smaller (table 3.5; manufacturing trade shares by industry are reported in appendix B, table B.7). These increased from 4.0 percent of total exports in 1963 to 35.8 percent in 1988. This increase was concentrated in engineering products (mainly electronics), textiles, and wood products.

The Philippines also reduced its reliance on the US and Japanese markets, whose combined share of Philippine exports fell from 72.8 percent to 55.8 percent over the period (table 3.6). The United States remains the principal export market, absorbing 35.7 percent of Philippine exports in 1988. On the import side, the major changes were the decline in imports originating in the United States and the increasing importance of imports from the NICs, possibly associated with their increased FDI in the Philippines. Otherwise, there has been little change in the geographical composition of trade in recent years.

Issues for the 1990s

To strengthen its export competitiveness, the Philippines needs to implement a variety of policy reforms. Some of these will enhance export competitiveness indirectly by improving the efficiency of domestic industry, whereas others will strengthen export competitiveness more directly by changing the

---

14. These achievements should not be underestimated. A constant-market-share analysis of exports of 156 products in 37 markets over the period 1967–83 found that, because of the concentration of the Philippines' export bundle in products facing relatively slow growing demand, the maintenance of constant export shares implied an income elasticity of demand for the Philippines' exports of 0.75 (Noland 1990a). In fact, exporters were able to successfully diversify into faster-growing product and geographical markets, and the Philippines' exports grew faster than trading-partner income, despite the government's poor policy performance.

Table 3.5 Philippines: composition of trade by major product group, 1963 and 1988 (percentages)

Industry	Exports 1963	Exports 1988	Imports 1963	Imports 1988
Fuels (SITC 3)	0.4	2.1	11.4	13.2
Nonfuel primary products	94.7	36.1	23.4	17.1
Food and live animals (SITC 0)	26.4	14.3	13.1	6.9
Beverages and tobacco (SITC 1)	1.8	0.5	0.3	1.1
Industrial raw materials (SITC 2, 4, 68)	66.5	21.4	10.0	9.1
Manufactures (industrial classification)	4.0	35.8	50.8	48.7
Textiles, apparel, and leather (ISIC 32)	0.4	8.2	1.7	4.1
Wood products and furniture (ISIC 33)	3.6	7.9	0.0	0.1
Paper and paper products (ISIC 34)	0.0	0.4	2.9	2.2
Chemicals (ISIC 35)	0.0	3.5	8.0	13.5
Nonmetallic mineral products (ISIC 36)	0.0	0.5	1.5	0.9
Iron and steel (ISIC 37)	0.0	1.1	6.4	6.1
Engineering products (ISIC 38)	0.0	11.2	29.9	21.4
Miscellaneous (ISIC 39)	0.0	3.1	0.5	0.4
Other products	0.9	26.0	14.4	21.0
Memorandum: trade in goods and nonfactor services as a share of GDP	16.5	27.2	15.4	30.2

SITC = Standard International Trade Classification.

ISIC = International Standard Industrial Classification.

Source: General Agreement on Tariffs and Trade. Memorandum data are from the World Bank.

relative prices within the tradeables sector of the domestic economy, and between Philippine exportables and those of its competitors.

From a welfare standpoint, the highest priority has to be increasing productivity in the agricultural sector. This is where most of the population and most of the poverty are. The single most important change would be to implement a genuine, widespread land reform.[15] This should be accompanied by improvements in basic rural infrastructure (especially roads), extension

---

15. It must be recognized that in some agriculture-related activities (such as crop spraying) significant economies of scale exist. It would be desirable to organize small landholders into cooperatives to facilitate the continuance of some of these efficient practices, now conducted at the plantation level.

Table 3.6 Philippines: geographical composition of trade, 1963 and 1988 (percentages)

Country	Exports		Imports	
	1963	1988	1963	1988
Developed countries	95.5	77.4	81.8	57.4
United States	45.5	35.7	41.1	21.0
Western Europe	22.3	18.3	18.1	13.6
Japan	27.3	20.1	17.0	17.4
Canada, Australia, New Zealand	0.5	3.2	5.7	5.4
Developing countries	4.2	22.2	18.3	41.9
Pacific countries (other than China)	3.0	16.9	8.3	24.1
East Asian NICs	2.9	13.2	2.0	18.7
Hong Kong	0.4	4.9	1.1	4.5
Singapore	0.1	3.1	0.3	4.1
Taiwan	1.5	2.8	0.5	6.1
Korea	0.9	2.3	0.1	4.0
Other ASEAN–4	0.1	3.8	6.3	5.4
Malaysia	0.0	1.7	2.1	2.9
Thailand	0.1	1.8	1.2	0.6
Indonesia	n.a.	0.4	3.0	1.9
China	n.a.	0.9	n.a.	3.1
Other developing countries	1.2	4.3	10.0	14.7
Other Asia	0.5	1.9	3.6	1.8
Africa	0.3	0.2	1.1	1.1
Europe[b]	0.0	0.1	n.a.	0.2
Middle East	0.0	1.4	3.8	9.6
Latin America	0.3	0.7	1.4	2.0
European socialist countries	n.a.	0.4	n.a.	0.8

n.a. = not available.

a. Regional aggregates may not sum to 100 percent because of inclusion in the world total of special categories and other countries not specified.

b. Principally Portugal, Greece, and Turkey.

Sources: International Monetary Fund, *Direction of Trade Statistics,* various issues.

services, and the provision of rural credit and other agricultural inputs. Investments in small-scale communal irrigation and rural electrification would also have high payoffs.

It must be recognized, however, that agrarian reform on this scale is unlikely to occur without considerable financial support from abroad. Paradoxically, the most comprehensive land reforms in the world since World War II have been produced either by communist revolution (China, Vietnam) or by military forces with little stake in the status quo (the United States in Japan and Korea, the nationalists from the mainland in Taiwan). It is difficult (indeed virtually impossible in a democracy) to mobilize sufficient political wherewithal to accomplish agrarian reform without revolution or occupation. The third alternative, buying off the rural elites, invariably requires the infusion of massive amounts of funds from outside (e.g., as in Zimbabwe). Serious agrarian reform in the absence of significant external support is extremely unlikely given the political and economic realities of the Philippines.

Unfortunately, such large-scale external support is unlikely to be forthcoming without further progress in resolving the Philippines' debt problem. The external debt is projected to exceed $30 billion (or more than twice GNP) in 1990 and 1991, and interest payments are expected to equal 16 percent to 17 percent of exports (World Bank 1990). Although these numbers are high, they represent a substantial improvement from the mid-1980s, when the debt–GNP ratio exceeded 300 percent and the interest-exports ratio reached 25 percent.

The Philippines' debt is divided roughly evenly between official and private creditors. In the autumn of 1989, on the heels of the Mexican debt-reduction agreement, the Philippines entered into debt-reduction negotiations with its commercial bank creditors and the international financial institutions. The Philippine government aimed to buy back $1.4 billion in loans from the banks at a 50 percent discount and receive $1 billion in new lending. The arrangements were proceeding reasonably well when the December 1989 coup attempt deeply shook investor confidence. The Philippine government, supported by the World Bank, the IMF, and Japan's Export-Import Bank, eventually retired $1.34 billion in debt at a price of $668 million in January 1990. Indeed, the buyback was oversubscribed. New money was less forthcoming, however, and estimates of additional lending for 1990 were reduced to $700 million to $750 million. Unlike the recent agreements in Mexico and Costa Rica, the Philippine package lacks an air of finality, and it is likely that the debt problem will remain a drag on the economy for the foreseeable future.

Within the industrial sphere, reforms are needed to strengthen property rights and remove the state from activities that could be more efficiently performed by private firms. This means pushing forward with the privatization program and ending subsidies to the public corporate sector. This would include completing the privatization of the Philippines National Bank and rehabilitating the commercial banking sector. Assistance should be provided to those banks that are fundamentally sound while encouraging the consolidation of those that are not viable in their current form. These reforms would facilitate the rationalization and more efficient use of existing productive assets.

Specific reforms needed in the financial sector include strengthening regulations on general and specific provisions against bad loans, lowering reserve requirements, increasing the interest paid on reserves, eliminating forced investment in agricultural reform bonds, and abolishing the 5 percent tax on the gross receipts of financial intermediaries (Balassa 1990). These reforms would increase the efficiency of financial intermediation and contribute to a reduction in the cost of capital.

Investment and industrial capacity should be increased. The most effective means of stimulating investment would be to reduce the cost of capital to private investors. This, in turn, requires lowering interest rates by reducing the government's borrowing demands and improving the efficiency of intermediation. The former can be achieved by reducing government spending (for instance, by halting subsidies to publicly owned firms) and improving the efficiency of tax collection, which is notoriously poor. An increase in the value-added tax rate should also be considered. The financial reforms already outlined would contribute to more efficient intermediation.

Physical infrastructure needs to be refurbished through complementary public investment. The transportation network, especially in outlying areas, needs improvement. Electrical generating capacity needs to be expanded. Charges to industrial users should be reduced by equalizing the rates charged to commercial and household users. Rebates to exporters should be introduced to ensure that they compete on an equal footing with exporters in the other East Asian developing countries. The government has recognized these problems and is planning to unify the rate structure faced by residential and industrial users. It also hopes to expand the system's capacity. The power sector currently accounts for 26 percent of the government's public investment program (Intal and Pante 1989).

Technological performance could also be strengthened. The Philippines needs to do a better job of attracting FDI, which would not only increase total investment but also encourage technology transfer and improve marketing and distribution links with world markets. Net FDI averaged $63 million per year from 1971 to 1982, then fell to $49 million per year during the economic crisis of 1983–85. Since then it has grown rapidly to $140 million in 1986,

$326 million in 1987, $986 million in 1988, and possibly $795 million in 1989.[16] The increases are due partly to the recent intensification of East Asian intraregional investment flows, and partly to the political and economic reforms undertaken in the Philippines. Nonetheless, the Philippines still lags well behind the other East Asian developing countries in accumulated FDI. Within the Philippines, the largest foreign investors are Japan, Taiwan, the United States, and Hong Kong. The single most important policy measure that could be undertaken is the abolition of the constitutional provision limiting foreign investors to 40 percent equity ownership in most sectors. This is a considerable disincentive to potential foreign investors, who require control over management to ensure quality control.

Technological upgrading would also be promoted by greater emphasis in the educational system on technical training and engineering. This could be accomplished by reallocating resources within the existing educational structure, and by the establishment of technical training centers in cooperation with private firms, along the lines of those in Singapore. Greater efforts at technological adaptation and development could be promoted through technology development centers and R&D tax credits.

Other reforms to strengthen trade performance would be desirable. Exchange rate management will become increasingly important as the Philippines moves into manufactured exports and competes more directly against the other East Asian economies. Since the Philippine peso floats, macroeconomic policy can be used to reduce the real exchange rate. A reduction of the fiscal deficit along with a relaxation of monetary policy would encourage lower interest rates and currency depreciation.

Export performance could be further enhanced by improving the structure of incentives and improving export promotion. As noted earlier, even after the trade liberalization, the Philippines' structure of protection still encourages import substitution. The industrial policy development programs should be eliminated. There is a need to further reduce the level and variation of tariff rates. A tariff ceiling of 25 percent should be considered. Existing quantitative controls should be converted to tariffs, and an interim system of auction quotas should be considered to determine the appropriate tariff conversions for existing quantitative restrictions. Infant-industry protection should be confined to tariff protection, subject to time limits. Domestic trade liberalization should be coupled with an external trade negotiation strategy, as will be discussed in chapter 5. Measures to improve export promotion should include streamlining and simplifying the duty exemption system as well as the fixed and individual drawback system; reforming the existing bonded warehouse

---

16. International Monetary Fund, *International Financial Statistics*, various issues.

system by establishing special warehouses and customs procedures; improving the efficiency of the export processing zone system; developing a preshipment export finance guarantee agency that would service small, infant, and indirect exporters; and consolidating the fragmented support for product development and marketing.

All of these problems are well recognized within the Philippines, and the Aquino government has been pursuing a broad (if unevenly implemented) program of economic reform. The key issue is implementation, which is made all the more difficult by the twin obstacles of debt and political instability.

Indonesia

Historical and Policy Background

Indonesia is an archipelagic state of over 13,500 islands straddling the equator from the southeast Asian coast to Australia. It was colonized by the Portuguese in the 16th century, conquered by the Dutch in the 17th century, and occupied by the Japanese during World War II. Nationalist leaders proclaimed independence in 1945, prevailing after four years of armed struggle over the Dutch, who withdrew in 1949. The Dutch possession of West New Guinea (Irian Jaya) came under Indonesian control in 1963, and Indonesia forcibly annexed the Portuguese Overseas Territory of East Timor in 1976.

Indonesia has a population of more than 185 million, making it the fifth most populous country in the world. Around 95 percent of the population is Malay; the remainder consists of various ethnic groups, most prominently the Chinese, who comprise approximately 2 percent of the population. Overall, the population is overwhelmingly (around 85 percent) Muslim, although the ethnic and religious composition of the population varies considerably from island to island. Geographically the population is distributed highly unevenly: the islands of Java, Madura, and Bali, which account for just over 7 percent of the land area, hold almost 65 percent of the population. The government is actively pursuing resettlement schemes to reduce this imbalance.

During the colonial period the Indonesian economy was based on the production of tin, rubber, coffee, and other agricultural cash crops, which were exported in return for manufactures and the staple food, rice. The country's first leader after independence, President Sukarno, emphasized the development of heavy industry in the context of a highly statist program. Foreign interests were nationalized and new state enterprises created to implement the industrialization strategy. The productive capacity destroyed during the wars was rebuilt, but eventually the program began to falter. In 1959 per capita income started falling. Sukarno declared martial law and began to assume increasingly dictatorial powers. In 1965 a group of army officers launched an attempted coup, allegedly in cooperation with the Indonesia Communist Party (PKI). The coup failed, and in its aftermath hundreds of thousands of Indonesians were killed in communal violence, many of them ethnic Chinese. Sukarno attempted to continue in power, but in 1966, with the economy at the point of collapse, he was removed from office, and Major General Suharto became the acting executive. Suharto was later elected president, a position that he continues to hold.

Although he introduced a number of reforms, President Suharto has largely maintained the statist economic program of his predecessor. Indonesia's strong ability to export primary products (especially crude oil) has provided officials with a large financial cushion against policy errors. However, the decline in the price of oil in the late 1980s and other adverse movements in the terms of trade have put considerable pressure on the authorities for policy reform and have encouraged diversification away from oil.

Nearly three-quarters of the population of Indonesia live in rural areas, and agriculture directly provides employment to nearly 60 percent of the population. The food crop subsector, which is the most important component of Indonesian agriculture, is almost entirely composed of smallholders. In general, government policies have been supportive.

The government has made the expansion of rice production a very high priority. This has in effect meant implementing an ambitious program of expanding rural infrastructure and agricultural support services. Production has been increased by expanding the acreage under cultivation, as well as by increasing productivity though improved irrigation and increased use of modern inputs such as fertilizers, pesticides, and high-yield varieties of rice. As a result, Indonesia has shifted from being a major rice importer in the late 1970s to self-sufficiency, and most recently to an exporter of rice.

The other main thrust of agricultural policy has been the encouragement of investment in the neglected tree crop subsector. By the early 1980s, the Indonesian replanting program was the largest in the world. Rubber, oil palm, and coconut together account for one-third of the land under cultivation, provide employment and cash income to one out of eight people, and generate about 30 percent of agricultural earnings. Indonesia is the world's second-largest producer of all three of these crops, and the world's third-largest producer of coffee.

Indonesia is also a major producer of other primary products. Marine exports (especially shrimp and tuna) are increasingly important. Indonesia is also a major exporter of forest products, primarily timber. Beginning in 1980, authorities introduced a ban on log exports, which have been replaced by exports of processed wood. Lastly, Indonesia has considerable mineral resources. It is the world's second-largest producer of tin, and gold production has increased steadily in recent years. Bauxite, copper, and nickel are also mined in significant quantities.

The predominant primary product export, however, is oil. The early development of the Indonesian oil industry was slowed by the constitutional requirement that the state control all of the country's mineral resources, which led to the nationalization of existing foreign interests. Production-sharing contracts were subsequently introduced, under which foreign firms were granted the right to develop specified fields in return for a proportion of their output. As a consequence, foreign firms now dominate production, accounting for nearly 95 percent of output. Crude oil and petroleum products account for nearly half of total exports, and taxes on oil companies generate more than 40 percent of government revenues (Nasution 1989).

Manufacturing activities, promoted by government policies since independence, represent a small but growing share of output. The manufacturing share of GDP rose steadily from 7.4 percent in 1963 to 10.6 percent in 1973, 12.1 percent in 1981, and 13.9 percent in 1987 (Balassa 1990). Much of this has been accomplished through state enterprises, which at the end of 1987 numbered 214. These include 23 financial institutions and 191 nonfinancial institutions, of which 158 were fully state-owned. The state enterprises accounted for 20 percent of the establishments and more than 60 percent of the output in the manufacturing sector, although these shares have fallen over time. The state enterprises hold dominant positions in oil refining, petrochemicals, fertilizers, steel, aluminum, cement, basic chemicals, capital-goods manufacturing, and shipbuilding.

In general, the state enterprises have been less efficient than their private-sector counterparts, although in the absence of reliable data on financial flows between these enterprises and the government it is impossible to ascertain the extent of subsidization. The state enterprises are also promoted through protection from foreign competition and the provision of economic rents such as concessions, licenses, monopoly rights, preferential tax treatment, and preferential access to public procurement contracts. The relatively poorer economic performance of the state enterprises can be explained in part by extensive bureaucratic interference in their management and their charge to fulfill social, as well as economic, objectives. Output prices and permissible marketing channels are sometimes set by bureaucratic decree, and routine business decisions can require bureaucratic approval.

Each state enterprise under the Department of Industry has been assigned the task of transferring technologies to, and creating markets for, small and medium-sized enterprises, sometimes in wholly unrelated businesses.[17] As in Malaysia, the public sector has also been assigned the task of promoting the economic development of the indigenous Malay population, or *pribumi*. This is partly accomplished through an extensive system of procurement set-asides. *Pribumi* enterprises receive preferential access to credit through the state financial institutions, and special credit programs have been established to promote *pribumi* businesses.[18]

The state-owned nonfinancial enterprises exist in a symbiotic relationship with the state-owned financial enterprises. The state-owned banking system, consisting of the central bank and a group of seven commercial banks, is the core of Indonesian finance, accounting for more than 80 percent of the gross assets of the formal financial system (Nasution 1989). Before financial reforms were undertaken in 1988, government regulations effectively assured the state bank group a monopsony in the funds market and a monopoly in the credit market. Discriminatory tax regulations discouraged raising capital through alternative channels such as the stock and bond markets, and forced firms to rely on bank finance. Moreover, until 1983, the government controlled the lending of these banks through a variety of interest ceilings and direct rationing mechanisms. As might be expected, this induced rent seeking on a massive scale, as close relationships with the government regulatory and financial bureaucracies were essential to business success.

Recent Reforms

Financial reforms undertaken in 1983 abolished the credit ceilings and controls on the state banks' interest rates, resulting in a sharp rise in interest rates and a dramatic increase in bank deposits. A new monetary instrument was introduced to facilitate control of the money supply through open market operations, complemented by a system of rediscount facilities and the adoption of measures to strengthen the financial markets. Because of the shallowness of the domestic financial markets, the government had been unable to float bonds domestically, and as a consequence relied on foreign aid and borrowing to finance its budget deficit.

During the 1980s, foreign aid and loans have accounted for about 10

---

17. Nasution (1989) cites the examples of a state-owned cement plant which was assigned the task of developing marketing channels for local cinnamon producers, and a fertilizer plant which was ordered to create markets for local handicrafts.

18. The recent substitution of the term *Indonesia asli*, or Indonesian national, for *pribumi* could be expected to dilute the impact of these measures, however.

percent of GDP, 80 percent of the current account deficit, and 90 percent of the government deficit (Nasution 1989). Most of this is government debt on concessional terms from official sources. Not only did this heavy reliance on external finance imply considerable transfers from domestic residents to foreigners; it also exposed the Indonesian economy to additional terms-of-trade shocks. The largest share of the debt (40 percent) is denominated in yen, and the spectacular appreciation of the yen starting in 1985 caused a considerable increase in the real financial burden, with the interest-exports ratio peaking at 18 percent in 1986. This ratio has been on a declining path ever since, however, and Indonesia has avoided the periodic reschedulings that have plagued the Philippines.

Further reforms were enacted in 1988 to increase competition within the financial sector and to integrate the domestic financial system with the international financial centers. The 1988 measures permitted the entry of new banks (including joint ventures with foreign banks), the expansion of existing banks through the establishment of additional branches, and the relaxation of restrictions on nonbank financial institutions, effectively ending the state banks' monopsony in the funds market. The reforms also permitted more institutions to deal in foreign exchange and promoted closer integration with the international financial system. Deregulation of the stock market encouraged the rejuvenation of the languishing Jakarta stock exchange. A second, over-the-counter exchange was established in 1989.

At the same time the government was introducing reforms to strengthen the financial markets, it was implementing a comprehensive tax reform to reduce its reliance on oil taxes, increase revenues, and thereby reduce its dependence on external finance. The system in existence prior to the 1983–85 reforms had become "a complex maze of virtually unenforceable, if not unintelligible, amendments, decrees, and regulations" (Gillis 1989). Individual income taxes were assessed at steeply progressive rates starting at 5 percent and rising to 50 percent. The base was so full of exemptions and exclusions, however, that the effective rate of income tax for individuals in the top 5 percent of the income distribution was only 4 percent. Similarly, the business tax was levied at graduated rates rising from 20 percent to 45 percent, but because of exemptions, exclusions, and abatements only about 12 percent of the large foreign firms and 8 percent of the large domestic firms paid the maximum rate (Gillis 1989).[19]

---

19. Gillis (1989) reports that the tax code contained provisions to encourage the purchase of life insurance, to encourage the construction of bowling alleys, to finance tournament travel for chess players, and to promote the use of public accountants. Perhaps the most galling exemption was that for income of civil servants, which meant that the tax collectors themselves were not subject to income taxes.

The reforms undertaken in 1983–85 were systemic, encompassing not only the tax structure but also the instruments and institutions governing administration and compliance. The centerpiece of the reform was the introduction of a simple value-added tax of 10 percent on all manufactured items, applied at the manufacturer-importer level. Excluding wholesalers and retailers from the value-added tax greatly simplified its collection, since nearly two-thirds of the taxes could be assessed and collected at a few easily accessible bottlenecks: the customs house for imports, PERTAMINA (the state oil enterprise) for petroleum products, and the remaining 200-odd state enterprises for many manufactures. Business and individual taxes were combined, with rates set progressively at 14 percent, 25 percent, and 35 percent. Most exclusions were eliminated. The progressivity of the system was increased by raising the standard deduction, thus excluding most households (approximately 85 percent) from any income taxes at all. The former, differentiated-rate property tax system was replaced with a flat tax. Again, progressivity was ensured by combining this with a large exclusion, making virtually all rural housing and low-income urban housing exempt. Lastly, by simplifying the rules and reducing the number of payers in the system, authorities were able to concentrate auditing efforts on targets with potentially large payoffs, sometimes with astounding success.[20]

The new system has generated revenues beyond expectation. Nonoil tax revenues rose 164 percent between 1983 and 1988, with the nonoil tax share of GDP increasing from 6.3 percent to 9.3 percent. Yet this only partly offset the dramatic fall in oil tax revenues from 12.3 percent of GDP in 1983 to 6.3 percent in 1988.

The policies discussed thus far largely involve the state enterprises, the state institution–dominated financial system, and the system of public finance itself. Historically, the government has also exercised considerable influence over the investment decisions of private firms. When the government reformed the financial and tax systems, it also undertook reform of its investment regulations. Starting in 1985, the government began relaxing its investment and licensing system. Fields of investment open to private investors were delineated more precisely, and the range of economic activities open to them was increased markedly. Approved investments rose dramatically, from 3.7 trillion rupiahs (Rp) in 1985 to Rp14.9 trillion in 1988. Moreover, the share of export-oriented investment in domestic investment rose from 54 percent in 1986 to 74 percent in 1988 (Nasution 1989).

---

20. Gillis (1989) cites the example of a 30-person strike force established in 1986 at a cost of $200,000. In its first year of operation, this group generated $68 million in taxes, fines, and penalties, enough to pay for the entire cost of computer hardware and software introduced during the reform, and the overseas training of 75 junior tax officials.

The deregulation of investment has extended to FDI as well. During the Sukarno regime, Dutch-owned enterprises were nationalized, and investment controls discouraged FDI. The Suharto government adopted a more favorable stance. The Foreign Capital Investment Law of 1967 forswore nationalization and provided a variety of tax preferences for foreign investors.[21] These were curtailed following the violent protests that accompanied the visit of Japanese Prime Minister Kakuei Tanaka in 1974. A more restrictive set of rules was enacted stipulating that all new foreign investments were to be joint ventures, with Indonesian equity to be increased to 51 percent within 10 years. The list of industries closed to foreign investment was expanded, and the number of foreign management and technical personnel permitted to work on these ventures was reduced (Balassa 1990).

These restrictions, as well as additional performance requirements, were widely ignored in later years (Ariff and Hill 1985). In particular, the 10-year deadline for local majority equity ownership was never enforced (Balassa 1990). Starting in 1986, the rules were formally liberalized: the time limit for 51 percent Indonesian equity participation was extended to 15 years; for export-oriented and high-risk projects domestic equity obligations were reduced to 5 percent; for others a 20 percent share could be paid in over five years. Other changes were introduced to narrow the differences in treatment between foreign and domestic investors.[22]

The investment plans of foreign firms have been affected by local-content regulations in the form of the government's "deletion program," under which selected products, assemblies, or parts must be produced domestically. This policy has proved a costly and disruptive means of promoting domestic manufacturing: the specification of requirements in terms of specific components to be deleted, rather than as a proportion of output, encourages inflexible product substitution and the freezing of product design, raising costs and impeding technological improvements.

Initially the deletion program emphasized the motorcycle and automotive industries, but by the early 1980s the program had spread to cover a wide range of engineering products including construction machinery, agricultural machinery, motors, and machine tools. As part of the 1985 investment

---

21. Tax preferences for foreign investors included exemption from profit and dividend taxation for three years and carryover of losses into the post–tax holiday period; exemption from import duties on raw materials for two years; and free transfer of profits, depreciation funds, and proceeds from sale of shares to Indonesian nationals.

22. Under the 1986 reforms foreign investment is permitted in existing firms in priority sectors; foreign investment companies have been given the same access to export finance and foreign-exchange swap facilities as domestic firms; and foreign investment firms may now act as marketing channels for the exports of other firms.

reforms, a number of products on the deletion list were removed, and the deletion program for household appliances was postponed indefinitely. Administrative decrees further relaxed the deletion programs in 1986, 1987, and 1988.

In addition to the deletion programs, trade flows are affected by an extensive system of quantitative controls, import licensing requirements, tariffs, export prohibitions, and countertrade.[23] Like the tax preferences and deletion lists, quantitative import controls proliferated over time, so that by the mid-1980s 32 percent of tariff line items, accounting for 43 percent of imports and 41 percent of domestic production, were under some form of import licensing restriction.[24] These, coupled with already high tariffs, led to very high ERPs, favoring import substitution activities over export activities. In particular, the trade regime favored more capital- and foreign-exchange-intensive upstream industries over more labor-intensive downstream industries. ERPs in excess of 200 percent were estimated for a wide range of industries including motor vehicles, plastic products, glass and glass products, and wood pulp.

The government began a continuing program of comprehensive trade reforms in 1985. Tariffs were reduced across the board, although the reduction was partially offset by an increase in the number of items covered under import licensing restrictions. The number of tariff rate categories was reduced from 25 to 12, and the range of rates was narrowed, from zero to 225 percent before the reform to zero to 100 percent thereafter (with a special 200 percent tariff levied on sedans and station wagons). Most customs responsibilities were transferred to a Swiss firm, the Société Générale de Surveillance (SGS), reducing costs to both the government and traders as well as improving fee collection and reducing opportunities for corruption.[25]

In 1986 the Indonesian government began reducing the number of products covered under import licensing schemes. By the end of 1988 the extent of quantitative controls had been roughly halved, with the share of restricted products reduced to 16 percent of product types, 21 percent of import value, and 21 percent of domestic production (Nasution 1989). This resulted in a considerable decline in ERPs (table 3.7).

---

23. See Pangestu and Boediono (1986) for a historical description of the evolution of trade policy instruments in Indonesia.

24. There are five categories of importers: general importers, registered importers (approved to import specific goods under government direction), importer-producers (producers who can import goods similar to the ones that they produce), producer-importers (producers who import goods required in the production process), and sole agents.

25. The SGS contract is up for renewal in 1991, and there is concern that it will not be renewed, dealing a setback to the reform program.

Table 3.7 Indonesia: structure of protection, 1987 (percentages)

Industry	Effective rate of protection
Food crops	19
Estate and other crops	19
Livestock	23
Forestry	−25
Fishing	22
Food, beverages, and tobacco	37
Textiles, clothing, and footwear	49
Wood products	14
Paper products	14
Chemicals	45
Nonmetallic products	43
Basic metals	31
Engineering	48
Other manufacturing	40
Mining and quarrying	4
Oil and gas	−1

Source: Nasution (1989), table 13.

Reform of the system of protection was accompanied by export promotion reforms. Beginning in 1978, export subsidies had been granted to offset tariffs and taxes on imported inputs and the high costs of domestic inputs. Indonesia came under pressure from the United States over the subsidies, and in 1985 Indonesia signed the GATT Code on Subsidies and Countervailing Measures, obligating it to eliminate export subsidies. These were replaced by a duty drawback program, and the subsidy element in short-term export finance was phased out.

"Producer-exporters," defined as producers who export 85 percent or more of total production, were granted permission to import inputs free of restrictions and were exempted from import duties. This meant not only that exporters could obtain inputs at world prices, but unlike under the previous Export Certificate System they could bypass the networks of approved importers. The major beneficiaries have been the textile and garment producers (which have accounted for more than half the imports approved for exporters). Other significant participants have been exporters of processed foods, chemicals, and wood products.

The duty drawback system was also extended to indirect exporters. Its administration was also reorganized to eliminate face-to-face meetings between duty drawback applicants and officials and to reduce the abuses that had occurred under the Export Certificate System (Pangestu 1989). Additional measures to assist exporters included the establishment of an export insurance and guarantee company and the creation of an export supporting board for small and medium-sized exporters (Balassa 1990).

In 1987 the system of textile export quota allocation was reorganized. The changes were aimed at reducing costs and administrative discretion and increasing the vitality of the textile export sector. Although the quotas are still based on previous allocations, unused quotas can be transferred, and nonfulfillment of a quota allocation by a firm will result in a reduction of its quota in the following year (Pangestu 1989). Export identification numbers and licenses for exports to nonquota countries were abolished (Nasution 1989). Indonesia has also opposed the coffee export quota system imposed under the International Coffee Agreement.

Export processing zones were established in 1973 to promote exports and foreign investment. Warr (1986) concluded that the benefits of the Indonesian export processing zones slightly outweighed their costs. The main benefit derived from the unusually high rate of domestic sourcing of intermediate inputs (over 40 percent, mainly domestically produced textiles) by firms operating in the zones. If transfers to government officials (counted as a benefit) were disregarded, however, the net costs exceeded the net benefits. The export promotion scheme was expanded in 1990, when the government decided to treat inland industrial parks as bonded areas.

Indonesia's exports have been affected by the bans on the exportation of logs and rattan. The ban on logs was introduced in 1980 to encourage the location of wood products–processing industries in Indonesia. The export ban indeed encouraged investment in processing industries, especially plywood mills. However, it has been estimated that because these mills are relatively inefficient, and because of the price-depressing effects of the supply increase, for every real dollar of additional plywood exports, Indonesia lost eight dollars worth of log exports (Fitzgerald 1986). An export ban on raw and semiprocessed rattan was imposed in 1988. Evidence from a similar export ban in the Philippines suggests that losses from rattan exports forgone are likely to outweigh any increase in furniture exports.

In the area of services trade, reforms introduced in 1988 have expanded the access of foreign firms to the domestic insurance market. The market for foreign films remains highly restricted, however. A copyright law was passed in 1987, a patent law in 1989, and a trademark law is in the drafting stage. Overall, protection of intellectual property rights has been improving (US Trade Representative 1990).

Externally, Indonesia faces a variety of trade barriers. The most important are, first, the escalating barriers to wood products in the Japanese market and, second, the MFA. In the Japanese market, sawn timber and veneer are subject to 10 percent and 15 percent tariff rates, respectively (after the quota is exhausted), whereas tropical hardwood plywood is subject to duties of between 17 percent and 20 percent. Government support for the mills further discourages the importation of processed wood products.

Indonesian exports are also adversely affected by the MFA. Although Indonesia initially benefited from the relocation of production away from quota-constrained countries, the system now reduces Indonesian exports. According to Trela and Whalley (1988), removal of the quotas would cause textile and apparel exports to grow by 275 percent. Eliminating both the tariffs and the quotas would lead to an increase of 409 percent.

Exchange Rates

Prior to 1966, Indonesia maintained a complex system of multiple exchange rates. In that year the government began the process of dismantling this system, which culminated in its replacement in 1970 with a unified exchange rate pegged to the US dollar. The rupiah was subsequently devalued on several occasions. In 1978 the currency was devalued 34 percent against the dollar, and the official link with the dollar was severed. Since then the rupiah has been pegged to an undisclosed basket of currencies. The rupiah was devalued by 28 percent against the dollar in 1983, and by another 38 percent in 1986. In 1988 Indonesia announced its acceptance of Article VIII of the IMF's Articles of Agreement, signaling its intention of moving to a fully convertible currency. The real exchange rate indices shown in figure 3.4 indicate that the nominal devaluations have been accompanied by significant real depreciation, giving Indonesia's increasingly diversified export basket a competitive boost.

Trade Patterns

The commodity composition of Indonesian trade is shown in table 3.8 (manufacturing trade shares by industry are reported in appendix B, table B.8). On the export side the most dramatic changes were the fall in the share of nonfuel primary products from 61.2 percent of total exports in 1963 to 26.0 percent in 1987, and the rise in manufactured exports in the total from 0.3 percent to 25.1 percent over the same period. Fuels exports also increased, from 38.5 percent to 48.9 percent. Among the nonfuel primary products, the biggest decline occurred in industrial raw materials. Within this group, raw rubber exports fell dramatically (from 35.4 percent to 5.7 percent) as the

Figure 3.4 Indonesia: real effective exchange rates, 1970–88

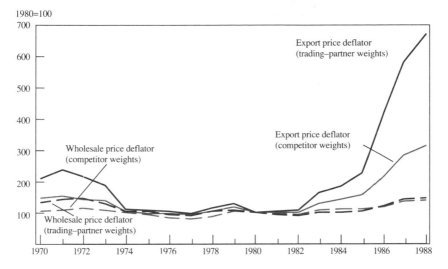

Note: The indices are defined as the local-currency price of foreign currency, so that a rise in the index signifies a depreciation.

nationalized rubber plantations fell into disrepair, and the export ban halted the exports of logs.

Among manufactures, wood products (mainly plywood) and furniture were the largest export category, with a 14.0 percent share in 1987. Apparel was next with 3.1 percent, while spinning and weaving accounted for 2.5 percent of exports. Footwear exports grew 10-fold between 1987 and 1989, largely as a result of inward direct investment from Taiwan and Korea. Basic metals exports have also grown rapidly over the last several years.

Data on the product composition of imports are unavailable for 1963. In 1987, nearly three-quarters of imports were manufactures. The largest component was chemicals (20.0 percent), followed by machinery (17.6 percent), indicating Indonesia's continued comparative disadvantage in capital goods, despite 40 years of promotional policies.

The geographical composition of trade is shown in table 3.9. The biggest change in the export pattern has been the declining importance of Europe and the growing significance of Japan. Missing data make assessing changes in the importance of the other East Asian developing countries impossible. On the import side, the United States, which had been Indonesia's leading import supplier in 1963, was displaced by both Japan and Europe. As with exports, changes in the importance of the East Asian developing countries cannot be ascertained because of missing data.

Table 3.8　Indonesia: composition of trade by major product group, 1963 and 1987 (percentages)

Industry	Exports		Imports	
	1963	1987	1963	1987
Fuels (SITC 3)	38.5	48.9	n.a.	9.0
Nonfuel primary products	61.2	26.0	n.a.	15.5
Food and live animals (SITC 0)	12.1	10.0	n.a.	3.9
Beverages and tobacco (SITC 1)	2.7	0.4	n.a.	0.3
Industrial raw materials (SITC 2, 4, 68)	46.3	15.6	n.a.	11.3
Manufactures (industrial classification)	0.3	25.1	n.a.	74.9
Textiles, apparel, and leather (ISIC 32)	n.a.	6.9	n.a.	1.8
Wood products and furniture (ISIC 33)	n.a.	14.0	n.a.	0.1
Paper and paper products (ISIC 34)	n.a.	0.6	n.a.	2.9
Chemicals (ISIC 35)	n.a.	1.2	n.a.	20.0
Nonmetallic mineral products (ISIC 36)	n.a.	0.6	n.a.	1.3
Iron and steel (ISIC 37)	n.a.	1.1	n.a.	5.6
Engineering products (ISIC 38)	n.a.	0.7	n.a.	42.8
Miscellaneous (ISIC 39)	n.a.	0.1	n.a.	0.4
Other products	0.0	0.0	n.a.	0.6
Memorandum: trade in goods and nonfactor services as a share of GDP	9.2	26	8.9	23.2

SITC = Standard International Trade Classification.

ISIC = International Standard Industrial Classification.

n.a. = not available.

Source: General Agreement on Tariffs and Trade. Memorandum data are from the World Bank.

Issues for the 1990s

Looking toward the future, it is imperative that Indonesia maintain high rates of employment growth to keep pace with its rapidly growing labor force. This, in turn, means emphasizing the continued expansion of the agriculture and labor-intensive manufacturing sectors. To accomplish this, Indonesia must remain internationally competitive in these sectors.

Overall competitiveness would be enhanced by strengthening the basic physical infrastructure. Because of the budgetary crunch of the early 1980s, associated with the fall in oil prices and hence in oil tax revenues, the Indonesian government drastically cut back funds devoted to the operation and

Table 3.9 Indonesia: geographical composition of trade, 1963 and 1988[a] (percent)

Country	Exports		Imports	
	1963	1988	1963	1988
Developed countries	68.6	71.4	68.2	67.8
United States	15.8	16.2	33.1	12.9
Western Europe	35.0	11.3	24.3	22.4
Japan	8.5	41.7	10.5	25.4
Canada, Australia, New Zealand	9.3	2.2	0.3	7.2
Developing countries	25.0	27.8	24.6	30.8
Pacific countries (other than China)	16.2	20.5	9.2	18.7
East Asian NICs	0.6	18.3	1.5	15.5
Hong Kong	0.5	2.9	1.5	1.0
Singapore	n.a.	8.5	n.a.	6.6
Taiwan	0.0	2.5	n.a.	4.6
Korea	n.a.	4.4	n.a.	3.3
Other ASEAN–4	15.7	2.2	7.7	3.2
Malaysia	12.2	0.9	4.2	2.2
Thailand	1.2	0.8	3.5	0.7
Philippines	2.3	0.4	n.a.	0.3
China	5.8	2.5	6.8	3.0
Other developing countries	3.0	4.8	8.6	9.0
Other Asia	2.0	1.2	6.8	0.9
Africa	0.2	0.9	n.a.	1.3
Europe[b]	0.0	0.2	0.0	0.2
Middle East	0.0	2.2	0.0	5.0
Latin America	0.7	0.2	1.8	1.6
European socialist countries	6.3	0.7	7.2	0.9

n.a. = not available.

a. Regional aggregates may not sum to 100 percent due to inclusion in denominator of special categories and other countries not specified.

b. Principally Portugal, Greece, and Turkey.

Source: International Monetary Fund, *Direction of Trade Statistics,* various issues.

maintenance of the physical infrastructure. Less than half of the national and provincial road network and an even lower share of local roads are in satisfactory condition. Irrigation systems, harbors, and bridges are likewise in poor condition. Electricity is a problem: the main provider, a state-owned company, is plagued by inefficiency and inadequate generating capacity.

Forty-one percent of the relevant age group attended secondary schools in 1986, the most recent year for which data are available. Seven percent were enrolled in institutional higher education. These enrollment ratios, although good for a low-income country, will have to increase if Indonesia is to join the ranks of the middle-income countries. At the same time there is a need to improve the quality of education at the primary and secondary levels, and to expand technical education opportunities.

These necessary improvements in the physical and social infrastructure require public investment. The tax reform of the mid-1980s has provided Indonesia with a good public revenue base, so that remaining efforts should be concentrated on reducing wasteful expenditure. The obvious place to start is with the subsidies to the extensive network of state-owned enterprises. Judicious liberalization and privatization would not only free these enterprises from bureaucratic overregulation, but free up government revenue for public investment as well. Continued efforts to strengthen the financial markets, in particular the bond and money markets, would also have a positive impact on public finance.

These broad policies to improve competitiveness should be complemented with sectoral policies to enhance efficiency. In agriculture this would involve building on the strong set of policies in place, to promote a greater capacity to respond flexibly to changing market conditions. This means strengthening agricultural research and extension services; encouraging greater private participation in production, processing, and marketing; and aligning public expenditures and charges more precisely with actual costs.

In the industrial sector there is a need to further deregulate investment, both foreign and domestic. The efficiency of investment could also be raised by eliminating the deletion programs and reforming the incentive system. In particular, recent trade reforms that have reduced the number of goods subject to quantitative restrictions or import licensing schemes should be extended, and the import restrictions replaced by tariffs. At the same time it would be desirable to lower tariffs and reduce their dispersion, to reduce effective rates of protection. This is especially important since the products receiving the highest ERPs tend to be of high capital and low labor intensity. As a consequence, resources are diverted into sectors that generate little employment at a time when Indonesia needs to maintain a rapid job creation rate. Further real currency depreciation, in conjunction with the tariff reductions, should also be considered.

4

Trade Prospects

The previous chapters reviewed the trade patterns and economic policy histories of the Pacific Basin developing countries. This chapter presents projections of their trade patterns in the year 2000. These are derived econometrically using a model in which a country's commodity composition of trade is a function of national income, technology, and relative factor endowments. This reflects the belief that, over the medium run, countries' patterns of trade *specialization* evolve in a reasonably systematic and predictable way. In contrast, countries' trade *balances* may change quite abruptly in response to prevailing macroeconomic conditions, and attempts to predict these over more than a short time horizon should be regarded with extreme skepticism. This chapter therefore focuses solely on prospective changes in the former and eschews predictions of the latter.

In a world of many products and factors of production, changes in trade specialization will not follow a simple ladder or path. Differences in relative factor endowments will affect the timing, extent, and pattern of such changes. In particular, countries with few or no natural resources (e.g., Hong Kong, Singapore) will specialize completely in the production of manufactures early in their development, and can be expected to shift quickly into exports of greater human and physical capital intensity as they accumulate those factors. Conversely, countries with significant natural resource endowments (e.g., Indonesia, Malaysia) can be expected to begin producing manufactures much later in their development, and as long as their natural resource–based industries exert resource pulls they will never specialize in manufactures to the extent the natural resource–scarce economies do. Within the manufactures sector, countries may exhibit a variety of patterns of specialization over time, depending on their particular patterns of factor accumulation.

Figure 4.1 Endowment triangle

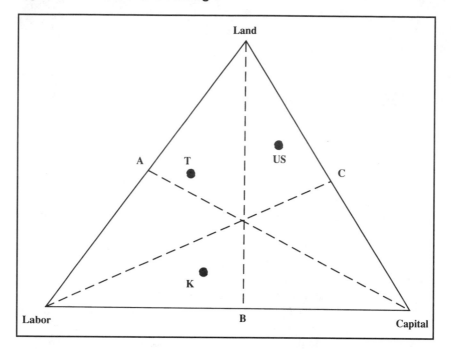

These ideas are illustrated graphically in figures 4.1 and 4.2.[1] Figure 4.1 is a three-factor (land, labor, and capital) endowment triangle. Its interpretation is straightforward. The dashed lines emanating from each corner of the triangle represent the average endowment of the other two factors. So, for example, the dashed line emanating from the land corner and running to the midpoint of the capital-labor side (point B) represents the average capital-labor ratio. As one moves away from point B toward the capital (labor) corner, the capital-labor ratio increases (decreases). Similarly, the dashed line from the labor corner to the land-capital midpoint (point C) represents the average land-capital ratio, and the line from the capital corner to point A is the average labor-land ratio.

Points within the triangle represent factor endowment bundles, in this case those of Korea (K), Thailand (T), and the United States (US). As represented

---

1. This discussion follows Leamer (1987).

Figure 4.2 Triangles of diversification

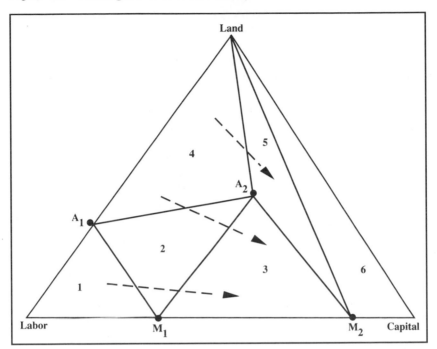

in the figure, the United States has a higher capital-labor ratio than Korea, which in turn has a higher capital-labor ratio than Thailand, since a line connecting point US to the land corner would lie to the right (toward the capital corner) of a line connecting K with the land corner, which in turn would lie to the right of a line connecting point T with the land corner. Similarly one can observe that the United States has the highest land-labor ratio of the three, followed by Thailand and then Korea, and that Korea has the highest capital-land ratio, followed by the United States and then Thailand. The important thing to remember is that every endowment point on a straight line emanating from one corner of the triangle has the same ratio of the other two factors.

Now suppose there are four goods: a labor-intensive agricultural product (A_1) that uses labor and land (but no capital) in production; a capital-intensive agricultural good (A_2) that uses all three factors in production; a labor-intensive manufacture (M_1); and a capital-intensive manufacture (M_2). The vector of inputs associated with each of these activities is shown in figure 4.2. A linear programming result shows that, given output prices for the four goods, the endowment triangle will be divided into six regions, or triangles of diversification. Within each region countries will produce the same subset of commodities, indicated by the corners of the triangles of diversification. An arbitrary division of the endowment triangle along these lines is shown in figure 4.2.

So, for example, countries in region 1 will produce the labor-intensive agricultural good (A_1) and the labor-intensive manufacture (M_1). In region 2, countries will produce both agricultural goods and the labor-intensive manufacture. In region 3, both manufactures and the capital-intensive agricultural product (A_2) will be produced. The patterns of specialization of the remaining regions can be similarly determined.

As they develop, countries will accumulate endowments and their patterns of specialization will change. This process is illustrated in figure 4.2 by the three arrows, which represent the accumulation of capital by countries starting from three different land-labor endowment points. The arrow nearest the bottom of the triangle indicates the path of development of a land-scarce country, such as one of the NICs. It begins in region 1, producing the labor-intensive agricultural good (A_1) and the labor-intensive manufacture (M_1). As it accumulates capital it moves successively through regions 2 and 3, beginning production of the capital-intensive agricultural good (A_2), then dropping production of the labor-intensive agricultural good (A_1) and starting production of the capital-intensive manufacture (M_2). Ultimately, if the country accumulates enough capital, it will reach region 6 and specialize completely in the capital-intensive manufacture.

The middle arrow represents the case of a country with an intermediate land-labor endowment (perhaps an ASEAN–4 economy). The country is initially in region 4, producing agricultural products and no manufactures. As it accumulates capital it moves into region 2 and begins producing the labor-intensive manufacture (M_1). Thus, the country with the larger land endowment begins producing manufactures later in its development (i.e., at a higher per capita income, or at a higher capital-labor ratio) than the land-scarce country. This is consistent with the pattern of development observed among the Pacific Basin developing countries. From this point on, the pattern of development for the intermediate country is similar to that of the land-scarce country.

The upper arrow in figure 4.2 represents the path of development of a land-abundant country (Australia or Canada, perhaps). Like the intermediate country, it begins in region 4, specializing in agricultural products. But as it accumulates capital it moves into region 5, dropping production of the labor-intensive agricultural product and starting production of the capital-intensive manufacture (M_2). Of the three countries it begins the production of manufactures the latest in its development, and unlike the other two it never produces the labor-intensive manufacture.

These examples illustrate a very important point: even in a very simple model (three factors, four goods) there are multiple paths of development. Indeed, in the examples above, the countries only accumulated capital—the other endowment ratios remained fixed. If the countries are allowed to accumulate (or deaccumulate) all productive factors, there can be an infinite number of development paths even in this simple model.

These examples should not be taken too seriously—the world is obviously characterized by more than three factors and four goods. Moreover, the division of the endowment triangle in figure 4.2 is entirely arbitrary; different output prices would give rise to a different set of triangles of diversification. Indeed, these prices are not static—as countries accumulated factors, product prices would change, and so too would the regions of specialization.

Thus, the analysis of actual paths of development is an empirical matter. This has been undertaken through the use of an econometric model of trade specialization in 46 industries encompassing the entire traded-goods sector. In this model the commodity composition of trade is a function of national income, technology, relative endowments of labor, physical capital, human capital, arable land, pasture land, forest land, oil, coal, other minerals, transportation costs, and (implicitly) real exchange rates. The model was estimated for a sample of 30 countries (the largest sample for which a complete data set could be constructed) over the period 1968–84. Details of the formal model, estimation techniques, and data sources are presented in appendix A.

The estimated coefficients of this model were then combined with forecasts of the Pacific Basin countries' economic characteristics to derive projections of their commodity composition of trade for the year 2000, using their actual trade in 1988 as a base.[2] For all industries the 1988 data and 2000 projections are expressed in 1980 relative prices. This reflects the assumption that the Pacific Basin countries are small in international trade terms, and therefore that changes in their trade specialization will not change world relative prices. A second and implicit assumption is that neither the Pacific Basin countries nor their major trade partners make major changes in trade policies over the forecast period. Departures from this assumption are discussed below as warranted.

---

2. The exception is the textiles and apparel industries, where the Multi-Fiber Arrangement (MFA) has seriously distorted the pattern of trade. For these industries the forecasts were generated using the results of the Trela and Whalley (1988) model under the assumption that the bilateral quotas are removed but existing tariff protection is retained and the adjustment of exports is spread over the entire 1988–2000 period. This was done to generate a pattern of growth rates similar to those currently observed (and thus reflecting the restrictive impact of the MFA), while reflecting actual differences in competitiveness among the Pacific Basin developing countries.

Trade Projections

For purposes of presentation, the forecasts for each of the 46 industries have been aggregated into 12 trade categories: fuels; food and live animals; beverages and tobacco; industrial raw materials; textile, apparel, and leather products; wood products and furniture; pulp and paper products; chemicals; nonmetallic mineral products; iron and steel; engineering products; and miscellaneous manufactures.[3]

Hong Kong

In the case of Hong Kong, two sets of projections have been used.[4] In the first scenario, the variables used to construct the trade forecasts took the values forecasted using conventional time-series techniques on the basis of historical data (scenario 2000A). Yet it must be recognized that the forthcoming transfer of sovereignty from the United Kingdom to China may cause significant changes in the Hong Kong economy that are not predictable on the basis of past history. As a consequence, another set of trade projections was generated under a second scenario, in which it is assumed that the majority of the college-educated population of Hong Kong emigrates, and the rate of physical capital accumulation falls to half its forecasted rate (scenario 2000B). Trade projections obtained under each of these scenarios, along with actual data for 1988, are presented in trade-share terms in table 4.1.

Under the first scenario, the model predicts a considerable decline in Hong

---

3. The fuels category consists of coal, oil, and natural raw gas. Industrial raw materials includes nonfood agricultural commodities, natural rubbers and gums, raw wood, crude minerals, nonferrous metals, and raw textile fibers. The category of textiles, apparel, and leather products consists of spinning and weaving, textile products, and footwear. Pulp and paper products includes printing and publishing. Chemicals consists of basic chemicals (excluding fertilizer), synthetic resins, other industrial chemicals, pharmaceuticals, other chemical products, rubber products, and plastic products. The nonmetallic minerals products category includes pottery, glass, and other nonmetallic minerals products. Engineering products consists of fabricated metal products; office and computing equipment; machinery; radio, television, and telecommunications equipment; other electrical machinery; shipbuilding and repairing; railroad equipment; motor vehicles; aircraft; motorcycles and bicycles; and professional goods. Miscellaneous manufactures consists of a variety of manufactured products such as jewelry, sporting goods, toys, and office supplies.

4. For Hong Kong and Singapore reexports are excluded from exports to filter out the influence of entrepôt trade.

Table 4.1 Hong Kong: composition of trade by major product group, 1988 and projected 2000[a] (percentages)

Industry	Exports			Imports		
	1988	2000A	2000B	1988	2000A	2000B
Total primary products	4.0	4.0	4.7	17.9	26.3	22.7
Fuels (SITC 3)	0.5	0.5	0.5	3.7	7.2	3.5
Nonfuel primary products	3.4	3.4	4.2	14.2	19.2	19.2
Food and live animals (SITC 0)	0.8	0.6	0.6	6.7	7.1	7.8
Beverages and tobacco (SITC 1)	1.1	1.1	1.2	1.9	1.4	1.9
Industrial raw materials (SITC 2, 4, 68)	1.6	1.7	2.4	5.6	10.7	9.5
Manufactures (industrial classification)	96.0	96.0	95.3	82.1	73.7	77.3
Textiles, apparel, and leather (ISIC 32)	41.2	16.7	25.6	26.3	17.5	17.0
Wood products and furniture (ISIC 33)	0.4	1.0	0.5	1.1	2.2	1.5
Paper and paper products (ISIC 34)	2.3	2.8	6.5	1.9	2.0	1.8
Chemicals (ISIC 35)	5.6	15.0	6.3	10.2	10.1	9.6
Nonmetallic mineral products (ISIC 36)	0.6	0.8	0.7	1.2	1.1	1.3
Iron and steel (ISIC 37)	0.1	0.5	0.2	2.3	3.3	3.0
Engineering products (ISIC 38)	38.6	45.1	47.6	33.5	30.7	37.3
Miscellaneous (ISIC 39)	7.3	14.3	7.9	5.6	6.8	5.8

SITC = Standard International Trade Classification.

ISIC = International Standard Industrial Classification.

a. The 1988 data in this table are based on 1980 constant relative prices, whereas those in table 2.1 are based on current prices.

Kong's share of textile, apparel, and leather exports. The largest export share increase is in the capital-intensive chemicals sector, whose share of Hong Kong's total exports rises from 5.6 percent to 15.0 percent. This change is mainly due to a large projected increase in plastics exports, from 3.7 percent to 11.9 percent. The next largest export share increases are in the miscellaneous manufactures category, which increases from 7.3 percent to 14.3 percent, and engineering products, whose share increases from 38.6 percent to

45.1 percent. Engineering products thus emerge as the largest export category, followed by textiles and chemicals. On the import side, the biggest share increases are in industrial raw materials (5.6 percent to 10.7 percent) and fuels (3.7 percent to 7.2 percent).

However, there is reason to believe that the evolution of Hong Kong's trade pattern may deviate from the model's prediction. Lack of space, environmental concerns, and the desires of the Chinese government to develop heavy industry on the mainland may all serve to retard the growth of capital-intensive manufacturing production in Hong Kong. Resources that might have otherwise gone into increasingly capital-intensive manufacturing activities may be channeled into the services sector instead. (Indeed, the share of manufacturing in GDP has been declining in recent years.) As a consequence the share of labor-intensive products in merchandise exports may not decline as rapidly as predicted by the model.

Moreover, considerably less export upgrading occurs under the second, less favorable scenario (2000B). The share of textiles, apparel, and leather products in exports falls, but not by as much in as the 2000A forecast. The major upgrading into chemicals exports is effectively halted. Strangely, there is an increase in the paper and paper products export share, as the printing and publishing share increases from 1.5 percent to 5.6 percent.

Singapore

Projections for Singapore are reported in table 4.2. Significant export share increases are forecast in the capital-intensive industries of chemicals and iron and steel. Within the chemicals group, the export share of basic chemicals is projected to increase from 2.3 percent to 4.4 percent. Engineering products and chemicals remain the two largest manufactures export categories; iron and steel supplants textiles as the third-largest. The major shift in imports is in fuels, whose import share is expected to rise from 27.0 percent to 32.0 percent. A number of categories switch net export signs: manufactured wood products, a net export category in 1988, is forecast to become a net import category in 2000. Obversely, four categories shift from net import to net export status: chemicals, iron and steel, engineering products, and miscellaneous manufactures.[5]

---

5. As in the case of Hong Kong, one may surmise that space constraints and future environmental concerns might limit the large-scale development of Singapore's chemical, paper, and iron and steel industries. On the other hand, Singapore has developed a large petroleum refining industry.

Table 4.2 Singapore: composition of trade by major product group, 1988 and projected 2000[a] (percentages)

Industry	Exports		Imports	
	1988	2000	1988	2000
Total primary products	39.0	34.2	40.6	44.9
Fuels	24.5	23.5	27.0	32.0
Nonfuel primary products	14.5	10.6	13.6	12.9
Food and live animals (SITC 0)	4.4	3.1	5.4	4.7
Beverages and tobacco (SITC 1)	0.9	0.7	1.0	0.9
Industrial raw materials (SITC 2, 4, 68)	9.2	6.8	7.3	7.3
Manufactures (industrial classification)	61.0	65.8	59.4	55.1
Textiles, apparel, and leather (ISIC 32)	5.2	2.7	5.6	4.0
Wood products and furniture (ISIC 33)	1.8	1.0	0.9	1.5
Paper and paper products (ISIC 34)	1.1	1.0	1.3	1.2
Chemicals (ISIC 35)	6.5	9.1	6.9	5.5
Nonmetallic mineral products (ISIC 36)	0.3	0.3	1.0	1.1
Iron and steel (ISIC 37)	0.8	7.2	2.6	1.3
Engineering products (ISIC 38)	44.3	42.7	40.0	39.5
Miscellaneous (ISIC 39)	1.1	2.0	1.1	1.0

SITC = Standard International Trade Classification.

ISIC = International Standard Industrial Classification.

a. The 1988 data in this table are based on 1980 constant relative prices, whereas those in table 2.3 are based on current prices.

Taiwan

Trade forecasts for Taiwan are shown in table 4.3. These projections show a decline of nearly 8 percentage points in the export share of textiles, apparel, and leather, from 24.4 percent of total exports to 16.7 percent, as export shares fall in each category (spinning and weaving, textile products, wearing apparel, leather products, and footwear). At the same time there is an increase of a similar magnitude in the chemicals share, from 9.6 percent to 18.2 percent; within this grouping the share of plastics is projected to increase from 5.1 percent to 11.2 percent, and the share of basic chemicals is forecast to grow from 1.0 percent to 3.8 percent. Chemicals, in fact, replaces textiles as the second-largest export category, behind engineering products. On the import side the share of fuels rises from 16.5 percent to 23.3 percent, the

Table 4.3 Taiwan: composition of trade by major product group, 1988 and projected 2000[a] (percentages)

Industry	Exports 1988	Exports 2000	Imports 1988	Imports 2000
Total primary products	9.2	7.2	37.2	46.8
Fuels	1.3	1.0	16.5	23.3
Nonfuel primary products	7.9	6.3	20.7	23.5
Food and live animals (SITC 0)	5.1	3.8	5.0	4.7
Beverages and tobacco (SITC 1)	0.1	0.2	0.7	0.6
Industrial raw materials (SITC 2, 4, 68)	2.7	2.2	15.1	18.1
Manufactures (industrial classification)	90.8	92.8	62.8	53.2
Textiles, apparel, and leather (ISIC 32)	24.4	16.7	3.7	3.1
Wood products and furniture (ISIC 33)	3.7	5.7	1.4	3.3
Paper and paper products (ISIC 34)	1.0	2.1	1.8	1.7
Chemicals (ISIC 35)	9.6	18.2	13.9	12.2
Nonmetallic mineral products (ISIC 36)	2.0	1.6	0.8	0.8
Iron and steel (ISIC 37)	1.5	2.5	5.6	6.2
Engineering products (ISIC 38)	41.5	37.2	34.9	25.3
Miscellaneous (ISIC 39)	7.2	8.8	0.7	0.6

SITC = Standard International Trade Classification.

ISIC = International Standard Industrial Classification.

a. The 1988 data in this table are based on 1980 constant relative prices, whereas those in table 2.5 are based on current prices.

share of industrial raw materials increases from 15.1 percent to 18.1 percent, and the share of wood products increases from 1.4 percent to 3.3 percent. Two capital-intensive categories, chemicals and paper, shift from net imports to net exports.[6]

---

6. Noland (1990b) reports alternative projections using a time-varying, country-specific parameter model of net exports. In these projections the shift from net imports to net exports in paper and paper products is reproduced (because of a large increase in net exports in printing and publishing), but the shift to net exports in the chemicals sector is not (although the amount of net imports declines).

Table 4.4 Korea: composition of trade by major product group, 1987 and projected 2000[a] (percentages)

Industry	Exports 1987	Exports 2000	Imports 1987	Imports 2000
Total primary products	9.3	7.2	43.8	57.9
Fuels	2.5	1.9	20.9	29.9
Nonfuel primary products	6.8	5.3	22.9	28.0
Food and live animals (SITC 0)	4.5	1.7	6.0	6.2
Beverages and tobacco (SITC 1)	0.2	0.7	0.1	0.6
Industrial raw materials (SITC 2, 4, 68)	2.1	2.8	16.8	21.2
Manufactures (industrial classification)	90.7	92.8	56.2	42.1
Textiles, apparel, and leather (ISIC 32)	34.1	17.8	6.1	5.3
Wood products and furniture (ISIC 33)	0.7	1.2	0.4	1.0
Paper and paper products (ISIC 34)	1.1	4.0	1.7	1.6
Chemicals (ISIC 35)	6.7	15.2	11.7	8.8
Nonmetallic mineral products (ISIC 36)	1.2	1.1	0.8	0.9
Iron and steel (ISIC 37)	5.0	14.8	4.1	3.1
Engineering products (ISIC 38)	38.3	35.6	30.9	21.0
Miscellaneous (ISIC 39)	3.6	3.0	0.5	0.4

SITC = Standard International Trade Classification.

ISIC = International Standard Industrial Classification.

a. The 1987 data in this table are based on 1980 constant relative prices, whereas those in table 2.7 are based on current prices.

Korea

Trade forecasts for Korea are presented in table 4.4.[7] According to the model there is a significant fall in the textiles, apparel, and footwear export share. As in the case of Taiwan, export shares of all subcategories (spinning and weaving, textile products, wearing apparel, leather products, and footwear) fall. Significant increases in export shares are predicted for the capital-intensive categories of iron and steel (from 5.0 percent of total exports to 14.8 percent),

---

7. Trade data for Korea, Malaysia, Thailand, and Indonesia were unavailable for 1988. Data for 1987 have been used instead.

chemicals (from 6.7 percent to 15.2 percent), and paper and paper products (from 1.1 percent to 4.0 percent).[8] Within chemicals, the export share of basic chemicals is expected to increase from 1.2 percent to 6.9 percent, while the plastics share is projected to increase from 2.2 percent to 5.4 percent. For imports the largest increases are in fuels (from 20.9 percent to 29.9 percent) and industrial raw materials (from 16.8 percent to 21.2 percent). Two categories, paper and paper products and chemicals, shift from net imports to net exports.[9]

Malaysia

Projections for Malaysia have been calculated under two scenarios. In the projections labeled 2000A, the variables used to construct the trade projections take the values obtained from the time-series analysis. In the projections labeled 2000B, investment and technology transfer associated with inward foreign direct investment are assumed to raise the rates of physical and human capital accumulation by 25 percent. These forecasts are reported in table 4.5.

Under the first scenario, there is a projected drop in the fuels export share from 26.0 percent in 1988 to 21.3 percent in 2000. In the manufacturing sector, the largest increase is in the engineering products category, where the export share of radio, television, and telecommunications equipment increases from 14.6 percent to 17.5 percent, and that of shipbuilding and repairing increases from 0.7 percent to 1.9 percent. On the import side the largest increases are in industrial raw materials (from 9.9 percent to 14.3 percent), fuels (from 11.6 percent to 14.6 percent), and iron and steel (from 4.1 percent to 5.1 percent).

The projections under the second scenario are broadly similar. The most noticeable difference in projected export share is in chemicals, whose share rises under scenario 2000B to replace textiles as the second-largest manufacturing export grouping.

---

8. In the cases of Taiwan and Korea the shift into paper products is a function of this industry's high capital intensity. Presumably Taiwan and Korea could import raw wood to produce paper if domestic supplies were unavailable.

9. These results can be contrasted with those obtained from a Heckscher-Ohlin model of net exports reported in Noland (1990c). The leading Korean net export sectors for 2000 were projected to be motor vehicles and radio, television, and telecommunications equipment. The biggest net export increases were predicted for motor vehicles; machinery; radio, television, and telecommunications equipment; iron and steel; and fabricated metals products.

Table 4.5 Malaysia: composition of trade by major product group, 1987 and projected 2000[a] (percentages)

Industry	Exports			Imports		
	1987	2000A	2000B	1987	2000A	2000B
Total primary products	67.6	60.5	57.5	30.8	37.6	41.9
Fuels	26.0	21.3	21.7	11.6	14.6	17.7
Nonfuel primary products	41.6	39.2	35.8	19.2	23.0	24.2
Food and live animals (SITC 0)	5.4	5.6	4.5	8.6	7.8	7.9
Beverages and tobacco (SITC 1)	0.2	0.4	0.6	0.8	0.9	1.1
Industrial raw materials (SITC 2, 4, 68)	36.1	33.2	30.6	9.9	14.3	15.2
Manufactures (industrial classification)	32.4	39.5	42.5	69.2	62.4	58.1
Textiles, apparel, and leather (ISIC 32)	4.4	4.1	3.8	5.4	3.6	3.2
Wood products and furniture (ISIC 33)	4.9	3.6	4.4	0.2	0.3	0.4
Paper and paper products (ISIC 34)	0.2	0.6	0.7	2.7	2.5	2.6
Chemicals (ISIC 35)	1.7	3.4	5.0	10.7	8.8	8.8
Nonmetallic mineral products (ISIC 36)	0.3	0.7	0.8	0.7	0.8	0.9
Iron and steel (ISIC 37)	0.7	1.1	1.3	4.1	5.1	4.9
Engineering products (ISIC 38)	19.4	24.9	25.3	44.3	40.1	36.2
Miscellaneous (ISIC 39)	0.7	1.1	1.3	1.1	1.0	1.1

SITC = Standard International Trade Classification.

ISIC = International Standard Industrial Classification.

a. The 1987 data in this table are based on 1980 constant relative prices, whereas those in table 3.1 are based on current prices.

Thailand

Trade projections for Thailand have been computed under the same set of scenarios. In both sets of projections, Thailand emerges as a net exporter of manufactures by 2000, with manufactures exports accounting for more than half of total exports. The biggest export share increase is in miscellaneous manufactures, from 7.7 percent in 1988 to 16.2 percent in 2000, making it the largest manufacturing export category. The export share of chemicals also

Table 4.6 Thailand: composition of trade by major product group, 1987 and projected 2000[a] (percentages)

Industry	Exports			Imports		
	1987	2000A	2000B	1987	2000A	2000B
Total primary products	52.4	49.7	43.3	37.7	47.8	52.5
Fuels	1.1	0.8	0.8	21.2	23.6	28.0
Nonfuel primary products	51.4	48.9	42.5	16.5	24.2	24.5
Food and live animals (SITC 0)	34.2	34.8	28.9	4.2	4.5	5.2
Beverages and tobacco (SITC 1)	0.5	0.5	0.6	0.6	0.5	0.6
Industrial raw materials (SITC 2, 4, 68)	16.7	13.6	13.1	11.7	19.2	18.8
Manufactures (industrial classification)	47.6	50.3	56.7	62.3	52.2	47.5
Textiles, apparel, and leather (ISIC 32)	21.1	11.1	9.5	4.3	2.5	2.2
Wood products and furniture (ISIC 33)	2.1	2.3	2.8	0.8	1.8	2.0
Paper and paper products (ISIC 34)	0.6	0.9	1.2	2.0	2.2	2.4
Chemicals (ISIC 35)	3.1	7.5	10.7	14.6	11.9	11.6
Nonmetallic mineral products (ISIC 36)	0.7	1.0	1.0	7.0	0.5	0.6
Iron and steel (ISIC 37)	0.7	1.1	1.2	7.0	6.1	5.8
Engineering products (ISIC 38)	11.6	10.2	12.0	30.9	23.9	19.4
Miscellaneous (ISIC 39)	7.7	16.2	18.2	2.1	3.3	3.5

SITC = Standard International Trade Classification.

ISIC = International Standard Industrial Classification.

a. The 1987 data in this table are based on 1980 constant relative prices, whereas those in table 3.3 are based on current prices.

increases; within this group the export share of plastics increases from 1.1 percent to 3.8 percent. The export share of textiles, apparel, and leather products falls from 21.1 percent to 11.1 percent. The biggest import share increase occurs in industrial raw materials (from 11.7 percent to 19.2 percent).

The projections under the second scenario exhibit a more pronounced shift toward manufacturing. Compared with the first set of projections, the 2000B forecasts show a significantly smaller export share for food products and significantly larger shares for chemicals and the miscellaneous manufactures category, which emerges as the second-largest, behind food products.

Table 4.7 Philippines: composition of trade by major product group, 1988 and projected 2000ᵃ (percentages)

Industry	Exports			Imports		
	1988	2000A	2000B	1988	2000A	2000B
Total primary products	54.2	41.8	32.8	50.2	57.7	63.9
Fuels	5.8	4.3	4.2	30.4	35.9	41.5
Nonfuel primary products	48.4	37.5	28.6	19.8	21.9	22.5
Food and live animals (SITC 0)	19.3	15.4	11.6	7.8	7.4	7.7
Beverages and tobacco (SITC 1)	0.7	1.2	1.6	1.4	1.4	1.4
Industrial raw materials (SITC 2, 4, 68)	28.4	21.0	15.4	10.6	13.1	13.3
Manufactures (industrial classification)	45.8	58.2	67.2	49.8	42.3	36.1
Textiles, apparel, and leather (ISIC 32)	10.6	8.5	7.4	5.6	4.5	3.3
Wood products and furniture (ISIC 33)	10.4	8.9	9.7	0.1	0.2	0.2
Paper and paper products (ISIC 34)	0.4	0.9	1.4	2.1	2.2	2.1
Chemicals (ISIC 35)	4.4	8.8	12.1	13.7	10.4	9.5
Nonmetallic mineral products (ISIC 36)	0.5	1.3	1.8	0.8	0.8	0.9
Iron and steel (ISIC 37)	1.3	1.7	2.3	6.1	5.7	5.1
Engineering products (ISIC 38)	13.5	21.9	26.3	20.7	18.0	14.5
Miscellaneous (ISIC 39)	4.7	6.2	6.2	0.6	0.6	0.5

SITC = Standard International Trade Classification.

ISIC = International Standard Industrial Classification.

a. The 1988 data in this table are based on 1980 constant relative prices, whereas those in table 3.5 are based on current prices.

The Philippines

Projections for the Philippines have likewise been calculated under two scenarios. The first set of forecasts (2000A) were constructed on the basis of time-series modeling techniques. These imply significantly lower rates of factor accumulation than observed in the other Pacific Basin developing countries. A second set of forecasts (2000B) were calculated under the assumption that policy reforms enable the Philippines to raise its rates of physical and human capital formation to the average for the other three ASEAN–4 economies. These projections are reported in table 4.7.

Under both sets of forecasts, manufactures exports account for more than half of total exports by 2000. In the 2000A projections, the largest export share increase is in engineering products (from 13.5 percent to 21.9 percent), followed by chemicals (from 4.4 percent to 8.8 percent). Both nonmetallic mineral products and paper and paper products more than double their shares. The export share of industrial raw materials falls from 28.4 percent to 21.0 percent, while its import share rises from 10.6 percent to 13.1 percent. The import share of fuels rises from 30.4 percent to 35.9 percent. Nonmetallic mineral products goes from net imports to net exports.

The alternative forecasts show even greater shifts in trade specialization away from primary products and toward manufactures. There are considerable declines in the export shares of industrial raw materials and food products and significant increases in the engineering products and chemicals shares, with the latter replacing wood products and furniture as the second-largest export category.

Indonesia

The projections for Indonesia are reported in table 4.8. As in the cases of Malaysia and Thailand, the projections have been done under two scenarios: one based on time-series projections (2000A) and another under the assumption that inward FDI increases the effective rates of physical and human capital formation by 25 percent (2000B). In either case, Indonesia displays the greatest transformation of trade specialization of any of the Pacific Basin developing countries, with the export share of manufactures projected to double to more than 40 percent.

According to the projections in scenario 2000A, the share of primary products in total exports will fall from 81.2 percent in 1987 to 58.7 percent in 2000, with the fuels share alone falling from 57.2 percent to 37.1 percent. Conversely, the manufactures share rises from 18.8 percent to 41.3 percent. Within the manufacturing category, the most dramatic increase is for engineering products, whose export share is projected to increase from 0.4 percent to 14.9 percent. Other rapidly growing export categories include iron and steel (from 0.8 percent to 4.6 percent) and chemicals (from 0.9 percent to 3.6 percent). On the import side the industrial raw materials share increases from 14.0 percent to 22.4 percent, and the fuels share increases from 14.1 percent to 23.9 percent. Four categories shift from net imports to net exports: nonmetallic minerals products, iron and steel, engineering products, and miscellaneous manufactures.

Table 4.8 Indonesia: composition of trade by major product group, 1987 and projected 2000[a] (percentages)

Industry	Exports			Imports		
	1987	2000A	2000B	1987	2000A	2000B
Total primary products	81.2	58.7	54.3	32.3	57.6	60.4
Fuels	57.2	37.1	33.5	14.1	23.9	26.6
Nonfuel primary products	24.0	21.6	20.8	18.2	33.7	33.9
Food and live animals (SITC 0)	7.5	4.3	3.4	4.0	9.4	10.1
Beverages and tobacco (SITC 1)	0.3	1.4	1.6	0.3	1.8	1.9
Industrial raw materials (SITC 2, 4, 68)	16.2	15.9	15.8	14.0	22.4	21.9
Manufactures (industrial classification)	18.8	41.3	45.7	67.7	42.4	39.6
Textiles, apparel, and leather (ISIC 32)	5.5	5.6	4.8	2.3	1.5	1.3
Wood products and furniture (ISIC 33)	10.3	9.3	10.0	0.1	0.1	0.1
Paper and paper products (ISIC 34)	0.4	1.7	2.1	2.6	2.9	3.0
Chemicals (ISIC 35)	0.9	3.6	4.5	19.7	13.9	13.3
Nonmetallic mineral products (ISIC 36)	0.4	1.4	1.5	1.1	1.4	1.5
Iron and steel (ISIC 37)	0.8	4.6	4.8	5.3	3.6	3.3
Engineering products (ISIC 38)	0.4	14.9	17.8	36.3	18.6	16.8
Miscellaneous (ISIC 39)	0.1	0.2	0.3	0.4	0.4	0.4

SITC = Standard International Trade Classification.

ISIC = International Standard Industrial Classification.

a. The 1987 data in this table are based on 1980 constant relative prices, whereas those in table 3.8 are based on current prices.

The forecasts computed under the assumption of faster physical and human capital accumulation (scenario 2000B) reveal an even greater shift into manufactures exports. There is a further fall in the fuels share of exports, and the shares of engineering products and chemicals show an even greater rise.

Overview

Overall, these projections forecast a continuing shift toward manufactured products in the trade specialization of the Pacific Basin developing countries.

Such a shift implies that the ASEAN–4 countries will manage to harness the resources, either domestic or foreign, to successfully upgrade their economies out of assembly-dominated manufacturing activities.

Perhaps the most striking aspect of the projections is the consistent decline (except in Indonesia) in the export share of the textiles, apparel, and leather products group. This result is in part due to the assumption that textiles and apparel exports will continue to be significantly restricted by tariff protection in developed-country markets, and as a consequence grow more slowly than exports overall (without, however, declining in absolute terms). If, however, significant trade liberalization were achieved in this sector, textile and apparel exports would accelerate accordingly, and export growth in other parts of the economy would slow as resources were pulled into the textile and apparel industries.

On the import side, the share of manufactures in imports falls for each country. This reflects substitution of local manufactures for imports and the predominance of Heckscher-Ohlin-type interindustry trade.

These observations point to two important caveats. First, the projections implicitly assume that there are no dramatic changes in the sectoral trade policies of either the Pacific Basin developing countries themselves or their trade partners. If there were a significant liberalization in textiles and apparel, or increased restrictions in steel, for example, trade patterns would change in ways not captured by the model. Second, the data are expressed in 1980 relative prices. If there were significant shifts in relative prices, such as a large change in the price of oil, the current price composition of trade could look considerably different from these projected values. However, with the exception of the textile and apparel industries (where export growth is inhibited by the MFA), the Pacific Basin developing countries (even as a whole) are small in international trade terms, and hence changes in their exports and imports are not expected to systematically affect world prices.

Complementarity or Competition?

Thus far the trade prospects of each Pacific Basin developing country have been considered individually, but it also is of interest to analyze the impact these prospective changes would have on patterns of competition within the group as a whole. As a starting point, indices of export product similarity between pairs of countries have been computed for all eight Pacific Basin developing countries, as well as for the other countries used to estimate the econometric model. The index varies between 0 and 1, with 0 indicating

Table 4.9 Export similarity indices, 1968[a]

Country	Hong Kong	Singapore	Taiwan	Korea	Malaysia	Thailand	Philippines	Indonesia
Hong Kong	1.00							
Singapore	0.45	1.00						
Taiwan	0.58	**0.62**	1.00					
Korea	**0.67**	0.49	**0.68**	1.00				
Malaysia	0.22	0.54	0.46	0.41	1.00			
Thailand	0.47	0.48	0.57	**0.64**	0.41	1.00		
Philippines	0.15	0.29	0.32	0.36	**0.63**	0.36	1.00	
Indonesia	0.25	**0.44**	**0.44**	0.30	0.38	0.27	0.21	1.00

a. See text for definition of the index. Numbers in boldface are the highest index values for each country.

Table 4.10 Export similarity indices, 1988[a]

Country	Hong Kong	Singapore	Taiwan	Korea	Malaysia	Thailand	Philippines	Indonesia
Hong Kong	1.00							
Singapore	0.46	1.00						
Taiwan	0.68	0.60	1.00					
Korea	0.63	0.53	**0.70**	1.00				
Malaysia	0.41	**0.62**	0.49	0.54	1.00			
Thailand	**0.72**	0.45	**0.70**	**0.73**	0.48	1.00		
Philippines	0.54	0.52	0.57	0.60	**0.64**	**0.64**	1.00	
Indonesia	0.29	0.21	0.31	0.40	0.39	0.41	**0.47**	1.00

a. See text for definition of the index. Numbers in boldface are the highest index values for each country.

Table 4.11 Export similarity indices, 2000[a]

Country	Hong Kong	Singapore	Taiwan	Korea	Malaysia	Thailand	Philippines	Indonesia
Hong Kong	1.00							
Singapore	0.52	1.00						
Taiwan	**0.75**	0.59	1.00					
Korea	0.59	**0.61**	**0.68**	1.00				
Malaysia	0.45	0.57	0.51	0.52	1.00			
Thailand	0.64	0.39	**0.68**	0.57	0.42	1.00		
Philippines	0.53	0.53	0.61	0.58	**0.65**	0.57	1.00	
Indonesia	0.30	0.40	0.44	**0.56**	0.50	0.38	0.50	1.00

a. See text for definition of the index. Numbers in boldface are the highest index values for each country.

complete dissimilarity and 1 indicating identical export compositions.[10]

Export similarity matrices for the Pacific Basin developing countries for 1968, 1988, and 2000 are reported in tables 4.9, 4.10, and 4.11, respectively.[11] The Pacific Basin developing countries are arranged in the matrices in (declining) order of per capita income, and the maximum value of the index for each country is in boldface. If countries' trade specialization followed a simple ladder or stages pattern, one would expect the maximum values of the export similarity index to appear just below the matrix diagonal. That is to say, Hong Kong's maximum value would be with Singapore, Singapore's maxima would be with Hong Kong and Taiwan, Taiwan's with Singapore and Korea, and so on. The tables do not provide a lot of evidence to support this notion, however. Indeed, this should not be unexpected—in a world with many goods and three or more factors, there are a multiplicity of paths, not a single ladder. In particular, Malaysia has considerable natural resources, which contribute both to per capita income and to dissimilarity in trade specialization in comparison to the natural resource–scarce NICs. If one transposes Malaysia and Thailand in these matrices, the evidence for the existence of a simple export ladder appears greater.

The indices can also be used to compare export similarity across different points in time (these noncontemporaneous indices were calculated for a number of countries and years but are not presented in the tables because of space considerations). On this basis, the Pacific Basin developing countries appear to fall into three groups. The first group consists of Singapore alone. With its heavy concentration in engineering products and petrochemicals, its export pattern is more akin to those of developed countries such as the United States and Japan than to any of the other Pacific Basin developing countries.

The second group of countries consists of Hong Kong, Taiwan, Korea, and Thailand. Hong Kong's highest contemporaneous export similarity pairing in 1968 was with Korea (0.67), in 1988 with Thailand (0.72), and in 2000 the

---

10. The index is defined as

$$S(a,b) = \sum_i \min(X_{ia}, X_{ib})$$

where X_{ia} (X_{ib}) is the industry i export share in country a's (b's) exports. This measure was originally proposed by Finger and Kreinin (1979). See also Kellman and Schroeder (1983) and Pearson (1989).

11. The 46-industry sample has been used to calculate the export similarity indices. For the projected values, the 2000A forecasts have been used.

highest value is predicted to be with Taiwan (0.75). In turn, Taiwan's highest values are registered with Korea (0.68 in 1968 and 0.70 in 1988), Thailand (0.70 in 1988), and Hong Kong (0.75 in 2000).

Similarly, Korea's closest contemporaneous export similarity pairings are with Taiwan (0.68) and Hong Kong (0.67) in 1968, with Thailand (0.73) and Taiwan (0.70) in 1988, and with Spain (0.72), Austria (0.69), Taiwan (0.70), and Italy (0.67) in 2000. This last result suggests that Korea will be a developed country, at least in international trade terms (as will Taiwan), by 2000. Perhaps the most striking result of this entire exercise is that the highest export similarity pairing for Korea in 2000 is with the Japanese export pairing in 1968.[12]

Thailand's highest contemporaneous index values are with Korea (0.64 in 1968 and 0.73 in 1988) and Taiwan (0.68 in 2000). But when noncontemporaneous values are taken into account, Thailand's export pattern in 1988 is more similar to Hong Kong's in 1968 (0.79), and to those of Korea and Taiwan in 1976 (both 0.78), suggesting that Thailand is following these three countries along a similar development path.

The third group of countries consists of Malaysia, the Philippines, and Indonesia. Malaysia's highest contemporaneous export similarity pairings are with the Philippines (0.63 in 1968, 0.64 in 1988, and 0.65 in 2000). Noncontemporaneous pairings yield higher values with Singapore, however. The pairing of Malaysia in 1988 and Singapore in 1980 is 0.72. Likewise the projected export pattern in 2000 is more similar to that of Singapore in 1976, 1980, 1984, and 1988 (with the 1980 pairing taking the highest value of all, at 0.77), than with its contemporaneous competitors. These results suggest that Malaysia is specializing in a set of industries similar to that of its neighbor Singapore, perhaps because of the investment links and overall integration of the two economies.

The export similarity pairings of the Philippines show a muddled picture. Perhaps this should not be surprising in light of the high degree of policy intervention in sectoral resource allocation in the Philippine economy. In 1968 and 1988 the Philippines' export similarity indices with Malaysia are 0.63 and 0.64, respectively. In 1988 it had an export similarity index of 0.64 with Thailand, and in 2000 the maximum is with Malaysia (0.65). However, with respect to both Taiwan and Thailand the index for the Philippines takes higher values in noncontemporaneous pairings. For 1988, the Philippines' export similarity index is higher in pairings with Taiwan in 1968, 1972, and 1976, and with Thailand in 1976; the highest value of all is that with Taiwan

---

12. Pearson (1989), comparing export similarity and correlation indices over the period 1962–86, also obtained the result that Korea, but not Taiwan, appears to be "following" the development path of Japan.

in 1972 (0.71). For the 2000 projection, the 1972 pairing with Taiwan takes a higher value (0.67) than the contemporaneous maximum. These comparisons suggest that the Philippines' export pattern is contemporaneously most similar to that of Malaysia, but is even more similar to earlier patterns of specialization exhibited by Taiwan and later by Thailand.

Indonesia's heavily natural resource–based export pattern is not particularly similar to the contemporaneous patterns of any of the other Pacific Basin developing countries. Its export pattern in 1988 was more similar to those of (in increasing order) Thailand in 1968 and 1976, Korea in 1968, Brazil in 1968, Taiwan in 1968, the Philippines in 1972, and Malaysia in 1972 (the highest at 0.75) than any contemporaneous pairing. Similarly, Indonesia's export pattern in 2000 is forecast to be more similar to Brazil's in 1968 or 1972 than to any other country in any given year.

Taken together, these indices reveal a number of interesting patterns. Korea appears to be following Japan in its development path. Thailand (and possibly the Philippines) is following the path of Taiwan, Hong Kong, and Korea. Lastly, Indonesia with its natural resources appears to be following the more natural resource–oriented economies of Malaysia, the Philippines, and Brazil.

One obvious inference is that the "follower" countries are natural candidates for FDI and offshore production as costs rise in the "leader" countries. This would imply that one might expect to observe close investment and technology transfer links between Korea and Japan; between Thailand (and possibly the Philippines) and Taiwan, Hong Kong, and Korea; and between Indonesia and the rest of the Pacific Basin developing countries.

Tables 4.9 through 4.11 also reveal a clear increase in overall values between 1968 and 1988; seven of the eight maximal values for 1988 are greater than or equal to their counterparts in 1968. This suggests a convergence among the Pacific Basin developing countries, possibly due to the widespread shift into manufactures exports during this period. A similar trend toward convergence does not appear in the 2000 projections; if anything the trade patterns appear to diverge. The exception is Indonesia, whose shift into manufactures steadily increases its degree of trade specialization similarity with the other Pacific Basin developing countries.

This suggests that fears of "congestion," as countries specialize too narrowly in similar products, is unwarranted (with the possible exception of Indonesia's entry into manufactures markets). In any event, such problems could be mitigated by intraindustry trade in differentiated products. It is frequently argued that intraindustry trade facilitates economic integration by reducing the sectoral adjustment costs associated with a given expansion of trade.

Values of the index of intraindustry trade in manufactures are reported in table 4.12. This index ranges in value from 0 (indicating pure interindustry trade) to 1 (indicating pure intraindustry trade). The extent of intraindustry

Table 4.12 Intraindustry trade indices, 1968, 1988, and 2000[a]

Country	1968	1988	2000
Hong Kong	0.35	0.39	0.32
Singapore	0.48	0.70	0.64
Taiwan	0.31	0.54	0.61
Korea	0.16	0.53	0.51
Malaysia	0.15	0.48	0.47
Thailand	0.07	0.39	0.34
Philippines	0.06	0.34	0.30
Indonesia	0.07	0.17	0.42
Memoranda:			
United States	0.61	0.66	n.a.
Japan	0.50	0.42	n.a.

n.a. = not available.

a. The conventional intraindustry trade index is:

$$IIT_i = 1 - [(X_i - M_i)/|X_i + M_i|],$$

where the subscript i refers to the ith industry and X and M refer to exports and imports, respectively. The aggregate indices reported here are trade-weighted averages of the disaggregated 46 industry indices. This index will be biased if aggregate (manufactures) trade is not balanced; as a consequence, the Balassa (1986) adjustment has been performed.

trade tends to be correlated with the level of development or per capita income, as shown in table 4.12. The forecasts for 2000 generally do not reveal dramatic changes in intraindustry trade. The exception is Indonesia, which is projected to experience a large increase in intraindustry trade (its index increases from 0.17 in 1988 to 0.42 in 2000). Such a development may ameliorate adjustment problems vis-à-vis its trade partners' economies arising from its move into manufactures exports.

Conclusions

Myriad development paths are possible. In this chapter econometric forecasts have been used to attempt to divine the future prospects of each of the Pacific Basin developing countries. The trade composition projections indicate a considerable upgrading into sectors of greater human and physical capital intensity in the export patterns of these countries. This implies that the ASEAN–4 will be successful in obtaining, through domestic efforts or transfer from abroad, the technological prowess necessary to make this possible.

In the case of Hong Kong the degree of upgrading depends critically on the nature of the transition from British to Chinese rule. Emigration of educated workers could effectively halt the development process in Hong Kong. The trade restrictions of the MFA slow the growth of textiles and apparel exports, and with the exception of Indonesia, this group of industries declines in importance for the Pacific Basin developing countries.

There was a considerable increase in the similarity in product composition of exports among the Pacific Basin developing countries between 1968 and 1988. However, the projections do not indicate a continuation of this trend for most of the countries, suggesting that fears of "congestion" may be unwarranted. Nevertheless, the analysis does reveal some similarities in development paths across time. Korea, for example, appears to be following (with around a 30-year lag) the development path of Japan. Thailand appears to be following the paths of Taiwan, Hong Kong, and Korea, while Indonesia appears to be following in the paths of a number of countries, including Malaysia, the Philippines, and Brazil. It is possible that the followers will become natural recipients of FDI and technology transfer as production costs rise in the leaders.

It should be reiterated that these projections are conditioned on the maintenance of constant relative prices and trade policies similar to those currently observed. Dramatic changes in trade policy (such as a major liberalization of the MFA or new restrictions on steel trade) could affect trade patterns in ways not captured in these projections. It is to this topic that we now turn.

5

Regional and Global Economic Cooperation

The economic fortunes of the Pacific Basin developing countries will be influenced not only by their own actions but also by their external environment. This chapter will examine the prospects for regional economic cooperation, and for global cooperative initiatives that would have particular impact on these countries, as well as the implications for these countries of policies pursued unilaterally in other countries of the region.

Regional Cooperation

Several new institutions have been formed in recent decades to attempt to coordinate the economic policies of the Pacific Basin countries. There have been proposals for a Pacific Free Trade Area (PAFTA) and for an organization along the lines of the Organization for Economic Cooperation and Development, to be called the Organization for Pacific Trade and Development (OPTAD), but neither progressed beyond the proposal stage. There exist a variety of informal organizations that lack official governmental representation, such as the Pacific Economic Cooperation Council (PECC), the Pacific Basin Economic Council (PBEC), and the Pacific Trade and Development Conference (PAFTAD). The Economic and Social Commission for Asia and the Pacific (ESCAP), a United Nations organization, has official government representation, but the diversity of its membership and the very comprehensiveness of its mission have limited its relevance to economic policy.[1]

---

1. See Drysdale (1988, chapter 8) for an exhaustive discussion of these organizations.

The Association of Southeast Asian Nations

Historically, almost the only notable international organization in East Asia from an economic policy standpoint has been the Association of Southeast Asian Nations (ASEAN).[2] Its founding members in 1967 were Indonesia, Malaysia, the Philippines, Singapore, and Thailand. Brunei later joined the group. According to ASEAN's founding document, the Bangkok Declaration, the goal of the organization would be:

> to accelerate economic growth, social progress and cultural development in the region through joint endeavor in the spirit of equality and partnership in order to strengthen the foundation for a prosperous and peaceful community of Southeast Asian Nations" (quoted in Krause 1982, 6).

In the economic sphere, the founding document called for cooperation on the development of basic commodities (particularly food and energy), industrial cooperation, cooperation in trade, and a joint approach to international commodity problems and other world economic problems. The program of action further included political, social, cultural, and security issues.

To date, ASEAN has had little success in cooperative trade and industrial ventures. Cooperation in trade was to be served by the establishment of preferential trading arrangements. These took the form of product-by-product negotiations for tariff reductions on intra-area trade and across-the-board tariff reductions on small items. In practice, tariff reductions have been small, and there have been numerous exceptions, so that only about 5 percent of intra–ASEAN trade is covered by preferential tariff arrangements. Trade creation has been negligible (Ariff 1989); intraregional trade was only 16.3 percent of member states' trade in 1988.

Industrial cooperation was to be promoted by the establishment of large-scale ASEAN industrial plants, particularly to meet regional requirements in essential commodities. Initially, five projects were to be undertaken: urea plants in Indonesia and Malaysia, a superphosphates plant in the Philippines, a diesel-engine plant in Singapore, and a soda ash plant in Thailand. These projects failed for the most part. The urea plants were eventually constructed. In the Philippines, the superphosphates project was replaced by a pulp and paper project, which in turn was replaced by a copper-fabrication plant, as yet unbuilt. Thailand decided to liquidate the soda ash plant. In Singapore, the diesel-engine project was scrapped because Indonesia wished to undertake a similar project. In the end, Singapore chose a small hepatitis B vaccine project

---

2. One other regional organization of note has been the Asian Development Bank (ADB), which mobilizes concessionary and commercial funds to finance specific development projects in the region.

and reduced its equity participation in the other projects from 10 percent to 1 percent (Krause 1982).

At the 1976 Bali summit, ASEAN members called for complementary agreements involving joint ventures among private firms in a regional context. Eventually only seven such projects were approved, and only a few of these were implemented. New rules adopted at the Manila summit of 1987 should make these private cooperative ventures more feasible in the future (Ariff 1989).

The Bali summit also called for the creation of an ASEAN Finance Corporation. This corporation was set up by 140 commercial banks and individual shareholders to promote economic cooperation among member countries. It was not particularly successful, and was restructured in 1987–88; the corporation now acts as a merchant bank, with limited funds available to lend to bankable projects.

Although ASEAN has made little progress in the trade and industrial fields, it has established modest cooperative ventures in areas covered by its 11 permanent committees. These include food and agriculture; shipping; civil air transportation; communication, air traffic services, and meteorology; finance; commerce and industry; transportation and telecommunications; tourism; science and technology; sociocultural activities; and mass media.

ASEAN has also acted as a political force. In particular, its strong opposition to Vietnam's occupation of Cambodia helped facilitate negotiations undertaken between the warring parties and Vietnam's eventual withdrawal.

The future of ASEAN is likely to lie less in intraregional trade matters than in increasing the bargaining power of its member countries through joint action in global trade forums. Similarly, industrial projects are likely to be oriented toward world, rather than regional, markets. Nonetheless, ASEAN may play a positive role by acting as a pressure group in trade negotiations with industrial countries and in the General Agreement on Tariffs and Trade (GATT). ASEAN has been successful in inducing the European Community to modify its trade preference system; lobbying for increased aid flows, especially from Japan; and supporting the inclusion of the United States in the Asia Pacific Economic Cooperation (APEC).

Cooperation Among the Newly Industrializing Countries

Intra-area trade among the East Asian NICs is even less than that among the ASEAN countries. The share of this trade was 8.7 percent in 1973, 10.0 percent in 1981, and 10.5 percent in 1988. Moreover, a substantial part of intra-area trade involves trade through Hong Kong with China and, to a lesser extent, the Soviet Union. It is unlikely that the East Asian NICs would enter into preferential trade arrangements among themselves, if for no other reason than that Hong Kong and Singapore are practically free traders and there is consequently little scope for trade preferences.

Some have suggested, however, that the East Asian NICs would gain from adopting a common basket currency peg (see, e.g. Balassa and Williamson 1990). This would avoid the prisoners' dilemma under which each country is reluctant to revalue its currency for fear of losing markets to the others. Furthermore, revaluation would permit these countries to correct imbalances among themselves in trade and the current account.

Similarities in their geographical trade patterns support the establishment of a common basket peg. In addition, rapid productivity growth will engender the need for future appreciation of the currencies of the four countries, which would be facilitated by a common basket peg. Before adopting such an arrangement, however, the four East Asian NICs would have to correct their existing current account imbalances.

The East Asian NICs may also find it advantageous to join the Organization for Economic Cooperation and Development (OECD). Singapore and Hong Kong already have per capita incomes surpassing those of the United Kingdom, Italy, and Spain; Taiwan and Korea will reach similar income levels by the end of the century. The NICs already are major capital exporters and together account for more than 8 percent of world exports (compared with less than 5 percent for Japan when it entered the OECD).

OECD membership by Korea and Singapore should not encounter major obstacles, and the NICs have already been invited to participate in informal dialogues. Membership by Hong Kong and Taiwan could be politically problematic, although some sort of observer status might be possible.

Prospects for Regional Economic Cooperation

There has been growing interest in the Pacific region for an OECD–type organization to serve as a forum for consultation on issues of regional interest, as a pressure group to promote greater international openness to trade, and possibly as a means to pursue some regional infrastructure projects (e.g., telecommunications, transportation, and energy). Attention has coalesced around the proposal of Australian Prime Minister Bob Hawke for an Asia-Pacific dialogue involving the United States, Canada, Australia, New Zealand, and Japan, in addition to the Pacific Basin developing countries.[3] A similar

---

3. The original Hawke proposal did not include the United States and Canada, and consequently did not generate much enthusiasm in the smaller states, which feared Japanese domination of such an organization.

proposal by Japan's Ministry of International Trade and Industry (MITI) was incorporated into the Hawke initiative (Schott 1989), and in November 1989 government officials from the region met in Canberra, Australia, to launch the Asia Pacific Economic Cooperation (APEC).

The only specific policy issue addressed in this first meeting was strong support for the GATT multilateral trading system. It is doubtful that APEC would foster a preferential trading area on the model of the European Community, given the widely disparate levels of economic development, the dissimilar trade regimes, and the divergent political structures of the potential member countries. It is more likely that APEC would develop into a consultative forum, perhaps initially focusing on trade policy issues, and later extending its domain to encompass broader economic issues, cultural exchange, and environmental concerns (Baker 1989). Specifically, Preeg (1990) outlines five broad policy objectives APEC could pursue:

- Promoting multilateral trade liberalization and strengthening the GATT;

- Coordinating economic policies not covered under the GATT;

- Liberalizing trade and investment flows on an Asian and Pacific regional basis beyond the requirements of multilateral commitments;

- Avoiding a Japan-centered East Asian economic bloc and mercantilist rivalry across the Pacific with North America, and providing Japan and the United States a neutral forum for the discussion of issues of mutual interest in the region;

- Developing common approaches to evolving economic security interests in the region.

The multilateral character of the forum also would shield the smaller countries of the region from bilateral pressure from either the United States or Japan. In this way it could serve as a useful complement to existing organizations, especially the GATT.

Global Economic Cooperation

The Pacific Basin developing countries are highly dependent on international trade, and therefore they have a great interest in the maintenance of an open international trade regime and in a well-functioning GATT. The interests of these countries encompass the entire set of issues currently under discussion in the Uruguay Round of multilateral trade negotiations under the GATT. They have a special interest in maintaining the openness of trade in manufactured goods, particularly through a strong Safeguards Code that ensures that import controls are temporary and degressive, through outlawing protectionist measures outside the GATT such as "voluntary" export restraints (VERs), and through restricting the use of antidumping measures and countervailing duties. The Pacific Basin developing countries (particularly Korea and Taiwan) have been increasingly pressured into VERs and other forms of discriminatory trade restrictions.

The single most important source of trade restrictions in manufactured goods has been the Multi-Fiber Arrangement (MFA), which consists of a set of bilateral quotas (imposed by the developed countries excluding Japan) covering trade in textiles and apparel, mainly between the developed and the developing countries. MFA quota allocations do not reflect current production costs and thus discriminate against newer, low-cost producers to the benefit of long-standing, high-cost producers. Also, the MFA provides rents to the quota recipients, and the international inefficiencies are reproduced at the firm level in the exporting countries through the domestic allocation of quotas.

The rents derived from the quota system are dwarfed by the limitations imposed on the exporting countries under the MFA, and the Pacific Basin developing countries would gain significantly from the liberalization of trade in textiles and clothing. One recent study (Trela and Whalley 1988) concluded that all of the Pacific Basin countries would gain from a global liberalization of textile and apparel trade (table 5.1). Elimination of tariffs and quotas under the MFA would result in increases in the value of textile and apparel exports ranging from a low of 46 percent for Hong Kong to 409 percent for Indonesia. Even if only the bilateral quotas were eliminated, export value would increase anywhere from 25 percent for Hong Kong to 275 percent for Indonesia.

The Pacific Basin developing countries, and in particular the East Asian NICs, also face the imposition of antidumping measures and countervailing subsidies by developed-country importers, particularly the European Community.[4] The issues here are complex and center on reconciling the desire to protect importers from unfair trade practices with the need to prevent the application of trade laws from becoming a convenient way for import-competing industries to harass efficient exporters.[5]

The potential negative impact of these measures on the Pacific Basin developing countries is substantial. An example of the drift toward unilateralism is the US Omnibus Trade and Competitiveness Act of 1988, which expanded

---

4. Antidumping duties have been assessed recently against Taiwan (chemicals and polyester yarn and fiber), Korea (chemicals, polyester yarn, videocassette recorders, and videocassettes and tape), and Hong Kong (videocassettes and tape).

5. For an excellent treatment of these issues see Finger and Nogués (1987).

Table 5.1   Impact of discontinuing the Multi-Fiber Arrangement on textile and apparel exports

| | Percentage increase in exports due to: | |
Country	Removing bilateral quotas but not tariffs	Removing bilateral quotas and tariffs in all developed countries
Hong Kong	24.5	45.6
Singapore	51.6	88.4
Taiwan	138.6	207.8
Korea	184.8	241.0
Malaysia	146.5	189.6
Thailand	36.9	63.4
Philippines	113.6	179.3
Indonesia	275.4	409.1

Source: Trela and Whalley (1988), tables 5 and 6.

the scope of unfair trade practices, relaxed the criteria for affirmative findings, increased the automaticity of retaliation, and created the Super 301 provision. This is the type of trade policy that the Pacific Basin developing countries seek to prevent by strengthening multilateral disciplines on unilateral action.

In agriculture, the interests of the Pacific Basin developing countries vary widely, as some are principally importers of agricultural commodities while others are exporters.[6] For exporters, agricultural protection has a substantial impact. For example, a recent study concluded that agricultural protection in the European Community and Japan cost Thailand nearly $1 billion a year in net foreign-exchange earnings (Anderson and Tyers 1987). Subsidization of domestic producers in the United States and the European Community has also depressed world market prices, reducing the agricultural export receipts of several Pacific Basin developing countries.

The interests of the Pacific Basin developing countries diverge in the area of services as well. Korea has comparative advantage in some labor-intensive construction and engineering services, and Singapore and Hong Kong have comparative advantage in financial services. These NICs might benefit from liberalization in services trade. However, in other countries of the area, financial services are weak and domestic development is a first priority. Thus, although the Pacific Basin developing countries should support the development of a liberal international trading regime for financial services, the ASEAN–4, and perhaps Taiwan and Korea as well, will want special and differential treatment over the short term.

---

6. Four of these countries—Indonesia, Malaysia, the Philippines, and Thailand—are participants in the Cairns Group of agricultural exporters in the GATT.

Likewise, it is in the long-run self-interest of the Pacific Basin developing countries to strengthen intellectual property rights. Indeed, partly as a result of pressure from the United States, several have begun to do so. Although this will involve costs in the short run, strengthening of intellectual property rights will facilitate the smooth transfer of technology. In addition, several Pacific Basin developing countries, in particular Taiwan and Korea, are becoming producers of intellectual property (including computer software), and will want to have their firms' intellectual property rights protected.

Nonetheless, enforcing intellectual property rights may impose substantial explicit and implicit costs on the net importers of intellectual property. And in the context of the Uruguay Round of GATT negotiations, adherence to stricter standards of intellectual property protection could be considered a trade concession and used to extract quid pro quos from the developed countries. For example, there may be a variety of potential bargains that would combine stricter intellectual property rights standards with a mechanism for sharing enforcement and adjudication costs. Possibilities include the reform of national codes to increase allowable damage awards in civil suits, and the establishment of a common fund to subsidize enforcement costs. Thus, by agreeing to stricter standards, the Pacific Basin developing countries could reduce the costs to the proprietary firm of the technology transfer, while enforcement costs could be spread internationally.

Pacific Basin developing countries have pursued a variety of policies with regard to trade-related investment measures (TRIMs). Export-performance requirements are trade-distorting and may well deter investment projects that are economically desirable. Local-content requirements are essentially a form of protection for domestic parts manufacturers, although it is difficult to quantify their economic effects and the magnitude of distortion they cause in investment decisions. Such requirements should be eschewed (on purely self-interest grounds) in favor of explicit tariff protection when protection is considered desirable.

The countries of the region have offered a variety of incentives for foreign direct investment. In some cases, competition among potential recipients has led to foreign firms receiving preferential treatment over domestic firms, especially through tax benefits. One way to avoid such investment bidding wars would be to harmonize investment codes globally (or at least regionally) and to ensure equal treatment to domestic and foreign investors.

Another global trade issue important to the Pacific Basin developing countries is the future of the Generalized System of Preferences (GSP), the unilateral provision of tariff preferences by a number of developed countries. Under the GSP, certain developing-country exports enter developed-country markets duty-free. Although trade under the GSP is substantial, the impact of the program is less certain. First, the effect of the GSP should be measured in terms of the additional trade it creates, which may not be large (cf. Baldwin and Murray 1977; Ray 1987). Second, preferences granted under the GSP are not bound but may be withdrawn at any time. Meanwhile developed countries have imposed both product and source ceilings, many of which are binding. Moreover, several product categories of particular importance to the Pacific Basin developing countries, such as textiles, apparel, and footwear, are excluded from the GSP.

Finally, there is the issue of graduation. In principle, as countries develop, their preferential access is withdrawn, so as to limit trade preferences to those countries in greatest need of it. In January 1989, the United States withdrew GSP privileges from Hong Kong, Korea, Singapore, and Taiwan, affecting $10 billion of US imports from these countries. Although the four East Asian NICs clearly have developed into highly successful exporters of manufactured goods, the removal of their GSP privileges may have been spurred more by US trade deficits than by the principle of graduation. In a separate action, the United States also partially suspended GSP privileges to Thailand in a dispute over intellectual property rights. GSP privileges in the European Community have also been withdrawn from Korea, although this was done because of a trade dispute, not on graduation principles. In fact, the uncertainty surrounding the GSP due to the arbitrary determination by developed countries of product exclusion, ceilings, and graduation may have reduced the program's benefits by discouraging investment in the affected countries and industries.

Thus, it would be in the interest of the Pacific Basin developing countries to secure greater adherence to internationally recognized principles and rules in the conduct of trade policy. But the same lack of commitment to internationally recognized standards emerges on the other side of the ledger in relation to the "special and differential" provision of the GATT. This provision also provides an excuse for developed countries to apply discriminatory measures against developing-country exports. As long as developing countries insist on special and differential treatment (including the Article XVIII balance of payments provision in the GATT), it may be difficult to negotiate greater discipline in developed-country trade practices. As Bergsten has noted, this situation has "enabled LDCs to apply far-reaching restrictions of their own, and frustrated all GATT efforts to achieve meaningful liberalization of LDC trade barriers" (Bergsten 1988, 141). Thus, it may well be in the interest of the Pacific Basin developing countries to give up special and differential treatment in merchandise trade if such a move would secure a commitment to greater discipline and liberalization from the developed countries in the Uruguay Round.

There is a further need to increase reliance on multilateral forums in trade disputes. A case in point is the US–Korean negotiations on intellectual property rights. The United States secured retroactive protection that in some cases exceeded the protection afforded Korean firms. Although the United States achieved its narrow negotiating goals, the agreements are widely regarded in Korea as unfair and may actually impede the liberalization of intellectual property rights. It may be added that when the Korean government rejected the European Community demand for equal treatment, the Community suspended Korea's GSP privileges. These cases support the argument for strengthening the multilateral system by developing safeguards, creating rules to address issues not currently covered (including services, intellectual property, etc.), and improving adjudication.

Influence of Other Regional Powers

The Pacific Basin developing countries will be affected not only by their domestic policies and their participation in international organizations, but also by economic developments in other countries of the region. In particular, developments in five Communist countries—the Soviet Union, Vietnam, Laos, Cambodia, and North Korea—could present both opportunities and competition for the Pacific Basin developing countries.

The Soviet Union east of the Urals is rich in natural resources and is a potentially important source of supply for the manufacturing economies of East Asia. In turn, the Soviet Union may become a market for the products of these countries if it makes progress in its own economic reforms. Vietnam, now one of the world's poorest countries, could become an exporter of agricultural goods, oil, and labor-intensive manufactures and an importer of machinery and equipment if current economic reforms progress. Vietnam has recently improved its macroeconomic performance, reformed its agricultural policies, and emerged as a major exporter of rice. It already receives limited amounts of foreign direct investment, mostly from Japan, the East Asian NICs, and the ASEAN–4. The US trade and investment embargo against Vietnam remains a significant handicap to growth, however. Neighboring Laos has also undertaken economic reforms and has begun receiving aid from the United States and Japan (among others), as well as private investment, mostly from Thailand. Cambodia, if it resolves its internal political problems, could also become a more active participant in international trade.

The economic fortunes of North Korea may be intimately tied to progress in normalization of relations with the South. Such normalization could also have an appreciable impact on South Korea by providing a new outlet for trade and investment and by permitting a reduction in military expenditures.

Growth in trade between any of these five Communist countries and the other Pacific Basin developing countries is highly contingent on the successful implementation of fundamental economic reforms. It is by no means clear as yet that such reforms will indeed be implemented, and in any case these countries are unlikely to become major factors in Pacific Basin trade before the end of the century.

Complementarity in economic structure and geographic proximity make Australia and New Zealand natural trading partners for the Pacific Basin developing countries. Indeed, the greatest contribution Australia and New Zealand could make to the economic fortunes of the Pacific Basin developing countries would be to continue their current policy of reducing their historically high tariff rates on manufactured goods. Even so, trade with these countries will probably would remain a relatively small percentage of the overall trade of the Pacific Basin developing countries for the foreseeable future.

China

China's size, its ongoing economic reforms, and its assumption of sovereignty over Hong Kong in 1997 ensure that, unlike the other Communist countries in the region, it will have an important impact on the Pacific Basin developing countries over the next decade. China looms large in the trade of several of these countries, although the official figures understate its importance because of the substantial extent of China's unreported trade with Korea and Taiwan (in 1988, China's trade may have reached a combined $2.5 billion with Korea and Taiwan).

Since its establishment in 1949, the Chinese Communist government has maintained a centrally planned economic system, including centralized determination of firms' output targets, material allocation, employment, investment, and foreign trade. Targets were set in physical terms, with prices serving only an accounting function. Through the 1970s living standards stagnated as agricultural, industrial, and service output barely kept pace with population growth. Economic reforms were begun in the late 1970s. In agriculture, these included the establishment of the family responsibility system, the reduction of procurement targets, and the freeing of some agricultural prices. The result was a dramatic rise of production and real income in the agricultural sector. Since 1984, however, agricultural growth has slowed, as the maintenance of low prices on major crops and the reduction of funds available for investment have discouraged the expansion of production. The slowdown of agricultural growth, together with rising population and urban incomes, has forced China to increase its agricultural imports. China has become the world's third-largest agricultural importer, behind Japan and the Soviet Union, and some projections foresee its becoming the leading food importer during the next decade. Although this development would favorably affect the food-exporting developing countries elsewhere in the region, it will also put pressure on China to generate foreign exchange through the export of manufactured goods, thereby creating increased competition for the Pacific Basin developing countries in this sector.

Industrial-sector reforms in China have included changes in the allocation and incentives system, the establishment of special export-oriented zones, and the encouragement of foreign direct investment through the establishment of 14 "open cities" and five "special economic zones" on the coast. China has approved foreign investment in approximately 18,000 businesses, with a total contractual investment of over $30 billion (*The Economist*, 24 June 1989). A substantial number of these enterprises involved Hong Kong–based firms, and more recently there have been investments by Taiwanese and Korean firms.

The East Asian NICs are interested in investing in China to offset their own rising labor costs. From the Chinese point of view, such ventures are advantageous in that they involve the transfer of simpler and more appropriate technology than investments by the developed countries, while also bringing in the expertise of the East Asian NICs in marketing and distributing labor-intensive manufactures worldwide. But funds are moving both in and out of China: Guangdong province, adjacent to Hong Kong, absorbs one-half of foreign investment in China and reportedly also controls 3,000 firms in Hong Kong (*The Economist*, 10 December 1988).

The piecemeal and incomplete reforms in the industrial sector have been less successful than the earlier reforms in agriculture. Although under the family responsibility system there is a close correspondence between performance and reward, this link is less direct in industry. Firm managers attempt to increase profits by negotiating higher prices, lower planning targets, higher material allocations, and increases in subsidies or reductions in taxes, rather than by cutting costs.

Industrial efficiency has been further hampered by the lack of competition and the prevalence of sellers' markets in the Chinese industrial sector. These incentive problems have been compounded by a fragmented and irrational pricing system in which multiple prices for the same good coexist, none reflecting true scarcity value.

This incomplete liberalization has generated excess demand by creating supernormal profit opportunities on the one hand, while leaving loss-making activities uncurtailed, on the other. An unplanned investment boom has been undertaken by regional and local authorities and financed by local bank lending, and as a result the central bank eventually lost control of the money supply. By August 1988 the money supply was rising at an annual rate of 40 percent. In 1989 the rate of inflation attained 30 percent, and foreign debt reached $52 billion, with a peak repayment period expected to begin in 1992.

These developments prompted the Chinese authorities to initiate austerity measures to reduce aggregate demand and to roll back some of the reforms. The new measures were successful at reducing aggregate demand and slowing inflation, but at a considerable cost in the form of new administrative regulations and bottlenecks. According to China's State Statistical Bureau, GNP growth slowed to 4 percent in 1989, down from 11 percent in 1988. The estimated inflation rate for 1989 was 18 percent, although by December the year-on-year rate had fallen to less than 7 percent. Some Western analysts claimed that the growth estimate masked the fact that by the end of the year growth was zero or negative, while the actual inflation rate was closer to 25 percent, and the unemployment rate was forecast to double in 1990.

The economic difficulties were compounded following the violent repression of political unrest in June 1989. First, the immediate fall in tourism revenues worsened the external deficit problem, sparking internal debate on the need for further devaluation (in fact, the yuan was devalued by 21 percent in December 1989). Second, in response to the June events, the multilateral development banks and bilateral development agencies suspended or delayed loans. This was accompanied by the cancellation of private loans (or increased borrowing costs) in response to slowing demand and the perception of increased political risk. All this exacerbated China's external financing problems. At the same time, the June events slowed China's progress toward accession to the GATT, which would presumably enhance China's long-run access to foreign markets. The subsequent political retrenchment and movement away from economic liberalization further cloud China's prospects.

Future Chinese political and economic policies will have ramifications beyond their immediate domestic impact. With China scheduled to assume sovereignty over Hong Kong in 1997, any diminution in the city-state's economic vitality due to events in China is against China's long-run interest. China already receives a large share of its foreign-exchange earnings through trade with Hong Kong, which also provides essential entrepreneurial and marketing services. Indeed, the existence of a modern, sophisticated market economy in Hong Kong strongly aids the Chinese reforms.

China also maintains a claim of sovereignty over Taiwan. The Chinese government recently announced a policy of reunification by the year 2000, and with sovereignty over Hong Kong to be transferred to China in 1997, and the small Portuguese colony of Macao reverting to Chinese rule in 1999, Taiwan will remain the only outstanding claim. It is unlikely, however, that the Chinese government would attempt to seize Taiwan by force. Taiwan maintains a considerable defensive capability, and given the growing economic ties between the two, any diminution of Taiwan's economic vitality would ultimately be against China's self-interest.

The impact of prospective developments in China on the other Pacific Basin developing countries could be quite substantial. Successful reform of the Chinese economy would create further opportunities for trade and investment for the East Asian NICs. Rising incomes in China would generate greater demand for agricultural imports—a boon for agricultural exporters in the region. However, successful reforms of the Chinese economy would also lead to increases in the exports of labor-intensive manufactures, putting pressure on exporters of these products elsewhere in the region. World Bank projections show a slight rising trend in China's foreign-trade share of income, implying a total trade turnover of $210 billion in 2000 (World Bank 1985). Total trade turnover was $87 billion in 1988, the most recent year for which data are available, which means that Chinese exports and imports might be expected to grow by approximately $5 billion a year each, or less than 2 percent of the annual increment to world trade; this suggests that the growth of Chinese trade would probably not be disruptive (in most sectors, at least).

Japan

Japan will be increasingly important for the economies of the Pacific Basin developing countries. Japanese direct investment in the eight countries examined in this study increased nearly sixfold between fiscal 1985 (April to March) and fiscal 1989, reaching $7.8 billion in the latter year. Investment in this area has traditionally gone into trade-related operations, including natural resource–extracting industries and manufacturing.

Investment in extractive industries has generally been undertaken with a view to supplying the Japanese market, frequently with Japanese government support. In manufacturing, investment followed Japan's declining comparative advantage, initially in unskilled labor-intensive sectors, and more recently in more capital-intensive sectors such as metals, machinery, and automobiles. Once established, Japanese firms have tended to export a greater share of output back to their home market than do non-Japanese firms. Whereas indigenous manufacturing firms in the Pacific Basin developing countries have encountered considerable difficulties in penetrating the Japanese market, Japanese-based firms have used their knowledge of the home market and access to distribution channels to export successfully back to Japan. In 1980 the Asian subsidiaries of Japanese firms exported 9.8 percent of their output back to Japan; by 1987 this share had risen to 16.7 percent.

The flow of private money to the Pacific Basin developing countries has been accompanied by increasing flows of official funds to the less developed of these countries. Japan's foreign aid budget has grown considerably in recent years, and Japan is by far the biggest bilateral contributor of aid in the region.

The Japanese aid programs consist mainly of yen-denominated loans. The 50 percent appreciation of the yen against the US dollar between 1985 and 1988 caused repayment difficulties for aid recipients in East Asia, whose exports are mostly denominated in dollars. Moreover, Japan has been criticized by the Development Assistance Committee of the OECD for tying loans either directly or indirectly by concentrating development assistance in capital-intensive projects. Nearly 35 percent of Japanese aid is earmarked for public utilities, and another 10 percent for mining and manufacturing projects. Implementing these projects often involves purchasing sophisticated equipment from the donor country, especially in the areas of power generation, transportation, and telecommunications.

Although efforts have been made in Japan to increase aid to Africa and Latin America, rising concern about the possible fragmentation of world trade into regional blocs has encouraged the Japanese in their historical tendency to target aid to Southeast Asia, reinforcing private investment there. The desire to enhance regional influence has contributed to the establishment of the $2 billion aid package to ASEAN announced in December 1987 and to the Japanese determination to further increase its dominance over the Asian Development Bank. Ideas for Japanese-led regional economic schemes such as a preferential trade area or an Asian currency system modeled after the European Monetary System have also been floated.

Although such ideas have gained a small following in Japan, political sensitivities make it difficult to sell them in the Pacific Basin developing countries—and in the United States. Any attempt to create a regional preferential trade area involving trade diversion away from the United States would be viewed in negative terms in Washington, which could probably block any such initiative with a credible retaliatory threat.

Regional schemes aside, Japan's role in trade and investment in the Pacific Basin developing countries is bound to grow. Rising labor costs in Japan drive manufacturing firms offshore, while growing demand draws in imports, thereby creating increased opportunities for Pacific Basin exporters. At the same time, Japan will continue to be a major supplier of capital equipment and parts to the Pacific Basin developing countries. Whether firms based in these countries achieve greater success in penetrating the Japanese market, or whether this trade will be dominated by Japanese firms exporting back to Japan, is an open question. Either way, Japan's importance as a market will rise.

Conclusions

The only international organization of importance in East Asia is the Association of Southeast Asian Nations (ASEAN). Although ASEAN has made little progress in promoting joint trade and industrial ventures, it has been successful as a pressure group in trade negotiations with the developed countries. ASEAN's future role is likely to lie in maximizing the bargaining power of its member countries through joint action and limited schemes to promote regional cooperation.

Preferential trade arrangements are not likely to develop among the East Asian NICs, although they might gain from adopting a common basket currency peg once current imbalances in their balance of payments are corrected. They may also find it in their interest to join the OECD as full members or observers.

It would be desirable to establish an OECD–type organization within the Pacific Basin. Such an organization may include, in addition to the Pacific Basin developing countries, Japan, Australia, New Zealand, China and the United States. The organization would be oriented to a large extent toward trade issues, with a view to ensuring the openness of the international economic system. Indeed, the recently formed APEC may develop along these lines.

The critical point is that the Pacific Basin developing countries, being highly dependent on trade, have a great stake in the future of the international economic system. They are concerned over the entire set of issues under discussion in the Uruguay Round of multilateral trade negotiations, but have a particular interest in a strong Safeguards Code that would ensure that import controls are temporary and degressive, in outlawing protectionist measures outside of the GATT, and in limiting the use of antidumping measures and countervailing duties. And although the narrow mercantilist interests of the Pacific Basin developing countries differ in regard to agriculture and services, they should press for (or at least acquiesce in) liberalization in these areas.

One possible arrangement would be for the Pacific Basin developing countries to give up special and differential treatment in merchandise trade in exchange for a commitment from the developed countries to greater discipline and liberalization in the Uruguay Round. This would also involve placing increased reliance on multilateral forums for settling trade disputes.

Beyond their domestic policies and their participation in international organizations, the economic fortunes of the NICs and the ASEAN–4 will be affected by economic developments in other countries of the region. With the exception of China, none of the major Communist countries of the region have had major economic ties to the other Pacific Basin developing countries in the recent past. Such ties would increase if the Communist nations successfully implement fundamental economic reforms. Even so, these countries are unlikely to become major factors in the trade of the Pacific Basin developing countries before the end of the century.

In contrast, China's importance as a trading partner is expected to increase over time, although prospective changes will be greatly affected by the future course of its economic reform efforts. Successful reform of the Chinese economy would create opportunities for trade and investment for the East Asian NICs, and would also represent a boon for agricultural exporters in the region, as rising incomes lead to greater demands for agricultural imports. Successful reform of the Chinese economy would also lead to increased exports of labor-intensive manufactures from China, which would put pressure on other exporters in the Pacific Basin developing countries.

Trade with Australia and New Zealand is also likely to remain a small percentage of the overall trade of the Pacific Basin developing countries. Finally, Japanese trade with and investment in the Pacific Basin developing countries is bound to grow. Rising labor costs in Japan will continue to drive manufacturing firms offshore, while growing demand will continue to draw in imports. This will lead to significant changes in trade patterns, as Japanese firms integrate plants in the Pacific Basin developing countries into their international sourcing networks. As a consequence, Japan will remain the largest external source of private and official investment capital for the foreseeable future.

Under any scenario, however, the bilateral relations of the Pacific Basin developing countries with the United States will remain high on their policy agendas. It is to this topic that we now turn.

6

Economic Outlook and Implications for the United States

Prospects for the Pacific Basin Developing Countries

The eight countries examined in this study—Hong Kong, Singapore, Taiwan, Korea, Malaysia, Thailand, the Philippines, and Indonesia—are economically diverse, but their development paths show some important similarities. While there have been significant differences in the economic policies pursued by these countries, on the whole they have been more open to international trade than other developing countries. By exploiting the gains from trade they have achieved among the highest income growth rates in the world, and their per capita incomes are now comparable to those in the poorer countries of Europe.

The Pacific Basin developing countries' share of world trade has tripled over the past 25 years, and together these countries now account for a greater share of world trade than Japan. Historically, this trade has been oriented toward the United States, Japan, and Europe; there has been little trade integration among the Pacific Basin developing countries themselves. However, the emergence of balance of payments surpluses in Taiwan and Korea, exchange rate realignment in most of the countries, and the liberalization of investment restrictions in the ASEAN–4 (Malaysia, Thailand, the Philippines, and Indonesia) have led to an explosion of intraregional investment, which is in turn creating a more genuinely integrated regional market.

The Newly Industrializing Countries

The British Crown Colony of Hong Kong, the closest approximation to a laissez-faire economy in the world today, has experienced rapid growth for the past 30 years while absorbing millions of Chinese immigrants. Now Hong Kong faces two challenges. The first is to upgrade its industrial structure to include more high-value-added activities. This is being accomplished by product upgrading within existing industries (such as in apparel) and simultaneously by developing new industries.

The second challenge is how to cope with the transfer of sovereignty from the United Kingdom to China in 1997. Unless an acceptable modus vivendi can be negotiated, the flight of money and people from the colony is likely to accelerate from current high levels in the runup to 1997. The projections presented in chapter 4 indicate that this would effectively end the process of development in Hong Kong and have a serious impact on the economy of China as well.

Singapore, like Hong Kong, is an entrepôt hub and effectively a free trader, although the degree of government involvement in the economy is far higher. Singapore has gone much further than Hong Kong in developing its petroleum-refining and chemicals industries, and the projections presented in chapter 4 indicate further expansion of such capital-intensive sectors, particularly chemicals and iron and steel, subject to space limitations and possible environmental concerns. At the same time, Singapore is attempting to expand its role as an international financial center, in response to the uncertainty surrounding the future of Hong Kong. Its success in this endeavor will depend partly on its ability to negotiate the transition to a more open political system.

The economic history of Taiwan is proof of the feasibility of economic growth with equity. In the quarter-century after 1963, per capita real income grew at an average rate of 6.4 percent annually, while its income distribution remained possibly the most egalitarian among the market economies. The comprehensive agrarian reform undertaken in the late 1940s and early 1950s, the shift to labor-intensive manufactures, and the prevalence of small and medium-sized firms in the economy all contributed to this pattern. Now the rapid rise in asset prices (especially land) threatens to undermine Taiwan's egalitarian wealth distribution and to contribute to social and political tensions in this democratizing country. Taiwan faces the need to upgrade its industrial structure in the face of real appreciation of its currency, to modernize its financial system to achieve more efficient financial intermediation, and to reduce its large external imbalances. The trade projections presented in chapter 4 indicate that the share of textiles and apparel in Taiwan's exports could be expected to fall by nearly 8 percentage points from its 1988 level of about 24 percent, while the share of chemicals will rise by a similar amount, roughly doubling the export share of that sector.

Korea has pursued the most interventionist economic policies among the East Asian NICs. Although these policies have been consistent with rapid growth and strong trade performance, they have also contributed to a highly concentrated industrial structure and considerable popular discontent. Moreover, like Taiwan, Korea has seen an explosion of asset prices in recent years, with an accompanying rise in social tensions, in the midst of a transition toward more democratic rule. The creation and institutionalization of legitimate labor market dispute-resolution mechanisms is probably the single most important challenge to be met in ensuring Korea's continued strong external performance. The projections reported in chapter 4 indicate that the Korean trade pattern can be expected to undergo considerable change. Large increases can be expected in chemicals and iron and steel exports, and Korea is expected to go from being a net importer to a net exporter in two product categories, chemicals and paper and paper products. This changing trade pattern indicates that Korea is following the developmental path of Japan.

The four NICs have succeeded, through a variety of policies, at certain common tasks. They have been able to transform local productive potential into products demanded on world markets and to bring those products to world markets at competitive prices. They have demonstrated an ability to adapt to changing market conditions and establish apparently self-sustaining development. Now each of the four must confront internal demands for a more democratic political system.

The ASEAN-4

In the past quarter-century the Malaysian economy has undergone a tremendous transformation, with growth in oil and manufactures having eclipsed the traditional tin and rubber sectors. Yet it remains uncertain whether the manufacturing sector, which is dominated by state enterprise and assembly activity, has achieved self-sustaining momentum. A variety of reforms to improve the efficiency of resource allocation are advisable, but some (although not all) of these involve changes in the redistributive policies and institutions that have been central to the Malaysian government's economic agenda. In the end, the prospects for successful economic reform will hinge on the ability of the Malaysian political leadership to devise ways of reconciling the goals of wealth redistribution and economic efficiency.

Like Malaysia, Thailand has undergone considerable economic change in the past 25 years as the relative importance of agriculture in its economy has steadily declined. Although there have been some policy-inspired problems, these have been on a smaller scale than the counterpart policy failures in the other ASEAN–4 economies. Now the major policy challenge is to provide sufficient infrastructure investment for continued growth. According to the projections presented in chapter 4, Thailand should become a net exporter of manufactures by 2000.

In some respects the Philippines, with its plantation-style farming, protected manufacturing industries, large external debt, and political instability, more closely resembles a stereotypical Latin American economy than an East Asian one. And like some countries in Latin America, the Philippines is in the midst of a comprehensive liberalization program that at least holds the promise of improving the country's economic performance.

The highest priority in the Philippines' liberalization program, from a welfare standpoint, is improving productivity in the agricultural sector, in which most of the population works and where most of the poverty is. Agrarian reform on a scale large enough to transform the agricultural sector would require extensive financing from foreign governments, the international financial institutions, or most likely both.

In the industrial sector, the Philippine government has made considerable progress in dismantling the import substitution regime that has effectively strangled allocative efficiency. Nevertheless, a wide range of reforms will be needed to restructure the manufacturing sector, which is in reality two sectors: an assembly-dominated export enclave, and the still protected import-competing sector. Among the necessary reforms are privatization and a strengthening of property rights, infrastructure investment, and incentive reforms. Probably the most important steps are a further real devaluation of the currency and additional trade liberalization.

Indonesia is both the poorest and the most populous of the Pacific Basin developing countries examined in this study. Indonesian economic policy historically has put great emphasis on state control of the means of production, and, as in the case of Malaysia, public enterprises have been characterized by significant inefficiency. Beginning in the early 1980s, the government initiated a wide-ranging economic liberalization to correct some of these inefficiencies. The major challenge the government now faces is to maintain sufficient economic growth to absorb the rapidly increasing number of entrants into the labor market. This, in turn, necessitates the continuation of the ongoing liberalization program, in particular to encourage the growth of labor-intensive manufacturing activities, and the provision of public investment, to provide an adequate infrastructure for growth. The projections presented in chapter 4 indicate that a considerable transformation of Indonesia's trade composition is to be expected, with manufactured exports doubling to more than 40 percent of total Indonesian exports by 2000.

The ASEAN–4 must now seek to duplicate the success of the East Asian NICs in transforming local productive potential into products demanded on world markets, getting those products into world markets at competitive prices, adapting to changing market conditions, and establishing apparently self-sustaining development. How quickly they can achieve this level of economic sophistication is still an open question. Although they have recently registered impressive increases in manufactures exports, in many cases the relevant technology and skills have not been integrated into the wider economy. For example, in Malaysia and the Philippines the growth in manufactures exports has been largely due to export enclaves with few backward or forward linkages to the rest of the economy. In Indonesia the degree of integration between activities in export processing zones and the rest of the economy has been greater, but even here one study found that without informal transfers to government officials the zones would have been a net drag on the economy. This lack of integration raises questions about the ability of the ASEAN–4 ability to absorb technology and skills from abroad. This is compounded by the fact that the human capital embodied in their labor forces is significantly lower than that of the NICs, especially in engineering and management skills. At the same time, however, the recent explosion of intraregional investment presents the ASEAN–4 with a historic opportunity to appropriate technology and management and international marketing skills through inward FDI from the NICs.

Comparison of the export composition of all the Pacific Basin developing countries reveals some interesting patterns across time. Korea appears to be following a developmental path similar to Japan's, with a lag of about one generation. Thailand (and possibly the Philippines) appears to be following the paths of Taiwan, Hong Kong, and Korea. And Indonesia appears to be following the paths of several countries, including Malaysia, the Philippines, and Brazil. Because of similarities in industrial composition, the "followers" are natural recipients of FDI and technology transfers from the "leaders."

The Pacific Basin in International Trade

For the Pacific Basin developing countries as a whole, changes in the global trade regime have the potential either to facilitate or to hinder economic development over the next decade. These countries are small and highly dependent on trade and therefore have a major stake in an open, rules-based, multilateral system of trade.

The General Agreement on Tariffs and Trade

Policy interest consequently centers on the General Agreement on Tariffs and Trade (GATT), and, at the time of this writing, on the Uruguay Round of multilateral trade negotiations under the GATT's auspices. The Pacific Basin developing countries seek to promote open trade in manufactured goods, and several areas currently under negotiation are therefore of particular interest. They would benefit directly from liberalization of the Multi-Fiber Arrangement (MFA), creation of a GATT Safeguards Code to ensure that import controls are temporary and degressive, a tightening of discipline on countervailing and antidumping actions, elimination of protectionist measures outside the GATT such as voluntary export restraints, and adoption of measures banning discrimination in the application of trade restraints.

However, the Pacific Basin developing countries have, like other developing countries, used the "special and differential treatment" provision of the GATT to maintain practices that completely contravene the spirit of the agreement. One possibly useful negotiating stance for the Pacific Basin developing countries would be to offer to give up special and differential treatment in merchandise trade (including participation in the Generalized System of Preferences) in exchange for greater discipline on the use of safeguards measures and further liberalization by the developed countries.

There is less overlap of interests among the Pacific Basin developing countries in the other major areas under negotiation in the Uruguay Round. On some important issues, the narrow mercantilist interests of the individual countries conflict. In agriculture, the ASEAN-4 (and especially Thailand), which are net exporters of agricultural goods, would benefit from agricultural liberalization and the elimination of subsidies, whereas Korea, which maintains extensive protection of agriculture, would bear significant adjustment costs. In financial services, Hong Kong and Singapore might gain from liberalization, whereas the ASEAN-4, and perhaps Korea and Taiwan as well, will want special and differential treatment in the short run as they seek to develop their financial services sectors.

The narrow interests of the Pacific Basin developing countries are similarly split on the issues of intellectual property and trade-related investment measures. Most of the Pacific Basin developing countries are now overwhelmingly consumers of intellectual property and hosts of foreign direct investment, and they might not see the stricter regulation of intellectual property trade or a strengthening of the rules governing FDI in their immediate interest. However, the NICs are fast becoming producers of intellectual property and originators of FDI, and as highly outward-oriented economies it will be in their long-run interest to facilitate liberalization in the entire range of issues under discussion.

The Pacific Basin developing countries' shared interests in the area of manufactures trade, and the long-run convergence of their interests on other trade issues, argues for the development of a regional organization along the lines of the Organization for Economic Cooperation and Development. As outlined in chapter 5, such an organization could provide a useful consultative forum in place of the often acrimonious bilateral, and unwieldy global, forums. The recently formed Asia Pacific Economic Cooperation (APEC) could develop into such an organization.

Trade with the United States

The growing role of the Pacific Basin developing countries in the world economy will pose both adjustment and policy issues for the United States. Trade between the United States and the Pacific Basin developing countries exceeded $122 billion in 1988—nearly as much as US–Japan trade, and three-quarters the amount of US trade with the European Community—and is growing rapidly.

The Pacific Basin developing countries' exports to the United States are mainly labor-intensive products, including traditional light industries such as apparel and low-end electronics products, although these countries are also net exporters to the United States of iron and steel, and motor vehicles and parts. Their imports from the United States consist primarily of natural resource–based products, sophisticated engineering products, and chemicals.

The product composition of this trade is reported in table 6.1. The Pacific Basin developing countries' exports to the United States are concentrated in five categories, which together account for over half of the total: consumer electronics (16.9 percent); apparel (12.5 percent); office and computing equipment (11.1 percent); other manufacturing industries, including jewelry, toys, sporting goods, and musical instruments (5.9 percent); and petroleum and petroleum products (5.1 percent). More than half of US imports from these countries are in the following industries: electronics, including telecommunications equipment (15.2 percent); basic chemicals (9.2 percent); nonelectrical machinery (8.6 percent); office and computing equipment (6.5 percent); food crops (5.8 percent); electrical machinery (4.5 percent); and agricultural commodities (4.4 percent). The Pacific Basin developing countries run surpluses with the United States, in net export terms, in apparel, electronics, office and computing equipment, miscellaneous manufactures, and footwear; they run deficits in basic chemicals, animals and animal products, crude minerals, and synthetic resins. Considerable intraindustry trade occurs in the electronics industries.

The trade composition projections presented in table 6.1 for 2000 have been derived under the assumption that the United States maintains its

Table 6.1 Product composition of the Pacific Basin developing countries' trade with the United States, 1988 and 2000 (percentages of total)

Industry	Exports		Imports	
	1988	2000	1988	2000
Animals and animal products	0.1	0.1	4.1	5.9
Fish and preparations	1.4	1.0	0.5	0.4
Food crops	1.7	0.9	5.8	5.9
Tobacco and manufactures	0.0	0.0	2.3	1.9
Agricultural commodities	0.8	0.8	4.4	5.0
Beverages	0.0	0.1	0.1	0.1
Textile fibers	0.0	0.0	1.9	4.6
Natural rubber and gums	2.2	3.2	0.5	0.9
Raw wood	0.1	0.0	3.2	2.2
Crude minerals	0.0	0.0	3.6	5.1
Coal, coke, and briquettes	0.0	0.0	2.0	1.6
Petroleum and petroleum products	5.1	4.2	2.8	4.4
Nonferrous metals	0.4	0.3	0.8	1.3
Manufactures				
Spinning, weaving, etc. (ISIC 3211)	2.1	1.3	0.8	0.4
Textile products (ISIC 321 less 3211)	1.4	0.8	0.3	0.1
Wearing apparel (ISIC 322)	12.5	6.8	0.1	0.1
Leather and products (ISIC 323)	1.3	1.0	0.5	1.8
Footwear (ISIC 324)	4.8	3.5	0.1	0.2
Wood products (ISIC 331)	2.4	1.9	0.6	1.4
Furniture and fixtures (ISIC 332)	1.1	2.6	0.1	0.1
Pulp, paper, and products (ISIC 3411)	0.0	0.2	1.8	1.6
Paper products (ISIC 341 less 3411)	0.1	0.2	0.3	0.3
Printing and publishing (ISIC 342)	0.5	0.5	0.3	0.6
Basic chemicals, excluding fertilizer (ISIC 3511)	0.6	2.0	9.2	8.5
Synthetic resins (ISIC 3513)	0.5	0.3	4.0	3.3
Other industrial chemicals (ISIC 351 less 3511 and 3513)	0.0	0.0	0.0	0.1
Drugs and medicine (ISIC 3522)	0.0	0.0	0.3	0.2
Other chemical products (ISIC 352 less 3522)	0.2	0.4	2.1	1.4
Rubber products (ISIC 355)	0.8	0.7	0.4	0.3
Plastic products (ISIC 356)	3.8	9.1	0.5	0.2

Continued on next page

Industry	Exports		Imports	
	1988	2000	1988	2000
Manufactures				
Pottery, china, etc. (ISIC 361)	0.5	0.4	0.0	0.1
Glass products (ISIC 362)	0.4	0.3	0.3	0.3
Other nonmetallic products (ISIC 369)	0.1	0.1	0.2	0.2
Iron and steel (ISIC 371)	1.5	5.3	0.6	0.5
Fabricated metal products (ISIC 381)	3.9	8.8	1.5	1.0
Office and computing equipment (ISIC 3825)	11.1	6.6	6.5	7.4
Other machinery (ISIC 382 less 3285)	3.3	3.4	8.6	6.0
Radio, television, and telecommunications equipment (ISIC 3832)	16.9	14.0	15.2	10.6
Other electrical machinery (ISIC 383 less 3832)	3.3	3.4	8.6	6.0
Shipbuilding and repairing (ISIC 3841)	0.4	1.5	0.5	0.6
Railroad equipment (ISIC 3842)	0.1	0.1	0.0	0.0
Motor vehicles (ISIC 3843)	3.3	2.9	1.0	0.2
Aircraft (ISIC 3845)	0.2	0.1	3.2	5.7
Motorcycles and bicycles (ISIC 3844 and 3849)	1.5	1.7	0.0	0.0
Professional goods (ISIC 385)	2.6	1.8	3.5	3.6
Other industries (ISIC 390)	5.9	7.5	1.1	1.0

Source: General Agreement on Tariffs and Trade.

import and export market shares in each product category for each of the Pacific Basin developing countries. These figures should not be regarded as forecasts, but simply as indicators of how trade composition would change if constant market shares were maintained.

Under these assumptions, in 2000 more than half of the Pacific Basin developing countries' exports to the United States will be concentrated in consumer electronics, plastic products, fabricated metals products (including cutlery, hardware, and structural metal products), other manufacturing industries, apparel, and office and computing equipment. Together these account for more than half of total exports. From the standpoint of the Pacific Basin developing countries, the biggest increases in net exports would occur in plastic products, fabricated metal products, and radio, television, and tele-communications equipment; the biggest declines would occur in aircraft, animals and animal products, and crude minerals.

Again under the assumption of constant market shares, the Pacific Basin developing countries will continue to import natural resource–based and high-technology products from the United States; their imports will be concentrated in sophisticated electronics equipment (such as telecommunications equipment), basic chemicals, office and computing equipment, nonelectrical machinery, animals and animal products, food crops, and aircraft. Net imports from the United States will be the largest in animals and animal products, aircraft, crude minerals, basic chemicals, textile fibers (natural and synthetic), and food crops.

Table 6.2 reports US exports to the Pacific Basin developing countries as a proportion of US domestic traded-goods output, and US imports from these countries as a share of apparent US traded-goods consumption (output less net exports). According to these calculations, in 1988 exports to the Pacific Basin developing countries comprised 1.3 percent of US traded-goods output, and imports from the Pacific Basin countries accounted for 2.2 percent of apparent consumption. The products for which US exports to the Pacific Basin developing countries represented the greatest proportion of US traded-goods output were leather and leather products (5.5 percent), basic chemicals (5.1 percent), radio, television, and telecommunications equipment (4.2 percent), and electrical machinery (2.9 percent). The products for which US imports from the Pacific Basin developing countries were the highest share of US apparent consumption of traded goods were footwear (32.5 percent), leather products (17.2 percent), motorcycles and bicycles (15.1 percent), and wearing apparel (13.4 percent).

Under the constant-market-shares assumption, the importance to the US economy of trade with the Pacific Basin developing countries can be expected to increase dramatically over the next decade. The export share of traded-goods output would rise to 4.1 percent by 2000, while the import share of apparent consumption would increase to 6.5 percent.[1] These averages conceal considerable interindustry differences. Apart from the leather products industry, the export share of output would be the greatest in basic chemicals, electronics, and aircraft. The largest increases in the export share of output occur in basic chemicals and aircraft, along with shipbuilding, nonfuel primary products, electronics, and professional goods. The export share remains flat in motor vehicles, and declines in motorcycles and bicycles.

US imports of footwear and motorcycle and bicycle imports from the Pacific Basin developing countries will increase to more than half of domestic consumption under the constant-market-shares assumption. Because the trade projections assume that US textile and apparel imports will continue to be restricted, import growth is projected to be relatively slow in these industries,

---

1. Sectoral output is based on Bureau of Labor Statistics projections, which assume an overall real growth rate of 2.3 percent for the US traded-goods sector.

Table 6.2 Economic effects of US trade with the Pacific Basin developing countries, 1988 and 2000 (percentages)

Industry	Exports as a proportion of output		Imports as a proportion of apparent consumption[a]	
	1988	2000	1988	2000
Total	1.3	4.1	2.2	6.5
Total primary	1.1	5.1	0.7	2.1
Nonfuel primary	1.6	7.0	0.7	2.3
Fuels	0.4	2.1	0.7	1.9
Coal, coke, etc.	2.2	6.0	0.0	0.0
Petroleum and products	0.3	1.7	0.8	2.1
Total manufactures	1.3	3.6	3.0	8.6
Spinning, weaving, etc. (ISIC 3211)	0.8	1.6	3.6	8.0
Textile products (ISIC 321 less 3211)	0.3	0.5	2.3	4.3
Wearing apparel (ISIC 322)	0.1	0.2	13.4	22.4
Leather and products (ISIC 323)	5.5	83.8	17.2	42.7
Footwear (ISIC 324)	0.6	7.3	32.5	64.9
Wood products (ISIC 331)	0.3	2.7	2.3	6.0
Furniture and fixtures (ISIC 332)	0.1	0.6	2.4	17.3
Pulp, paper, and products (ISIC 3411)	1.6	4.0	0.0	1.0
Paper products (ISIC 341 less 3411)	0.2	0.6	0.1	0.7
Printing and publishing (ISIC 342)	0.1	0.7	0.3	1.0
Basic chemicals (ISIC 3511)	5.1	16.3	0.6	7.6
Other industrial chemicals (ISIC 351 less 3511 and 3513)	0.0	0.4	0.0	0.1
Drugs and medicine (ISIC 3522)	0.4	0.8	0.0	0.2
Other chemicals (ISIC 352 less 3522)	1.9	4.6	0.4	2.5
Rubber products (ISIC 355)	0.6	1.4	2.0	6.5
Plastic products and synthetic resins (ISIC 356)	1.7	3.8	2.9	17.4
Pottery, china, etc. (ISIC 361)	0.1	0.7	2.1	5.7
Glass products (ISIC 362)	0.7	2.8	1.8	5.1
Other nonmetallic products (ISIC 369)	0.3	1.1	0.3	1.0
Iron and steel (ISIC 371)	0.3	1.2	1.3	17.7

Continued on next page

Table 6.2   (continued)

Industry	Exports as a proportion of output		Imports as a proportion of apparent consumption[a]	
	1988	2000	1988	2000
Manufactures				
Fabricated metal products (ISIC 381)	0.4	1.0	1.9	15.1
Office and computing equipment (ISIC 3825)	1.3	2.2	4.0	3.3
Other machinery (ISIC 382 less 3825)	2.1	5.0	1.4	4.8
Radio, television, and telecommunications equipment (ISIC 3832)	4.2	8.5	7.6	17.0
Other electrical machinery (ISIC 383 less 3832)	2.9	6.3	4.6	9.9
Shipbuilding and repairing (ISIC 3841)	1.3	6.1	1.9	37.2
Railroad equipment (ISIC 3842)	0.5	0.8	1.6	5.3
Motor vehicles (ISIC 3843)	0.2	0.2	1.1	3.6
Aircraft (ISIC 3845)	1.4	8.4	0.2	0.2
Motorcycles and bicycles (ISIC 3844 and 3849)	0.2	0.1	15.1	59.8
Professional goods (ISIC 385)	2.1	6.3	2.9	5.3
Miscellaneous (ISIC 390)	1.2	4.7	9.1	39.3

a. Apparent consumption is equal to total output minus net exports. Because of differences in industry classifications, synthetic resins has been aggregated with plastics products, and nonfuel primary products could not be disaggregated.

Sources: Trade data from the General Agreement on Tariffs and Trade. US output and employment projections are from US Bureau of Labor Statistics.

and the import share of apparent apparel consumption only rises from 13.4 percent to 22.4 percent. Besides footwear and motorcycles and bicycles, the largest overall increases in import penetration will be in shipbuilding and repairing, miscellaneous manufactures, and leather products, while the most rapid growth will occur in furniture, iron and steel, plastics, and fabricated metal products. The most notable import increase is perhaps in iron and steel, where the import penetration ratio rises to 17.7 percent of domestic consumption.[2] In only one sector, office and computing equipment, does the share of imports from the Pacific Basin developing countries in apparent consumption decline.

---

2. This assumes that existing voluntary export restraints are abolished as scheduled.

Effects on US employment of the projected trade shifts are reported in table 6.3. These are the direct effects, calculated from the projected input-output table of the Bureau of Labor Statistics for the year 2000.[3] Exports to the Pacific Basin developing countries created 311,600 US jobs in 1988; imports replaced 755,900 potential jobs (that is, jobs that would have been created in the absence of such imports). Of the jobs created by exports to the Pacific Basin developing countries, 87,000 were in the nonfuel primary products sector; 60,100 were in radio, television, and telecommunications equipment; and 33,700 were in nonelectrical machinery. Potential jobs forgone because of imports were concentrated in apparel (173,700); radio, television, and telecommunications (122,400); footwear (78,500); and the miscellaneous manufactures category (53,700).

The constant-market-share calculations indicate that exports to the Pacific Basin developing countries will account for 1,021,200 US jobs in 2000, while imports from the Pacific Basin developing countries will cost the United States 2,198,400 potential jobs. The categories benefiting most from trade with the Pacific Basin developing countries will be nonfuel primary products (366,700) and radio, television, and telecommunications equipment (120,700). Imports from the Pacific Basin developing countries will primarily affect apparel (286,800); radio, television, and telecommunications equipment (270,200); fabricated metals products (206,800); and footwear (193,800).

Overall, there will be a net loss of 732,900 potential jobs due to trade with the Pacific Basin developing countries between 1988 and 2000. This net employment change can be decomposed into two parts: a technological-change effect (the change in the employment-output ratio at constant net exports) and a pure trade effect (the employment effect of the change in net exports calculated using the projected employment-output ratio). Technological change appears to create 207,500 US jobs between 1988 and 2000. This is due to the reduction in the employment-output ratio in net import industries and is therefore a reduction in potential jobs lost rather than a positive contribution to employment. The second part of the net employment change is that due purely to trade changes, a loss of 940,400 potential jobs. The largest employment gains are seen in nonfuel primary products (231,400) and aircraft (76,300). The largest net potential job losses occur in fabricated metals products (190,300), miscellaneous manufactures (179,800), and apparel

---

3. Unpublished data from the Office of Economic and Employment Projections, Bureau of Labor Statistics. Total (direct plus indirect) employment changes have not been calculated because some significant differences in the trade and input-output industry definitions could have propagated large errors throughout the calculations.

Table 6.3 Employment effects of US trade with Pacific Basin developing countries, 1988 and 2000[a] (thousands of jobs)

Industry	Employment				Decomposition of net employment changes		
	Exports		Imports		Techno-logical effects	Trade effects	Total effects
	1988	2000	1988	2000			
Total	311.6	1,021.2	−755.9	−2,198.4	207.5	−940.4	−732.9
Total primary	92.1	383.8	−45.3	−136.0	−34.4	235.4	201.0
Nonfuel primary	87.0	366.7	−39.7	−120.6	−32.6	231.4	198.8
Fuels	5.0	17.1	−5.6	−15.5	−1.9	4.0	2.2
Coal, coke, etc.	3.4	7.4	−0.0	0.0	−2.6	6.6	4.0
Petroleum and products	1.2	9.7	−5.6	−15.5	0.8	−2.6	−1.8
Total manufactures	219.5	637.4	−710.6	−2,062.4	241.9	−1,175.8	−933.9
Spinning, weaving, etc. (ISIC 3211)	3.2	5.5	−15.3	−28.3	5.0	−15.8	−10.7
Textile products (ISIC 321 less 3211)	1.5	2.2	−12.8	−20.4	5.2	−12.0	−6.8
Wearing apparel (ISIC 322)	0.9	1.3	−173.7	−286.8	60.1	−172.8	−112.7
Leather and products (ISIC 323)	3.2	38.6	−15.1	−37.0	0.9	12.6	13.5
Footwear (ISIC 324)	0.5	5.2	−78.5	−193.8	21.0	−131.6	−110.7
Wood products (ISIC 331)	2.5	22.0	−19.8	−51.5	4.4	−16.6	−12.2
Furniture, fixtures (ISIC 332)	0.6	3.3	−13.2	−99.9	10.8	−94.8	−84.0
Pulp, paper, etc. (ISIC 3411)	3.9	9.1	−0.1	−2.4	−2.5	5.5	3.0

| Industry | Employment | | | | Decomposition of net employment changes | | |
| | Exports | | Imports | | Techno-logical effects | Trade effects | Total effects |
	1988	2000	1988	2000			
Paper products (ISIC 341 less 3411)	0.8	3.0	-0.6	-3.2	0.0	-0.4	-0.4
Printing and publishing (ISIC 342)	1.9	12.1	-5.0	-17.6	0.7	-3.1	-2.4
Basic chemicals (ISIC 3511)	14.2	43.8	-1.7	-17.8	-4.7	18.3	13.5
Other industrial chemicals (ISIC 3513)	0.0	0.6	0.0	-0.1	-0.0	0.5	0.5
Drugs and medicine (ISIC 3522)	1.0	2.1	-0.1	-0.5	-0.3	0.9	0.6
Other chemical (ISIC 352 less 3522)	4.3	10.7	-0.9	-5.5	-0.7	2.4	1.7
Rubber products (ISIC 355)	1.3	2.7	-4.9	-13.3	2.4	-9.3	-6.9
Plastic products and synthetic resins (ISIC 356)	13.2	35.1	-23.1	-160.0	16.3	-131.3	-115.0
Pottery, china, etc. (ISIC 361)	0.3	1.4	-4.9	-12.6	2.1	-8.6	-6.5
Glass products (ISIC 362)	1.2	4.5	-3.1	-8.5	0.4	-2.6	-2.2
Other nonmetallic products (ISIC 369)	0.7	2.7	-0.8	-2.7	0.0	0.1	0.1
Iron and steel (ISIC 371)	1.3	4.7	-6.2	-83.4	2.6	-76.3	-73.8
Fabricated metal products (ISIC 381)	5.7	14.1	-27.8	-206.8	19.8	-190.3	-170.6
Office and computing equipment (ISIC 3285)	6.0	10.8	-19.0	-16.6	8.9	-1.6	7.3
Other machinery (ISIC 382 less 3825)	33.7	79.7	-23.8	-77.0	-1.3	-5.9	-7.2
Radio, television, and telecommunications equipment (ISIC 3832)	60.1	120.7	-122.4	-270.2	45.0	-132.1	-87.2

Continued on next page

Table 6.3 (continued)

| Industry | Employment | | | | Decomposition of net employment changes | | |
| | Exports | | Imports | | Techno-logical effects | Trade effects | Total effects |
	1988	2000	1988	2000			
Manufactures							
Other electrical machinery (ISIC 383 less 3832)	19.0	37.7	−33.0	−65.3	7.0	−20.6	−13.6
Shipbuilding and repairing (ISIC 3841)	2.5	10.6	−3.8	−48.4	3.9	−40.3	−36.4
Railroad equipment (ISIC 3842)	0.2	0.3	−0.5	−1.9	0.1	−1.3	−1.3
Motor vehicles (ISIC 3843)	1.9	1.5	−11.9	−31.7	5.8	−25.9	−20.1
Aircraft (ISIC 3845)	13.0	81.2	−1.8	−1.8	−8.4	76.6	68.2
Motorcycles and bicycles (ISIC 3844 and 3849)	0.1	0.0	−11.5	−31.4	12.1	−32.1	−20.0
Professional goods (ISIC 385)	15.6	52.0	−21.3	−45.2	−0.3	12.9	12.5
Other industries (ISIC 390)	5.3	18.1	−53.7	−220.7	25.6	−179.8	−154.2

a. Due to differences in industry classifications, synthetic resins has been aggregated with plastics products and nonfuel primary products could not be disaggregated.

Sources: Underlying trade data from the General Agreement on Tariffs and Trade. US employment projections are from US Bureau of Labor Statistics.

(172,800); net potential job losses are also significant in iron and steel (76,300) and in motor vehicles (25,900).

It must be stressed, however, that these are losses in potential jobs, and do not imply that any workers now in these industries would lose their current jobs. Since US imports are far more labor-intensive than US exports, balanced trade growth by definition implies a net loss of potential jobs. In fact, given the incremental increases in domestic consumption and in US exports, combined with normal turnover and attrition rates, it is possible that increases in import penetration even on this large a scale would generate no significant involuntary unemployment.

This loss of potential jobs therefore does not represent a national welfare loss. The losses are concentrated in declining light-industry sectors, and what appear to be large sectoral employment shifts actually represent welfare gains due to greater specialization along the lines of comparative advantage. Research by Hufbauer, Berliner, and Elliott (1986) indicates that the costs of attempting to preserve employment in these declining industries would greatly outweigh the economic benefits that these jobs provide.

Moreover, these calculations pertain only to merchandise trade and do not include services trade. Data limitations make it impossible to quantify the prospective impact on the US economy of trade in services with these countries, but the United States does have comparative advantage in many services, and employment gains there could offset losses in the merchandise trade sector.

Lastly, it should be reiterated that these computations are not predictions, but are simply calculations based on the assumption, for convenience's sake, that US market share in the exports and imports of the Pacific Basin developing countries remains unchanged. That may or may not happen. There are clearly cases in which the constant-market-share assumption is unlikely to be fulfilled. Increases or decreases in the fundamental competitiveness of US industry may affect the US share of the Pacific Basin developing countries' markets, for example. It is unlikely that the United States will maintain its current market share in leather products or footwear, for example. As a consequence, the calculations probably overstate US exports in these sectors. Conversely, high-technology markets may expand far more rapidly than these calculations imply, and as a result US exports to the Pacific Basin developing countries could increase rapidly, even with market share remaining constant, making these exports even more important than table 6.2 indicates.

At the same time, increases in the underlying competitiveness of the Pacific Basin developing countries may lead them to gain market share at the expense of other suppliers to the United States, such as Japan. This would result in an overstatement of the impact of imports on employment as presented in table 6.3, since the Pacific Basin developing-country imports would be displacing other imports, not domestic production. Similarly, the growing competitiveness of the Pacific Basin developing countries might lead to a diversification of their geographical markets, which would reduce their dependence on the United States. This is particularly likely if, as expected, domestic demand in Japan continues to grow much more rapidly than in the United States. This would reduce the share of Pacific Basin developing countries' exports coming into the United States, and the increase in import penetration reported in table 6.2 would be moderated.

The pattern of bilateral trade between the United States and the Pacific Basin developing countries may also change as a result of broader changes in the world economy. For example, most of the Pacific Basin developing countries are net importers of oil; most of them also run trade deficits with Japan. If there were a large change in the price of oil, or a dramatic change in the trading patterns of Japan, this would presumably be reflected in changes in the pattern of bilateral trade with the United States. Lastly, the trade shares are contingent on trade policies—most directly those of the Pacific Basin developing countries and the United States.

Impact of Policies in the United States

Economic relations between the United States and the Pacific Basin developing countries will be greatly affected by the efforts of the United States to reduce its global current account deficit. The US deficit fell from its peak of $143 billion in 1987 to $106 billion in 1989. There is reason to believe, however, that in the absence of further macroeconomic policy adjustments the deficit could begin rising again, particularly if the dollar again begins to rise, as it did between 1987 and 1989.

Cline (1989b) has analyzed the implications of the dollar's appreciation for the US external accounts, using a detailed model of the US current account and a multilateral trade model.[4] Cline conducted two sets of simulations: baseline simulations holding the real dollar exchange rate at its fourth-quarter 1987 level, and "strong dollar" simulations essentially holding the real exchange rate at its second-quarter 1988 level. In all cases the external deficits worsen in the future. According to his results, the central estimate of the baseline simulations is for the current account deficit to grow to $166 billion in 1992.[5] In the "strong dollar" case, the central estimate of the

---

4. These models are described fully in Cline (1989a).

5. However, there is a J-curve effect in the "strong dollar" case, which causes the 1989 trade balance to show greater improvement than in the baseline simulations. This effect is transitory, and by 1990 the external deficits are growing once again.

current account deficit in 1992 is $216 billion, a growth in the deficit of $50 billion from the baseline forecasts, and of more than $100 billion from the actual 1989 figure.

Thus, without major policy changes, the recent improvement in the US external accounts is likely to be reversed, with current account deficits possibly rising to over $200 billion. The Joint Economic Committee of the US Congress, among others, has urged that the United States reestablish a current account surplus so as to provide capital for developing countries. Others have argued for the more modest goal of stabilizing the net foreign debt–export ratio, which would be consistent with a current account deficit on the order of $50 billion to $75 billion. An intermediate target of achieving current account balance over the medium run would require deficit reductions of approximately $100 billion to $150 billion over four years (Bergsten 1988).

At the same time, because of mounting interest payments on the accumulated foreign debt, the improvement in the US merchandise trade balance would have to be even greater, on the order of $125 billion to $200 billion, to achieve the current account targets cited above. The change in the real volume of trade would have to be even larger still, depending on the extent of the dollar depreciation associated with the external adjustment, possibly in the range of $150 billion to $250 billion, or 3 percent to 5 percent of real GNP at its current level.

In this situation, a nonrecessionary adjustment would require continued dramatic increases in export growth combined with a substantial slowdown in the growth rate of imports. The necessary macroeconomic adjustment could be achieved by eliminating the US budget deficits through cuts in expenditures and increases in taxes, combined with depreciation of the dollar.

The reduction of the US trade deficit would have a considerable impact on the Pacific Basin developing countries, most of which rely on the United States as a major export market. The counterpart of US trade adjustment would be reductions in the surpluses of the Pacific Basin developing countries, in particular Korea and Taiwan, with the United States. Moreover, reductions in the Japanese surplus could change the triangular pattern of trade, with Japan becoming a more important market for the exports of the Pacific Basin developing countries.

In addition to reducing its global trade deficit, the United States faces three sets of policy questions in its relations with the Pacific Basin developing countries: exchange rate management, trade protection, and economic integration schemes.

Current US policy in all three areas is distinguished by a heavy reliance on bilateral, and public, actions to attempt to resolve disputes. This policy enables the United States to set the agenda unilaterally according to its priorities, and because of its bilateral orientation, it may help the United States extract

In addition, US authorities must make it clear to domestic import-competing industries that currency undervaluation by the East Asian NICs is not the principal source of import competition pressure, nor will the appreciation of these currencies end those industries' import competition problems. As the preceding analysis indicates, the less developed countries of the Pacific Basin are poised to move into market niches currently filled by the East Asian NICs, and even with currency adjustment the United States will continue to import substantial amounts of many categories of manufactures from Pacific Basin sources.

In the area of trade, the largely complementary pattern of specialization between the United States and the Pacific Basin countries means that the growth of trade, although beneficial to both groups, will likely involve significant adjustment costs to the domestic industries of both the United States and the Pacific Basin countries. These adjustments will inevitably generate demands for protection in the import-competing sectors of all of these economies.

The United States has a considerable interest in removing trade barriers in the Pacific Basin developing countries, and the current policy of bilateral pressure has had some successes, most notably in encouraging major liberalization efforts in Korea and Taiwan. At the same time, it has had the undesirable effect of elevating relatively minor trade issues (e.g., trade in turkey parts in Taiwan) into public political disputes. Moreover, public bilateral pressure can politically undermine reformist elements in target countries. Indeed, the argument is increasingly heard in these countries that liberalization should not be undertaken unilaterally; rather, it is better to wait and attempt to extract some quid pro quos during the inevitable negotiations with the United States.

Of course, protection is a two-way street. In recent years, the United States has initiated or tightened quantitative restrictions against imports from the Pacific Basin developing countries in a variety of industries, including textiles and apparel, steel, and machine tools. Protection of this sort is not in the long-run interest of the United States or the Pacific Basin developing countries. A more constructive US trade policy toward these countries would have several components.

First, the United States should move the locus of trade negotiations from bilateral to multilateral forums. The problems the United States faces are global, and so must be the solutions. The recent emphasis on bilateral negotiations cannot generate the necessary comprehensive solutions, and arguably it makes liberalization politically more difficult in the Pacific Basin developing countries. Indeed, the sector-by-sector bilateral approach shifts attention away from potentially more extensive multilateral liberalization and generates little external pressure on the United States for trade liberalization. Multilateral negotiations, such as the current Uruguay Round in the GATT, hold greater possibilities for extensive deprotection, which would be in all parties' interest. It is precisely the large potential gains from multilateral negotiations that justify trade concessions in domestic political terms.

Specifically, the United States should be willing to negotiate a strong Safeguards Code with guarantees to discipline the proliferation and use of informal quantitative barriers, and to ensure that protection is temporary and degressive. Such a policy would include the gradual elimination of the Multi-Fiber Arrangement and its replacement with a tariff-based system (see Cline 1990).

The quid pro quos the United States could expect to extract from the Pacific Basin developing countries are the liberalization of merchandise imports, selective liberalization in services, strengthened protection of intellectual property rights, and tightened export incentive rules. In particular, this would mean handling trade-related intellectual property regulation and enforcement in the GATT, rather than in the World Intellectual Property Organization (WIPO), as some in the Pacific Basin developing countries have suggested. It would also require the elimination of export incentives in Korea and Taiwan and the limitation of export incentives by the remaining Pacific Basin developing countries under the GATT Subsidies Code. This, it should be added, could be accomplished through clubs of like-minded members (the approach taken in the existing codes within the GATT), which would not necessarily be regional in orientation. These policies could go far to facilitate trade expansion to the benefit of all parties, and the need to reduce the US trade deficit makes it imperative that the United States seek solutions that are trade expanding rather than trade restricting.

Lastly, US policy must confront the issue of economic integration schemes. Free trade areas have been proposed as a second-best alternative to multilateral liberalization. The Pacific Basin developing countries (and Japan) are often proposed as candidates for bilateral free trade areas with the United States.[7] This is the wrong route to follow. Free trade areas cause trade diversion by granting exporters in the partner country preferential access to the importing country's market relative to other foreign suppliers. As a consequence, the conclusion of a free trade agreement between the United States and any of the Pacific Basin countries would immediately cause substantial foreign policy problems with the other Pacific Basin developing countries, which would be rightly concerned about injury due to trade diversion. Even if such arrangements were concluded between the United States and all of the Pacific Basin countries, the United States would still face major foreign policy problems in other regions of interest, particularly Latin America, where trade diversion

---

7. See Schott (1989) for an analysis of these proposals.

losses to Pacific Basin countries could greatly set back debt-reduction efforts. Simply put, extensive participation in trade preference schemes is incompatible with the US position as the linchpin of the open trading system.

As a third party, the United States should adopt a hands-off position in regard to regional integration schemes among Pacific Basin developing countries that would involve little significant trade diversion from the United States, but should move resolutely to block any that would involve significant trade diversion away from the United States (such as a free trade area between Japan and the Pacific Basin developing countries). A well-functioning multilateral system would make such an eventuality unlikely. However, if the Uruguay Round should fail, the United States would have to begin making such policy choices. This underlines the importance of the Uruguay Round negotiations.

Conclusions

The projected changes in the trade composition of the Pacific Basin developing countries are likely to result in increasing competition in traditional light industries, such as textiles, apparel, and leather products, as well as in manufacturing industries of increasing sophistication, such as motorcycles and bicycles, shipbuilding and repairing, furniture and fixtures, plastics products, and iron and steel. Assuming that the United States maintains its 1988 shares in the export and import markets of the Pacific Basin developing countries, US imports from these countries would increase from 2.2 percent of domestic traded-goods consumption in 1988 to 6.5 percent in 2000. At the same time, however, the Pacific Basin developing countries are likely to be increasingly important export markets for US producers of primary products, chemicals, aircraft, and sophisticated electronics equipment. Under the constant-market-share assumption, exports to these countries as a share of US output of traded goods would rise from 1.3 percent in 1988 to 4.1 percent in 2000. Trade-related employment gains would be nearly 250,000 jobs in the primary products sector, and 77,000 jobs in aircraft. It is unlikely that employment generated by the exports of these products will offset the potential jobs forgone in the more labor-intensive industries, however, and there would be a net loss of just under 1 million potential jobs in the merchandise trade sector (which would be at least partly offset by gains in the services sector); this poses an adjustment problem for the United States. The proper policy response in this situation is to encourage the reallocation of resources from the affected industries to more productive uses, not to frustrate the adjustment process by applying protectionist measures.

Obviously the critical assumption underlying these projections—that the US export and import shares in each country and each commodity will remain constant between 1988 and 2000—will not be fulfilled under a variety of plausible scenarios. Thus, these projections should be regarded more as reference points than as predictions. Nonetheless, they clearly indicate the shifting pattern of trade between the United States and the Pacific Basin developing countries.

These changes at the industry and sectoral level will be accompanied by balance of payments adjustments. Here the key variable is the extent to which the United States can reduce its trade deficit. Such an adjustment would imply counterpart reductions in the trade surpluses of the Pacific Basin developing countries (in particular Korea and Taiwan) with the United States, and would encourage a shift toward Japan as a market for Pacific Basin developing-country exports.

The need for the United States to increase its exports, and the growing importance of the Pacific Basin developing countries as markets for those exports, underline the need for the United States to pursue trade policies aimed at expanding trade and opening foreign export markets. This can best be achieved through multilateral, not bilateral, negotiations. US policy of late has been distinguished by a heavy reliance on bilateral, public action to open foreign markets. Although this policy has had some success (most notably in encouraging liberalization efforts in Korea and Taiwan), its heavy-handedness contributes to considerable political resentment in the target countries and in the long run may frustrate rather than facilitate the achievement of US policy goals.

In the area of trade, the United States should be willing to negotiate the elimination of the Multi-Fiber Arrangement and its replacement with a tariff-based system. It should also be willing to negotiate strong guarantees in the GATT Safeguards Code to inhibit the use of informal quantitative barriers and to ensure that protection is temporary and degressive. In return the United States could expect the Pacific Basin developing countries to agree to a liberalization of merchandise imports, a selective liberalization in services, a strengthening of the protection of intellectual property rights, and a tightening of export incentive rules. Such an agreement would be in the interest of both the United States and the Pacific Basin developing countries.

In monetary affairs, the United States should revise section 3004 of the 1988 trade act to end the practice of identifying countries as exchange rate manipulators. Although exchange rate regimes are a legitimate topic of international discussion, the economic analysis underlying the US Treasury implementation of this provision is flawed, and this is the kind of issue that would be better taken up in a multilateral forum.

In conclusion, the Pacific Basin developing countries can be expected to account for a growing share of international trade. With their increasingly important role in the global trading system, they will represent both new challenges and new opportunities for the United States.

Appendices

Appendix A
Statistical Methodology

To analyze the prospective changes in the trade composition of the Pacific Basin developing countries, estimates of the impact of resource endowments on trade flows derived from a cross-country econometric model have been combined with forecasts of future resource endowments to generate projections of future trade composition. The first step is to estimate the econometric model of trade composition. In order to analyze both net and gross trade flows, a Helpman-Krugman-type model of products differentiated by country of origin has been used. This approach employs the standard assumptions of microeconomic trade models (internationally identical, production functions with declining marginal products; nonreversibility of factor intensity rankings [either factor price equalization or endowment similarity]; factors that are immobile internationally and costlessly mobile between industries; pure competition in both goods and factor markets; internationally identical homothetic demand preferences, or else demand according to a linear expenditure system based on per capita income) to generate a reduced-form representation of a country's trade pattern based on available technology and its relative factor endowments. A country's output (Q) is produced from a factor use matrix (A) and a set of endowments (V):

(1) $Q = A^{-1}V.$

World output can be described similarly:

(2) $Q_w + A^{-1}V_w.$

Under the assumption of identical homothetic utility functions and factor price equalization, each country consumes each variety of the commodities in the same proportion:

(3) $C = sQ_w,$

where s is the country's share of world output, and C is its consumption vector.

Trade balance implies that the value of production is equal to the value of consumption, so that:

(4) $p'Q = p'C = sp'Q_w$,

where p is the price vector. Thus, if trade is balanced, the consumption share is the production share of world output:

(5) $s = p'Q/p'Q_w$.

The vector of imports is the difference between the country's production and consumption shares:

(6) $M = s(Q - Q_w)$.

Exports are the excess of domestic production over domestic consumption (including imports):

(7) $X = Q - sQ_w$.

Substituting expression (5) into expression (7) and dividing through by national income, one obtains:

(8) $X/p'Q = (Q/p'Q) - (Q_w/p'Q_w)$

$$= (A^{-1}V/p'Q) - (Q_w/p'Q_w),$$

which means that the commodity export share of national income is a function of national income, world income, technology, and factor endowments.

This model is similar to ones previously estimated by Leamer (1984) and Saxonhouse (1988). The following equation is estimated for each commodity group:

(9) X_{ij} or $M_{ij} = a + \sum_k b_{ik}V_{kj} + u_{ij}$,

where:

X_{ij} (M_{ij}) = the export (import) share of commodity i in national income of country j,
$\quad a$ = the industry share of world income (a constant term),
$\quad V_{kj}$ = endowments of resource k of country j as a share of national income,
$\quad b_{ik}$ = coefficients indicating the impact on the export share of commodity i of an increase in the kth endowment,
$\quad u_{ij}$ = a disturbance term.

Equation (9) was estimated for 46 commodity categories encompassing the whole of the traded-goods sector. The explanatory variables consisted of a constant term, nine factor endowments (labor, physical capital, human capital, arable land, pasture land, forest land, coal, oil, and minerals), and the ratio of c.i.f. (cost plus insurance and freight) traded-goods prices to f.o.b. (free on board) prices, which was used as a proxy for transport costs.[1] The country sample included 30 countries for which complete trade and endowment data sets could be constructed for the years 1968, 1972, 1976, 1980, and 1984.[2] Thus, this equation is a reduced-form representation of factor endowments (and real exchange rates) on trade patterns.

The trade data originate from the General Agreement on Tariffs and Trade. The labor endowment was defined as the economically active population; these data come from various issues of the *Yearbook of Labour Statistics,* published by the International Labour Organisation. The capital stock was calculated by summing and depreciating the purchasing power–adjusted gross fixed investment series found in Summers and Heston (1988). The asset life of capital was assumed to be 18 years and the depreciation rate 13 percent.

The human capital endowment was calculated by multiplying the economically active labor force by the Psacharopoulos index of per capita educational capital. The Psacharopoulos index is defined as the average per capita expenditure on education embodied in the labor force; it is calculated from data on the highest level of educational achievement, years of schooling at each level, and expenditures per year at each level normalized by the amount of expenditure for one year of primary school education. Data on educational achievement and schooling duration are found in the *Statistical Yearbook* published by the United Nations Educational Social and Cultural Organisation (UNESCO). Expenditure weights come from Psacharopoulos (1973).

Data on land endowments come from the *Production Yearbook* of the Food and Agricultural Organisation (FAO).

The coal endowment was measured by domestic production in thousands of metric tons and comes from the *Minerals Yearbook* of the US Bureau of Mines. (Data on coal mining capacity or reserves, a preferable measure of endowment, were unavailable for most countries.) The minerals index is the value of domestic production of 13 minerals; the production data are from the

---

1. Alternatively, one could think of geographical proximity to markets as an endowment.

2. The countries are Argentina, Austria, Brazil, Canada, Denmark, Finland, France, the Federal Republic of Germany, Greece, Hong Kong, Indonesia, Israel, Italy, Japan, the Republic of Korea, Malaysia, Mexico, Norway, Pakistan, Peru, the Philippines, Singapore, Spain, Sweden, Taiwan, Thailand, Tunisia, Turkey, the United Kingdom, and the United States.

Minerals Yearbook; the price data are from *International Financial Statistics* (IFS), published by the International Monetary Fund. The composition of this index was determined by taking the top 20 minerals (excluding oil, natural gas, and coal) by value of world output in 1984 and then dropping those for which price data could not be found. The oil endowment, defined as proven reserves, was taken from the *Oil and Gas Yearbook*, published by the American Petroleum Institute.

Lastly, the c.i.f. and f.o.b. data come from the IFS *Supplement on Trade Statistics*.

In some cases, data for Taiwan were unavailable from these sources and instead come from the *Taiwan Statistical Data Book*, published by the Council for Economic Planning and Development, Executive Yuan, Republic of China.

From an estimation standpoint, the application of the factor endowment model to the estimation of exports and imports presents both problems and opportunities. The most immediate problem is that the dependent variable (exports or imports) is truncated at zero, raising a well-known set of estimation problems.[3] On the other hand, the fact that the variables are effectively defined over a positive range means that functional forms involving logarithmic transformations of the variables can be explored.

Initially, the regressions were estimated for individual years, and a variety of diagnostic statistics were generated. Adjusted coefficients of determination (R^2) were typically quite high (a majority were over 0.9), and most of the estimated coefficients were statistically significant at conventional levels of testing. Lagrange multiplier tests revealed very little evidence of cross-sectiontional heteroskedasticity (Breusch and Pagan 1979). However, examination of influence statistics and a close look at the estimated coefficients suggested that concern for overfitting was warranted (Belsley et al. 1980). Since overfitting could have a seriously detrimental impact on the forecasts,

---

3. As it turns out, there were very few zero-valued observations in the data set. There were almost no zero-valued observations in the import data. In the export data, only three industries—railroad equipment (21 percent), natural rubber (20 percent) and coal (18 percent)—had sizable numbers of zero-valued observations. No individual country had more than 10 percent zero-valued observations for either imports or exports.

To investigate the implications of the dependent variable truncation for the parameter estimates, a Tobit estimation was done on the export and import equations of each industry. The presence of the truncated dependent variable appeared to have very minor effects on the parameter estimates when compared to conventional linear least squares estimates. Even in the cases of the three export equations with a significant number of zero-valued observations, the linear and Tobit estimates were virtually identical. Apparently, the zero-valued observations were scattered so randomly that the probit estimates used to form the Tobit estimates were almost entirely uninformative. It therefore seemed advisable to concentrate on the linear estimators while keeping the potential parameter bias problems in a few specific equations in mind.

the data were pooled to reduce the influence of individual observations on the parameter estimates.[4]

Application of ordinary least squares (OLS) regression techniques to pooled samples will generally yield inefficient, and possibly biased, coefficient estimates.[5] There are two basic methods of estimating coefficients from pooled time-series cross-sectional data sets. One, the fixed-effects (or dummy variable) estimator, treats the disturbance term as fixed and allows country- and time-specific intercept terms to vary; the other, the random-effects (or error components) estimator, treats the disturbance term as though it consists of random shocks in the country and time dimensions. Operationally the two methods are similar: one estimates regressions of the form:

$$y_{jt} - \hat{c}_j \hat{y}_j - \hat{c}_t \hat{y}_t = a + b(X_{jt} - \hat{c}_j X_j - \hat{c}_t X_t) + u_{ijt}$$

where the carets indicate sample means, and the subscript t indicates time.

In the case of the fixed-effects estimator, $\hat{c}_j = \hat{c}_t = 1$. In the case of the random-effects estimator, an OLS regression is estimated from the pooled data, and the disturbance term is decomposed into three components: one associated with time, one associated with the cross-sectional unit (in this case, the country), and a purely random component varying in both dimensions. The country- and time-related coefficients $(\hat{c}_j, \hat{c}_t)$ are then calculated as functions of the shares of the country- and time-specific disturbances in total variance. If the distributional assumptions underlying the variance decomposition are correct, and enough observations are available to estimate the variance components, the random-effects model will generally be more efficient than the fixed-effects estimator. However, if the disturbance term is correlated with the explanatory variables, the random-effects estimator will be biased, while the fixed-effects estimator will be unbiased, conditional on the sample means. Thus, in a rough sense, the choice between the two methods is a choice between robustness and efficiency.

It would be useful to have a statistical test to check whether the distur-

---

4. The trade data are reported in nominal US dollars, so pooling the data necessitated some adjustment for the rise in the price level over the sample period. The primary products trade data were deflated using price indexes constructed from commodity price data published in the IFS. For manufactures, international price data do not exist; the most complete national series on manufactures prices are those for the United States, published by the US Department of Commerce in its publication *Producer Price Indexes*. These were used in the absence of international price data on manufactures. Although this is a decidedly second-best procedure, it can be defended on the grounds that the United States is the world's single biggest import market, and world manufactures prices are undoubtedly highly correlated with US prices.

5. This discussion follows Judge et al. (1985, chapter 13).

bance term is correlated with the explanatory variables. Hausman (1978) developed such a test. Under the null hypothesis that the random-effects model is the correct specification, the difference between the random- and fixed-effects covariance matrices is distributed as chi-square. Rejection of the null hypothesis indicates that the fixed-effects estimator is preferred.[6] Moreover, Staiger (1988) has shown that this specification test can be interpreted as a test of the factor endowment model: if the Hausman test cannot be rejected, the exogeneity of the endowment matrix with respect to the trade vector is valid. If the Hausman test is rejected, then the endowment matrix and the trade vector may be related in ways not specified by the model. In this case the fixed-effects estimator is preferred. The estimation procedure here is consistent with this perspective.

Choice among alternative estimators was made on the basis of the Hausman tests and coefficients of determination. In some cases the power of the Hausman tests appeared to be weak, and the choice among estimators to be used for forecasting was done on a judgmental basis. Summary results of the regressions used in this exercise are reported in table A.1. Since the goodness-of-fit statistic is defined relative to sample variation after the country- and time-specific components have been removed, the coefficients of determination are considerably lower than those obtained from the simple cross-sectional regressions. What is ultimately of interest here, however, is the robustness of the coefficient estimates, and on this score the pooled estimates are clearly superior to those obtained from the simple cross-sectional estimates.

Having obtained estimates of the impact of factor endowments on trade, the next step is to generate forecasts of future endowments. The factor endowment forecasts were based on the longest sample available, usually 21 annual observations between 1968 and 1988. The logarithm of each variable was modeled using the autoregressive integrated moving average (ARIMA) process, and these models were tested by estimating an export forecasts and calculating Theil U statistics, the ratio of the root mean square error of the ARIMA process to the root mean square error of the "naive" forecast of no change in the variable. Selection between alternative models was on the basis of the Theil U; most of the models selected were either AR1 or AR2. In some cases no ARIMA model yielded a Theil U of less than unity; in these cases forecasts were generated on the basis of OLS regressions with jackknife slopes where necessary. These forecasts, along with the actual data for 1968 and 1988, are reported in table A.2.

---

6. Hausman warns, however, that problems due to errors in variables may invalidate the fixed-effects estimator.

These time-series forecasts are essentially sophisticated projections of historical relationships into the future. In some cases past history may be a poor guide to future developments (such as Hong Kong's forthcoming change in sovereignty). In these cases, alternative endowment vectors have been specified.

Trade projections have then been generated by combining the regression coefficients with estimates of the Pacific Basin developing countries' endowment vectors in 2000. They are expressed in 1980 relative prices, reflecting the twin assumptions that the Pacific Basin developing countries are small in international trade terms (and hence changes in their trade specialization do not affect relative prices), and that changes in the relative prices themselves are so unpredictable as to justify the modeling convenience of assuming their constancy.

Table A.1 Regression results[a]

Industry	Constant	Labor	Capital	Human capital	Arable land	Pasture land	Forest land	Coal	Oil	Minerals	Ratio of c.i.f. to f.o.b.	R^2	F statistic[b]
Animals and products													
Exports												.079	0.94
Imports	a		b			c						.156	2.02
Fish and preparations													
Exports		-c		c	a			-b	b		-c	.313	4.96
Imports	-a				-a						c	.202	2.77
Food crops													
Exports	-c	-c					c	c			c	.449	8.89
Imports			c		-c		c				c	.640	19.37
Tobacco and manufactures													
Exports	-c						-b	-c			c	.342	5.66
Imports		b	c		-c						c	.467	9.54
Agricultural commodities													
Exports	-b	a		-c		b	-b				c	.256	3.76
Imports	-c	-b	c	a			-c			-b	c	.485	10.28
Beverages													
Exports	b		c								c	.278	4.19
Imports			b		-c						c	.357	6.05
Textile fibers													
Exports		c		-c		c		-b			c	.398	7.21
Imports	c					c	b	a			-b	.225	3.17

Continued on next page

Industry	Constant	Labor	Capital	Human capital	Arable land	Pasture land	Forest land	Coal	Oil	Minerals	Ratio of c.i.f. to f.o.b.	R^2	F statistic[b]
Natural rubber and gums													
Exports	b		b		-b	-a	b				c	.565	14.14
Imports			b		-c						c	.447	8.83
Raw wood													
Exports							b			c		.263	3.90
Imports				a	-c	-c					c	.443	8.67
Crude minerals													
Exports		-b								c	c	.526	12.09
Imports	c		c			b	b				-b	.209	2.89
Coal, coke, etc.													
Exports	-b		c		-c				-b	-b		.294	4.54
Imports		-a	c			-a						.186	2.49
Petroleum and products													
Exports						b						.097	1.17
Imports	c		c	-a							a	.356	6.03
Nonferrous metals													
Exports		-b			a	-b	b		b	c		.356	6.02
Imports	a		c		-c	c	-c	-a	a		b	.498	10.80
Spinning, weaving, etc.													
Exports	c		b	c	a					a	-c	.318	5.08
Imports			a		-c						c	.306	4.81

Continued on next page

Table A.1 (continued)

Industry	Constant	Labor	Capital	Human capital	Arable land	Pasture land	Forest land	Coal	Oil	Minerals	Ratio of c.i.f. to f.o.b.	R^2	F statistic[b]
Textile products													
Exports	c		b	c			−c					.408	4.52
Imports	c	−c	a								c	.367	6.31
Wearing apparel													
Exports	b		b	b			−c				a	.404	7.38
Imports	−c	−c	b								a	.325	5.25
Leather and products													
Exports								−a				.068	0.71
Imports	−c	−c	−c				−b				c	.492	10.57
Footwear													
Exports								−b				.101	0.78
Imports	−c	−c										.298	4.62
Wood products													
Exports	b			b							a	.164	2.14
Imports	c	−c	c				−c				c	.488	10.37
Furniture and fixtures													
Exports	−c	−c									a	.357	6.05
Imports	−c	−c									c	.383	6.79
Pulp, paper, etc.													
Exports	−c	−c	b								a	.324	5.22
Imports	c	−a	b				−a				c	.328	5.32

Continued on next page

Industry	Constant	Labor	Capital	Human capital	Arable land	Pasture land	Forest land	Coal	Oil	Minerals	Ratio of c.i.f. to f.o.b.	R^2	F statistic[b]
Paper products													
Exports												.079	0.93
Imports	c	-c	c	b							c	.433	8.31
Printing and publishing													
Exports	-c				-a							.124	1.55
Imports			c				a				c	.237	3.39
Basic chemicals													
Exports	-c	-c	c	c	b	b	-c					.734	30.02
Imports	c		c		-b						c	.419	7.87
Synthetic resins													
Exports	-a				a			-b			-c	.219	3.06
Imports	c		b								c	.349	5.86
Other industrial chemicals													
Exports										c	b	.174	2.29
Imports		b	b									.173	2.28
Drugs and medicine													
Exports	-c		b				-b					.278	4.19
Imports	c		c								c	.531	12.32
Other chemicals													
Exports	c	-c	c	c			-c					.532	12.38
Imports	c		c		-c						c	.508	11.26

Continued on next page

Table A.1 (continued)

Industry	Constant	Labor	Capital	Human capital	Arable land	Pasture land	Forest land	Coal	Oil	Minerals	Ratio of c.i.f. to f.o.b.	R^2	F statistic[b]
Rubber products													
Exports			c									.209	2.88
Imports		b						-a			-c	.273	4.10
Plastic products													
Exports	c	-c	a	c								.486	10.31
Imports	-b				b		-c				-c	.378	6.61
Pottery, china, etc.													
Exports	a											.125	1.56
Imports			c								c	.250	3.64
Glass products													
Exports			b								b	.184	2.46
Imports	c	-c	c								c	.392	7.04
Other nonmetallic products													
Exports			a					c				.157	2.03
Imports					b						-c	.428	8.15
Iron and steel													
Exports	c	a	b		a	b	c				-c	.225	3.17
Imports			b		-c		-b				c	.240	3.45
Fabricated metal products													
Exports	c		c	c	b	a	b			a	-c	.313	4.96
Imports	c	-b	c								c	.394	7.09

Continued on next page

Industry	Constant	Labor	Capital	Human capital	Arable land	Pasture land	Forest land	Coal	Oil	Minerals	Ratio of c.i.f. to f.o.b.	R²	F statistic[b]
Office and computing equipment													
Exports	-c			-a	c						-c	.457	9.18
Imports	c	-c	b		-a	-b					b	.450	8.90
Other machinery													
Exports			a		b						-c	.283	4.29
Imports											-c	.235	3.34
Radio and television													
Exports					c						-c	.516	11.64
Imports	-a				c						-c	.577	14.85
Other electrical machinery													
Exports					c	a		-b			-c	.560	13.88
Imports	-a				b						-c	.400	7.26
Shipbuilding and repairing													
Exports			c						c			.234	3.32
Imports	c		c						b		c	.297	4.61
Railroad equipment													
Exports	-b		b								c	.262	3.86
Imports	-c					-c					c	.296	4.59
Motor vehicles													
Exports							a				a	.182	2.43
Imports					-b		-a	a				.261	3.85

Continued on next page

Table A.1 (continued)

Industry	Constant	Labor	Capital	Human capital	Arable land	Pasture land	Forest land	Coal	Oil	Minerals	Ratio of c.i.f. to f.o.b.	R^2	F statistic[b]
Aircraft													
Exports	−b										−c	.231	3.28
Imports	−c		c				−b					.331	5.39
Motorcycles and bicycles													
Exports			c		a			−c			−b	.275	4.14
Imports						−c						.243	3.49
Professional goods													
Exports					b						−c	.349	5.85
Imports	c	−b	c		−b						c	.473	9.78
Other industries													
Exports		b		c		b						.289	4.44
Imports	c	−c	a	c			−b				c	.531	12.33

a. The critical values of the t-statistics for a two-tailed test of the significance of the parameter estimates are (a) 10 percent significance = ±1.645; (b) 5 percent significance = ±1.96; (c) 1 percent significance = ±2.576. A minus sign indicates a negative coefficient.

b. The F statistic tests the null hypothesis that the joint value of the parameters is zero, with the critical values being: 5 percent significance = 1.91; 1 percent significance = 2.47.

Table A.2 The NICs: factor endowments and real GDP, 1968, 1988, and 2000[a]

Endowment	Hong Kong		Singapore		Taiwan		Korea	
Labor force (millions)								
1968	1.6		0.7		4.1		9.8	
1988	2.7	(2.6)	1.2	(2.7)	8.2	(3.5)	16.4	(2.6)
2000	4.1	(3.6)	1.9	(3.9)	10.7	(2.2)	18.9	(1.2)
Capital stock (millions of 1980 PPP dollars)								
1968	7,141		9,770		13,687		21,121	
1988	77,670	(12.7)	52,982	(8.8)	119,942	(11.5)	303,380	(14.3)
2000	387,491	(14.3)	147,940	(8.9)	541,752	(13.4)	1,676,529	(15.3)
Psacharopoulos index								
1968	1,172.0		1,024.0		1,097.0		1,013.0	
1988	2,119.4	(3.0)	2,213.0	(3.9)	2,043.3	(3.2)	2,410.9	(4.4)
2000	2,913.2	(2.7)	2,427.0	(0.8)	2,575.3	(1.9)	3,538.7	(3.2)
Arable land (thousands of hectares)								
1968	13.0		12.0		535.0		2,319.0	
1988	7.0	(−3.0)	4.0	(−5.3)	495.0	(−0.4)	2,135.2	(−0.4)
2000	5.0	(−2.8)	2.0	(−5.6)	480.0	(−0.3)	2,044.0	(−0.4)

Continued on next page

Table A.2 (continued)

Endowment	Hong Kong		Singapore		Taiwan		Korea	
Pasture land (thousands of hectares)								
1968	0.0		0.0		365.0		24.0	
1988	1.0	(n.a)	0.0	(n.a.)	382.8	(0.2)	92.8	(7.0)
2000	1.0	(0.0)	0.0	(n.a.)	389.0	(0.1)	231.0	(7.9)
Forest land (thousands of hectares)								
1968	11.0		3.0		2,224.0		6,631.0	
1988	12.0	(0.4)	3.0	(0.0)	1,836.5	(−1.0)	6,499.0	(−0.1)
2000	12.0	(−0.0)	3.0	(0.0)	1,527.0	(−1.5)	8,084.0	(1.8)
Coal reserves (thousands of metric tons)								
1968	0.0		0.0		5,014.1		10,242.2	
1988	0.0	(n.a.)	0.0	(n.a.)	1,424.5	(−6.1)	25,123.1	(4.6)
2000	0.0	(n.a.)	0.0	(n.a.)	773.0	(−5.0)	43,493.0	(4.7)
Oil reserves (millions of barrels)								
1968	0.0		0.0		18.8		0.0	
1988	0.0	(n.a.)	0.0	(n.a.)	4.7	(−6.7)	0.0	(n.a.)
2000	0.0	(n.a.)	0.0	(n.a.)	4.0	(−1.3)	0.0	(n.a.)

Continued on next page

Endowment	Hong Kong		Singapore		Taiwan		Korea	
Minerals production (thousands of 1980 dollars)								
1968	0.0		0.0		22,759.7		83,352.1	
1988	0.0	(n.a.)	0.0	(n.a.)	31,799.5	(1.7)	214,05.6	(4.8)
2000	0.0	(n.a.)	0.0	(n.a.)	36,004.3	(1.0)	304,294.9	(3.0)
Ratio of c.i.f. to f.o.b. prices								
1968	1.100		1.064		1.085		1.092	
1988	1.100	(0.0)	1.060	(−0.02)	1.095	(0.05)	1.054	(−0.18)
2000	1.100	(0.0)	1.055	(−0.04)	1.095	(0.00)	1.033	(−0.17)
Real GDP (millions of 1980 PPP dollars)								
1968	11,626		4,644		18,591		30,772	
1988	61,259	(8.7)	31,250	(10.0)	85,672	(7.9)	157,614	(8.5)
2000	145,906	(7.5)	74,432	(7.5)	204,053	(7.5)	392,511	(7.9)

n.a. = not applicable

a. Numbers in parentheses represent annual growth rates.

Sources: see text.

Table A.3   The ASEAN-4: factor endowments and real GDP, 1968, 1988, and 2000[a]

Endowment	Malaysia		Thailand		Philippines		Indonesia	
Labor force (millions)								
1968	3.1		16.2		11.8		38.3	
1988	6.1	(3.4)	30.8	(3.3)	23.3	(3.5)	78.9	(3.7)
2000	9.0	(3.3)	44.2	(3.1)	29.6	(2.0)	131.0	(4.3)
Capital stock								
(millions of 1980 PPP dollars)								
1968	15,785		28,441		28,176		27,190	
1988	123,496	(10.8)	127,567	(7.8)	92,850	(6.1)	301,662	(12.8)
2000	447,661	(11.3)	335,329	(8.4)	246,247	(8.5)	1,530,944	(14.5)
Psacharopoulos index								
1968	563.0		213.0		1,030.0		296.0	
1988	1,227.8	(4.0)	1,026.4	(8.2)	2,030.8	(3.5)	925.8	(5.9)
2000	1,338.2	(0.7)	1,854.3	(5.1)	2,835.1	(2.8)	1,633.1	(4.8)
Arable land								
(thousands of hectares)								
1968	5,533.0		13,300.0		6,992.0		15,050.0	
1988	4,337.3	(−1.2)	18,459.4	(1.7)	8,061.0	(0.7)	21,378.1	(1.8)
2000	4,153.0	(−0.4)	28,370.0	(3.6)	8,597.0	(0.5)	23,370.0	(0.7)

Continued on next page

Endowment	Malaysia		Thailand		Philippines		Indonesia	
Pasture land (thousands of hectares)								
1968	26.0		308.0		851.0		12,450.0	
1988	27.1	(0.2)	762.5	(4.6)	1,236.5	(1.9)	11,780.3	(−0.3)
2000	28.0	(0.3)	930.0	(1.7)	1,770.0	(3.0)	11,547.0	(−0.2)
Forest land (thousands of hectares)								
1968	23,440.0		22,500.0		16,662.0		123,200.0	
1988	19,286.7	(−1.0)	14,131.0	(−2.3)	10,764.9	(−2.2)	121,490.0	(−0.1)
2000	16,092.0	(−1.5)	11,129.0	(−2.0)	8,771.0	(−1.7)	121,453.0	(−0.0)
Coal reserves (thousands of metric tons)								
1968	0.0		304.8		31.8		176.0	
1988	0.0	(n.a.)	7,441.9	(17.3)	1,205.3	(19.9)	3,034.3	(15.3)
2000	0.0	(n.a.)	17,531.0	(7.4)	2,076.0	(4.6)	6,973.0	(7.2)
Oil reserves (millions of barrels)								
1968	500.0		0.2		0.0		8,850.0	
1988	2,941.8	(9.3)	82.2	(35.1)	15.6	(n.a.)	8,169.2	(−0.4)
2000	3,005.0	(0.2)	124.0	(3.5)	16.0	(0.2)	7,858.0	(−0.3)

Continued on next page

Table A.3 (continued)

Endowment	Malaysia		Thailand		Philippines		Indonesia	
Minerals production (thousands of 1980 dollars)								
1968	794,910.0		216,081.2		472,827.6		200,574.0	
1988	866,236.5	(0.4)	501,099.4	(4.3)	1,108,950.0	(4.4)	1,090,892.6	(8.8)
2000	1,087,888.0	(1.9)	811,187.7	(4.1)	1,780,335.0	(4.0)	1,804,418.0	(4.3)
Ratio of c.i.f. to f.o.b. prices								
1968	1.056		1.108		1.113		1.111	
1988	1.108	(0.24)	1.108	(0.00)	1.070	(−0.20)	1.120	(0.04)
2000	1.150	(0.31)	1.110	(0.02)	1.036	(−0.27)	1.120	(0.00)
Real GDP (millions of 1980 PPP dollars)								
1968	14,721		15,075		36,394		54,625	
1988	68,352	(8.0)	69,094	(7.9)	88,471	(4.5)	252,197	(7.9)
2000	181,931	(8.5)	183,906	(8.5)	176,017	(5.9)	594,006	(7.4)

n.a. = not applicable.

a. Numbers in parentheses represent annual growth rates.

Sources: see text.

Appendix B
Manufacturing Trade Shares by Industry

Table B.1 Hong Kong: composition of manufactures trade by industry, 1963 and 1988 (percentages of total trade)

Industry	Exports		Imports	
	1963	**1988**	**1963**	**1988**
Spinning, weaving, etc. (ISIC 3211)	15.2	5.3	13.2	10.9
Textile products (ISIC 321 less 3211)	1.9	6.9	1.3	2.1
Wearing apparel (ISIC 322)	27.6	25.9	1.2	6.3
Leather and products (ISIC 323)	0.7	0.9	0.5	2.7
Footwear (ISIC 324)	2.2	0.6	0.3	0.9
Wood products (ISIC 331)	0.7	0.2	0.3	0.7
Furniture and fixtures (ISIC 332)	0.0	0.2	0.0	0.5
Pulp, paper, and products (ISIC 3411)	0.0	0.1	0.5	1.7
Paper products (ISIC 341 less 3411)	0.1	0.8	0.1	0.2
Printing and publishing (ISIC 342)	0.6	1.8	0.2	0.3
Basic chemicals, excl. fertilizer (ISIC 3511)	0.4	0.1	1.6	2.5
Synthetic resins (ISIC 3513)	0.1	1.2	2.0	4.3
Other industrial chemicals (ISIC 351 less 3511 and 3513)	0.0	0.0	0.5	0.0
Drugs and medicine (ISIC 3522)	0.1	0.1	0.8	0.8
Other chemicals (ISIC 352 less 3522)	0.4	0.4	1.3	1.6
Rubber products (ISIC 355)	0.3	0.1	0.4	0.4
Plastic products (ISIC 356)	2.2	4.0	0.4	1.8
Pottery, china, etc. (ISIC 361)	0.1	0.1	0.3	0.4
Glass products (ISIC 362)	0.1	0.5	0.4	0.5
Other nonmetallic products (ISIC 369)	0.0	0.1	1.2	0.6
Iron and steel (ISIC 371)	0.7	0.1	2.8	2.5
Fabricated metal products (ISIC 381)	4.5	3.4	0.9	2.1
Office and computing equipment (ISIC 3825)	0.0	5.8	0.3	2.6
Other machinery (ISIC 382 less 3825)	0.1	3.6	2.8	5.7
Radio, television, and telecommunications equipment (ISIC 3832)	1.8	10.2	1.9	12.7
Other electrical machinery (ISIC 383 less 3832)	1.8	5.7	1.8	5.0
Shipbuilding and repairing (ISIC 3841)	0.0	0.1	0.1	0.1
Railroad equipment (ISIC 3842)	0.0	0.0	0.1	0.1
Motor vehicles (ISIC 3843)	0.0	0.1	1.7	1.8
Aircraft (ISIC 3845)	0.0	0.0	0.3	0.4
Motorcycles and bicycles (ISIC 3844 and 3849)	0.0	0.9	0.2	0.4
Professional goods (ISIC 385)	0.6	9.8	2.8	5.9
Miscellaneous (ISIC 390)	9.7	6.1	3.5	4.9

Source: General Agreement on Tariffs and Trade.

Table B.2 Singapore: composition of manufactures trade by industry, 1963 and 1988 (percentages of total trade)

Industry	Exports 1963	Exports 1988	Imports 1963	Imports 1988
Spinning, weaving, etc. (ISIC 3211)	4.0	1.4	6.1	2.4
Textile products (ISIC 321 less 3211)	0.5	1.1	0.9	1.0
Wearing apparel (ISIC 322)	1.1	2.5	2.1	1.3
Leather and products (ISIC 323)	0.2	0.2	0.1	0.5
Footwear (ISIC 324)	0.2	0.1	0.2	0.2
Wood products (ISIC 331)	0.1	1.6	0.2	0.8
Furniture and fixtures (ISIC 332)	0.2	0.3	0.1	0.3
Pulp, paper, and products (ISIC 3411)	0.3	0.5	0.9	1.1
Paper products (ISIC 341 less 3411)	0.3	0.2	0.3	0.2
Printing and publishing (ISIC 342)	0.7	0.6	0.6	0.4
Basic chemicals, excl. fertilizer (ISIC 3511)	0.7	2.5	0.9	2.2
Synthetic resins (ISIC 3513)	0.2	2.4	0.3	2.4
Other industrial chemicals (ISIC 351 less 3511 and 3513)	0.6	0.0	0.4	0.0
Drugs and medicine (ISIC 3522)	0.4	0.5	0.8	0.4
Other chemicals (ISIC 352 less 3522)	1.1	1.2	1.9	2.0
Rubber products (ISIC 355)	0.7	0.3	1.0	0.5
Plastic products (ISIC 356)	0.2	0.7	0.4	0.7
Pottery, china, etc. (ISIC 361)	0.1	0.0	0.3	0.3
Glass products (ISIC 362)	0.4	0.2	0.2	0.5
Other nonmetallic products (ISIC 369)	0.7	0.1	0.7	0.6
Iron and steel (ISIC 371)	1.6	0.9	2.5	3.1
Fabricated metal products (ISIC 381)	1.9	1.5	2.1	2.2
Office and computing equipment (ISIC 3825)	0.3	13.8	0.3	5.3
Other machinery (ISIC 382 less 3825)	2.3	5.7	2.9	8.7
Radio, television, and telecommunications equipment (ISIC 3832)	0.7	20.2	1.9	17.0
Other electrical machinery (ISIC 383 less 3832)	1.1	4.8	1.6	6.8
Shipbuilding and repairing (ISIC 3841)	0.4	1.7	0.2	1.8
Railroad equipment (ISIC 3842)	0.1	0.0	0.1	0.3
Motor vehicles (ISIC 3843)	4.2	0.8	4.4	2.3
Aircraft (ISIC 3845)	0.0	0.8	0.1	1.9
Motorcycles and bicycles (ISIC 3844 and 3849)	0.4	0.3	0.5	0.2
Professional goods (ISIC 385)	0.5	2.2	1.6	3.1
Miscellaneous (ISIC 390)	0.8	1.0	1.3	1.0

Source: General Agreement on Tariffs and Trade.

Table B.3 Taiwan: composition of manufactures trade by industry, 1963 and 1988 (percentages of total trade)

Industry	Exports		Imports	
	1963	1988	1963	1988
Spinning, weaving, etc. (ISIC 3211)	8.7	5.4	0.3	1.9
Textile products (ISIC 321 less 3211)	0.6	4.0	0.3	0.4
Wearing apparel (ISIC 322)	0.0	6.2	0.0	0.3
Leather and products (ISIC 323)	0.0	2.1	0.0	0.5
Footwear (ISIC 324)	0.0	5.1	0.0	0.1
Wood products (ISIC 331)	0.0	2.1	0.0	1.3
Furniture and fixtures (ISIC 332)	0.0	1.8	0.0	0.1
Pulp, paper, and products (ISIC 3411)	0.0	0.4	0.0	1.3
Paper products (ISIC 341 less 3411)	0.0	0.2	0.0	0.6
Printing and publishing (ISIC 342)	0.0	0.5	0.0	0.2
Basic chemicals, excl. fertilizer (ISIC 3511)	0.3	1.0	0.8	9.7
Synthetic resins (ISIC 3513)	0.0	2.4	0.0	3.0
Other industrial chemicals (ISIC 351 less 3511 and 3513)	0.6	0.0	0.8	0.0
Drugs and medicine (ISIC 3522)	0.0	0.1	1.9	0.5
Other chemicals (ISIC 352 less 3522)	0.0	0.4	0.3	1.2
Rubber products (ISIC 355)	0.3	0.9	0.0	0.3
Plastic products (ISIC 356)	0.9	5.6	0.0	0.4
Pottery, china, etc. (ISIC 361)	0.0	1.1	0.0	0.1
Glass products (ISIC 362)	0.3	0.8	0.0	0.5
Other nonmetallic products (ISIC 369)	3.9	0.5	0.0	0.4
Iron and steel (ISIC 371)	1.8	1.6	5.5	6.3
Fabricated metal products (ISIC 381)	0.3	5.5	0.8	1.4
Office and computing equipment (ISIC 3825)	0.0	8.9	0.0	2.8
Other machinery (ISIC 382 less 3825)	0.0	6.0	1.1	11.0
Radio, television, and telecommunications equipment (ISIC 3832)	0.0	10.9	0.0	11.3
Other electrical machinery (ISIC 383 less 3832)	0.3	5.1	0.3	4.1
Shipbuilding and repairing (ISIC 3841)	0.0	0.5	0.6	1.0
Railroad equipment (ISIC 3842)	0.0	0.2	0.3	0.0
Motor vehicles (ISIC 3843)	0.0	1.5	0.8	4.7
Aircraft (ISIC 3845)	0.0	0.0	0.6	0.5
Motorcycles and bicycles (ISIC 3844 and 3849)	0.0	2.5	0.0	0.4
Professional goods (ISIC 385)	0.0	2.5	0.0	2.7
Miscellaneous (ISIC 390)	0.0	6.2	0.0	0.6

Source: General Agreement on Tariffs and Trade.

Table B.4 Korea: composition of manufactures trade by industry, 1963 and 1987 (percentages of total trade)

Industry	Exports 1963	Exports 1987	Imports 1963	Imports 1987
Spinning, weaving, etc. (ISIC 3211)	9.1	7.4	5.2	3.6
Textile products (ISIC 321 less 3211)	0.0	3.6	0.2	0.4
Wearing apparel (ISIC 322)	5.7	13.7	0.0	0.0
Leather and products (ISIC 323)	0.0	2.2	0.0	1.2
Footwear (ISIC 324)	0.0	4.8	0.0	0.1
Wood products (ISIC 331)	6.8	0.5	0.0	0.4
Furniture and fixtures (ISIC 332)	0.0	0.3	0.0	0.1
Pulp, paper, and products (ISIC 3411)	0.0	0.5	0.4	1.4
Paper products (ISIC 341 less 3411)	0.0	0.2	0.0	0.5
Printing and publishing (ISIC 342)	0.0	0.5	0.2	0.2
Basic chemicals, excl. fertilizer (ISIC 3511)	1.1	1.1	3.0	7.4
Synthetic resins (ISIC 3513)	0.0	1.2	0.9	2.9
Other industrial chemicals (ISIC 351 less 3511 and 3513)	0.0	0.0	8.9	0.0
Drugs and medicine (ISIC 3522)	0.0	0.1	0.7	0.3
Other chemicals (ISIC 352 less 3522)	0.0	0.2	0.7	1.2
Rubber products (ISIC 355)	1.1	1.7	0.2	0.4
Plastic products (ISIC 356)	1.1	2.3	0.0	0.2
Pottery, china, etc. (ISIC 361)	0.0	0.3	0.0	0.1
Glass products (ISIC 362)	1.1	0.3	0.0	0.6
Other nonmetallic products (ISIC 369)	0.0	0.8	1.1	0.4
Iron and steel (ISIC 371)	13.6	5.1	5.9	4.6
Fabricated metal products (ISIC 381)	1.1	3.3	3.0	1.5
Office and computing equipment (ISIC 3825)	0.0	3.4	0.2	2.0
Other machinery (ISIC 382 less 3825)	1.1	3.4	8.4	13.0
Radio, television, and telecommunications equipment (ISIC 3832)	0.0	16.3	0.9	9.4
Other electrical machinery (ISIC 383 less 3832)	1.1	2.9	2.7	3.9
Shipbuilding and repairing (ISIC 3841)	0.0	2.5	0.9	1.1
Railroad equipment (ISIC 3842)	0.0	0.7	3.6	0.1
Motor vehicles (ISIC 3843)	2.3	6.9	1.8	2.4
Aircraft (ISIC 3845)	0.0	0.5	0.2	1.6
Motorcycles and bicycles (ISIC 3844 and 3849)	0.0	0.7	0.0	0.1
Professional goods (ISIC 385)	0.0	1.5	0.7	3.2
Miscellaneous (ISIC 390)	1.1	3.1	0.2	0.5

Source: General Agreement on Tariffs and Trade.

Table B.5 Malaysia: composition of manufactures trade by industry, 1963 and 1987 (percentages of total trade)

Industry	Exports 1963	Exports 1987	Imports 1963	Imports 1987
Spinning, weaving, etc. (ISIC 3211)	0.2	1.3	3.3	2.7
Textile products (ISIC 321 less 3211)	0.1	0.6	0.6	1.1
Wearing apparel (ISIC 322)	0.0	2.8	0.0	0.3
Leather and products (ISIC 323)	0.0	0.0	0.2	0.1
Footwear (ISIC 324)	0.0	0.2	0.0	0.1
Wood products (ISIC 331)	0.1	5.6	0.1	0.1
Furniture and fixtures (ISIC 332)	0.0	0.1	0.0	0.1
Pulp, paper, and products (ISIC 3411)	0.0	0.1	0.5	2.3
Paper products (ISIC 341 less 3411)	0.0	0.1	0.3	0.2
Printing and publishing (ISIC 342)	0.1	0.1	0.8	0.5
Basic chemicals, excl. fertilizer (ISIC 3511)	0.0	0.6	1.1	3.9
Synthetic resins (ISIC 3513)	0.0	0.3	0.3	3.0
Other industrial chemicals (ISIC 351 less 3511 and 3513)	0.0	0.0	1.5	0.0
Drugs and medicine (ISIC 3522)	0.2	0.1	0.8	0.9
Other chemicals (ISIC 352 less 3522)	0.6	0.4	1.0	1.8
Rubber products (ISIC 355)	0.2	0.4	0.8	0.4
Plastic products (ISIC 356)	0.0	0.4	0.2	0.9
Pottery, china, etc. (ISIC 361)	0.0	0.1	0.3	0.2
Glass products (ISIC 362)	0.0	0.2	0.4	0.3
Other nonmetallic products (ISIC 369)	0.0	0.2	0.7	0.3
Iron and steel (ISIC 371)	0.1	0.8	3.4	4.2
Fabricated metal products (ISIC 381)	0.1	0.5	1.6	2.6
Office and computing equipment (ISIC 3825)	0.0	0.2	0.3	1.2
Other machinery (ISIC 382 less 3825)	0.2	1.6	3.6	9.2
Radio, television, and telecommunications equipment (ISIC 3832)	0.1	19.6	1.0	22.6
Other electrical machinery (ISIC 383 less 3832)˙	0.1	1.5	1.6	5.1
Shipbuilding and repairing (ISIC 3841)	0.0	1.0	0.4	1.6
Railroad equipment (ISIC 3842)	0.0	0.0	0.2	0.4
Motor vehicles (ISIC 3843)	0.8	0.2	5.0	2.7
Aircraft (ISIC 3845)	0.0	0.7	0.3	1.7
Motorcycles and bicycles (ISIC 3844 and 3849)	0.0	0.1	0.3	0.2
Professional goods (ISIC 385)	0.0	0.8	0.4	2.7
Miscellaneous (ISIC 390)	0.2	0.8	0.5	1.0

Source: General Agreement on Tariffs and Trade.

Table B.6 Thailand: composition of manufactures trade by industry, 1963 and 1987 (percentages of total trade)

Industry	Exports		Imports	
	1963	1987	1963	1987
Spinning, weaving, etc. (ISIC 3211)	0.4	4.6	10.0	2.4
Textile products (ISIC 321 less 3211)	0.0	2.5	2.1	0.6
Wearing apparel (ISIC 322)	0.2	11.5	0.5	0.1
Leather and products (ISIC 323)	0.0	1.8	0.0	0.2
Footwear (ISIC 324)	0.0	1.6	0.0	0.0
Wood products (ISIC 331)	0.0	1.5	0.0	0.7
Furniture and fixtures (ISIC 332)	0.0	0.8	0.2	0.1
Pulp, paper, and products (ISIC 3411)	0.0	0.3	1.3	1.6
Paper products (ISIC 341 less 3411)	0.0	0.2	0.3	0.3
Printing and publishing (ISIC 342)	0.0	0.1	0.8	0.2
Basic chemicals, excl. fertilizer (ISIC 3511)	0.0	0.6	2.6	7.0
Synthetic resins (ISIC 3513)	0.0	0.5	0.7	3.6
Other industrial chemicals (ISIC 351 less 3511 and 3513)	0.0	0.0	1.5	0.0
Drugs and medicine (ISIC 3522)	0.0	0.1	2.3	1.0
Other chemicals (ISIC 352 less 3522)	0.0	0.3	2.1	1.8
Rubber products (ISIC 355)	0.0	0.6	2.8	0.7
Plastic products (ISIC 356)	0.0	1.2	0.7	0.8
Pottery, china, etc. (ISIC 361)	0.0	0.2	0.3	0.3
Glass products (ISIC 362)	0.0	0.3	0.5	0.2
Other nonmetallic products (ISIC 369)	0.7	0.4	0.5	0.3
Iron and steel (ISIC 371)	0.0	0.8	6.9	7.4
Fabricated metal products (ISIC 381)	0.0	1.1	4.8	2.1
Office and computing equipment (ISIC 3825)	0.0	1.3	0.3	3.2
Other machinery (ISIC 382 less 3825)	0.0	1.8	10.0	10.2
Radio, television, and telecommunications equipment (ISIC 3832)	0.0	5.9	3.1	4.9
Other electrical machinery (ISIC 383 less 3832)	0.0	2.4	4.3	6.2
Shipbuilding and repairing (ISIC 3841)	0.0	0.0	0.7	0.6
Railroad equipment (ISIC 3842)	0.0	0.0	0.2	0.1
Motor vehicles (ISIC 3843)	0.0	0.2	9.1	5.6
Aircraft (ISIC 3845)	0.0	0.0	0.8	0.1
Motorcycles and bicycles (ISIC 3844 and 3849)	0.0	0.2	1.5	0.3
Professional goods (ISIC 385)	0.0	0.8	1.2	1.9
Miscellaneous (ISIC 390)	0.4	7.3	0.8	1.9

Source: General Agreement on Tariffs and Trade.

Table B.7 Philippines: composition of manufactures trade by industry, 1963 and 1988 (percentages of total trade)

Industry	Exports		Imports	
	1963	1988	1963	1988
Spinning, weaving, etc. (ISIC 3211)	0.0	0.5	1.1	2.5
Textile products (ISIC 321 less 3211)	0.4	2.1	0.5	1.3
Wearing apparel (ISIC 322)	0.0	4.7	0.0	0.1
Leather and products (ISIC 323)	0.0	0.3	0.2	0.2
Footwear (ISIC 324)	0.0	0.5	0.0	0.0
Wood products (ISIC 331)	3.6	6.1	0.0	0.1
Furniture and fixtures (ISIC 332)	0.0	1.8	0.0	0.0
Pulp, paper, and products (ISIC 3411)	0.0	0.3	2.1	1.5
Paper products (ISIC 341 less 3411)	0.0	0.0	0.2	0.4
Printing and publishing (ISIC 342)	0.0	0.1	0.6	0.3
Basic chemicals, excl. fertilizer (ISIC 3511)	0.0	1.8	3.5	5.8
Synthetic resins (ISIC 3513)	0.0	0.5	0.6	4.0
Other industrial chemicals (ISIC 351 less 3511 and 3513)	0.0	0.0	1.1	0.0
Drugs and medicine (ISIC 3522)	0.0	0.1	0.6	1.3
Other chemicals (ISIC 352 less 3522)	0.0	0.4	1.4	1.4
Rubber products (ISIC 355)	0.0	0.1	0.6	0.6
Plastic products (ISIC 356)	0.0	0.7	0.3	0.4
Pottery, china, etc. (ISIC 361)	0.0	0.2	0.3	0.1
Glass products (ISIC 362)	0.0	0.2	0.5	0.4
Other nonmetallic products (ISIC 369)	0.0	0.1	0.8	0.4
Iron and steel (ISIC 371)	0.0	1.1	6.4	6.1
Fabricated metal products (ISIC 381)	0.0	0.4	3.8	1.3
Office and computing equipment (ISIC 3825)	0.0	0.3	0.9	0.8
Other machinery (ISIC 382 less 3825)	0.0	0.4	13.7	6.7
Radio, television, and telecommunications equipment (ISIC 3832)	0.0	7.5	1.5	5.1
Other electrical machinery (ISIC 383 less 3832)	0.0	1.3	3.0	1.8
Shipbuilding and repairing (ISIC 3841)	0.0	0.0	1.7	0.2
Railroad equipment (ISIC 3842)	0.0	0.0	0.3	0.0
Motor vehicles (ISIC 3843)	0.0	0.2	3.6	2.9
Aircraft (ISIC 3845)	0.0	0.0	0.3	1.3
Motorcycles and bicycles (ISIC 3844 and 3849)	0.0	0.1	0.3	0.2
Professional goods (ISIC 385)	0.0	1.0	0.8	0.8
Miscellaneous (ISIC 390)	0.0	3.1	0.5	0.4

Source: General Agreement on Tariffs and Trade.

Table B.8 Indonesia: composition of manufactures trade by industry, 1987 (percentages of total trade)

Industry	Exports	Imports
Spinning, weaving, etc. (ISIC 3211)	2.5	1.4
Textile products (ISIC 321 less 3211)	0.9	0.3
Wearing apparel (ISIC 322)	3.1	0.0
Leather and products (ISIC 323)	0.3	0.0
Footwear (ISIC 324)	0.1	0.0
Wood products (ISIC 331)	13.8	0.0
Furniture and fixtures (ISIC 332)	0.1	0.0
Pulp, paper, and products (ISIC 3411)	0.5	2.2
Paper products (ISIC 341 less 3411)	0.1	0.5
Printing and publishing (ISIC 342)	0.0	0.2
Basic chemicals, excl. fertilizer (ISIC 3511)	0.5	9.8
Synthetic resins (ISIC 3513)	0.1	5.9
Other industrial chemicals (ISIC 351 less 3511 and 3513)	0.0	0.0
Drugs and medicine (ISIC 3522)	0.1	0.8
Other chemicals (ISIC 352 less 3522)	0.3	2.9
Rubber products (ISIC 355)	0.2	0.5
Plastic products (ISIC 356)	0.1	0.2
Pottery, china, etc. (ISIC 361)	0.0	0.2
Glass products (ISIC 362)	0.2	0.3
Other nonmetallic products (ISIC 369)	0.4	0.8
Iron and steel (ISIC 371)	1.1	5.6
Fabricated metal products (ISIC 381)	0.1	3.7
Office and computing equipment (ISIC 3825)	0.0	0.7
Other machinery (ISIC 382 less 3825)	0.1	17.6
Radio, television, and telecommunications equipment (ISIC 3832)	0.1	3.1
Other electrical machinery (ISIC 383 less 3832)	0.1	4.9
Shipbuilding and repairing (ISIC 3841)	0.1	2.0
Railroad equipment (ISIC 3842)	0.0	0.2
Motor vehicles (ISIC 3843)	0.0	6.2
Aircraft (ISIC 3845)	0.1	1.1
Motorcycles and bicycles (ISIC 3844 and 3849)	0.0	0.7
Professional goods (ISIC 385)	0.1	2.5
Miscellaneous (ISIC 390)	0.1	0.4

Source: General Agreement on Tariffs and Trade.

References

Ajanant, Juanjai, and Paitoon Wiboonchutikula. 1988. "Thailand." In *Foreign Trade Barriers and Export Growth*. Manila: Asian Development Bank.

Akrasanee, Narongchai, and Juanjai Ajanant. 1986. "Manufacturing Industry Protection in Thailand: Issues and Empirical Studies." In Christopher Findlay and Ross Garnaut, eds., *The Political Economy of Manufacturing Protection: Experiences of ASEAN and Australia*. Sydney: Allen & Unwin.

Alavi, Hamid. 1988. "Human Resources and Technology Data Base." Washington: World Bank (mimeographed).

Alburo, Florian, Erlinda Medalla, and Filologo Pante, Jr. 1988. "Trade Policy Options for the Philippines." In Mohamed Ariff and Tan Loong-Hoe, eds., *The Uruguay Round: ASEAN Trade Policy Options*. Singapore: Institute for Southeast Asian Studies.

Anand, Sudhir. 1983. *Inequality and Poverty in Malaysia*. New York: Oxford University Press.

Anderson, Kym, and Rod Tyers. 1987. "Japan's Agricultural Policy in International Perspective." *Journal of the Japanese and International Economies* 1, no. 2 (June):131–46.

Ariff, Mohamed. 1989. "The Changing Role of ASEAN in the Coming Decades: Post Manila Summit Perspectives." In Miyohei Shinohara and Fu-chen Lo, eds., *Global Adjustment and the Future of Asian-Pacific Economy*. Kuala Lumpur: Asian and Pacific Development Center.

———, and Hal Hill. 1985. "Industrial Policies and Performance in ASEAN's 'Other Four'." Paper presented at the Fifteenth Pacific Trade and Development Conference, Tokyo, 26–29 August.

Baker, James A., III. 1989. "A New Pacific Partnership: Framework for the Future." Address to the Asia Society, New York, 26 June.

Balassa, Bela. 1986. "Intra-Industry Trade Specialization: A Cross-Country Analysis." *European Economic Review* 30:27–42.

———. 1990. *Economic Policies in the Pacific Area Countries*. Houndmills, UK: Macmillan (forthcoming).

———, and John Williamson. 1990. *Adjusting to Success: Balance of Payments Policy in the East Asian NICs*, rev. ed. POLICY ANALYSES IN INTERNATIONAL ECONOMICS 17. Washington: Institute for International Economics.

Baldwin, Robert E., and Tracy Murray. 1977. "MFN Tariff Reductions and Developing Country Trade Benefits under GSP." *Economic Journal* 87 (March):30–46.

Bautista, Romeo M. 1989. "Impediments to Trade Liberalization in the Philippines." *Thames Essay* no. 54. London: Trade Policy Research Centre.

Belsley, David A., Edwin Kuh, and Roy E. Welsch. 1980. *Regression Diagnostics*. New York: Wiley.

Bergsten, C. Fred. 1988. *America in the World Economy: A Strategy for the 1990s*. Washington: Institute for International Economics.

Bhattacharya, Amarendra, and Johannes F. Linn. 1988. "Trade and Industrial Policies in the Developing Countries of East Asia." *World Bank Discusssion Paper* no. 27. Washington: World Bank.

Breusch, T.S., and A.R. Pagan. 1979. "A Simple Test for Heteroskedasticity and Random Coefficient Variation." *Econometrica* 47:1287–94.

Chan, Paul. 1989. "Malaysia." Paper presented at the Seminar on Manufactured Export Expansion of Industrializing Economies in East Asia, Hong Kong, 7–9 June.

Chen, Edward K.Y. 1989. "Economic Liberalization and Restructuring in the Asian NIEs: Implications for the Asia-Pacific Region." Paper presented at the Bangkok Conference on the Future of Asia-Pacific Economies, organized by APDC/TDRI, Bangkok, 8–10 November.

————, and K.W. Li. 1989. "Manufactured Export Expansion and Economic Growth in Hong Kong: Experience and Prospects." Paper presented at the Seminar on Manufactured Export Expansion of Industrializing Economies in East Asia, Hong Kong, 7–9 June.

Chen, Po-chih, and Chi Schrive. 1990. "Past Strategies Won't Work Now." *Free China Journal*, 26 April.

Cho, Soon. 1989. "Overview of Economic Development." Washington: Institute for International Economics (unpublished).

Cline, William R. 1989a. *United States External Adjustment and the World Economy.* Washington: Institute for International Economics.

————. 1989b. "Impact of the Strong Dollar on Trade." Washington: Institute for International Economics (mimeographed).

————. 1990. *The Future of World Trade in Textiles and Apparel,* 2nd ed. Washington: Institute for International Economics.

Dornbusch, Rudiger, and Yung Chul Park. 1987. "Korean Growth Policy." *Brookings Papers on Economic Activity* 2:389–444.

Drysdale, Peter. 1988. *International Economic Pluralism.* New York: Columbia University Press.

Finger, J. Michael, and Julio Nogués. 1987. "International Control of Subsidies and Countervailing Duties." *World Bank Economic Review* 1, no. 4:707–26.

————, and M. E. Kreinin. 1979. "A Measure of 'Export Similarity' and Its Possible Uses." *Economic Journal* 89:905–12.

Fitzgerald, Bruce. 1986. "An Analysis of Indonesian Trade Policies: Countertrade, Downstream Processing, Import Restrictions and the Deletion Program." *CPD Discussion Paper* no. 1986-22. Washington: World Bank.

Gillis, Malcolm. 1989. "Comprehensive Tax Reform: The Indonesian Experience, 1981–1988." In Malcolm Gillis, ed., *Tax Reform in Developing Countries.* Durham, NC: Duke University Press.

Haggard, Stephan. 1990. *Pathways from the Periphery: The Politics of Growth in the Newly Industrializing Countries.* Ithaca, NY: Cornell University Press.

Hausman, J.A., 1978. "Specification Tests in Econometrics." *Econometrica* 46:1251–72.

Hooley, Richard. 1985. *Productivity Growth in Philippine Manufacturing: Retrospect and Future Prospects. Monograph Series* no. 9. Manila: Philippine Institute of Development Studies.

Hou, Chi-ming. 1987. "Strategy for Industrial Development." *Conference on Economic Development in the Republic of China on Taiwan.* Taipei: Chung-Hua Institution for Economic Research.

Hufbauer, Gary Clyde, Diane T. Berliner, and Kimberly Ann Elliott. 1986. *Trade Protection in the United States: 31 Case Studies.* Washington: Institute for International Economics.

Institute of International Finance. 1990. *Financial Sector Reform: Its Role in Growth and Development.* Washington: Institute of International Finance.

Intal, Ponciano S., Jr., and Filologo Pante, Jr. 1989. "Can the Philippines Grow Out of Debt?" Paper presented at the Bangkok Conference on the Future of the Asia-Pacific Economies, organized by APDC/TDRI, Bangkok, 8–10 November.

Judge, George, W.E. Griffiths, R.C. Hill, H. Lütkepohl, and T.C. Lee. 1985. *The Theory and Practice of Econometrics.* New York: Wiley.

Kamal, Salih, Mohamed Haflah Piei, and M. Sahathavan. 1988. "Trade Policy Options for Malaysia." In Mohamed Ariff and Tan Loong-Hoe, eds., *The Uruguay Round: ASEAN Trade Policy Options.* Singapore: Institute for Southeast Asian Studies.

Kellman, Mitchell, and Tim Schroeder, 1983. "The Export Similarity Index: Some Structural Tests." *Economic Journal* 93:193–98.

Kng, Chng Meng, Linda Low, and Toh Mun Heng. 1988. "Trade Policy Options for Singapore." In Mohamed Ariff and Tan Loong-Hoe, eds., *The Uruguay Round: ASEAN Trade Policy Options.* Singapore: Institute for Southeast Asian Studies.

Koh, Ai Tee. 1987. "Linkages and the International Environment." In Lawrence B. Krause, Koh Ai Fee, and Lee (Tsao) Yuan, eds., *The Singapore Economy Reconsidered.* Singapore: Institute for Southeast Asian Studies.

Krause, Lawrence B. 1982. *U.S. Economic Policy Toward the Association of Southeast Asian Nations: Meeting the Japanese Challenge.* Washington: Brookings Institution.

———, Koh Ai Fee, and Lee (Tsao) Yuan. 1987. "Challenges Facing Singapore." In Lawrence B. Krause, Koh Ai Fee, and Lee (Tsao) Yuan, eds., *The Singapore Economy Reconsidered.* Singapore: Institute for Southest Asian Studies.

Kravis, Irving, Robert, Summers, and Heston, Alan. 1988. "International Comparisons of Real Product and Its Composition." *Review of Income and Wealth* 34, no. 1 (March).

Kwon, Jene K. 1986. "Capital Utilization, Economies of Scale, and Technical Change in the Growth of Total Factor Productivity." *Journal of Development Economics* 24:75–89.

Leamer, Edward E. 1987. "Paths of Development in the Three-Factor, n-Good General Equilibrium Model." *Journal of Political Economy* 95, no. 5:961–99.

———. 1984. *Sources of International Comparative Advantage.* Cambridge: MIT Press.

Lee, Kiong Hock. 1986. "The Structure and Causes of Malaysian Manufacturing Sector Protection." In Christopher Findlay and Ross Garnaut, eds., *The Political Economy of Manufacturing Protection: Experiences of ASEAN and Australia.* Sydney: Allen & Unwin.

Lee, T.H., and Kuo-shu Liang. 1982. "Taiwan." In Bela Balassa and associates, *Development Strategies for Semi-Industrial Economies.* Baltimore: Johns Hopkins University Press.

Leipziger, Danny M. 1988. "Industrial Restructuring in Korea." *World Development* 16, no. 1:121–35.

Liang, Kuo-shu. 1987. "Financial Reform, Trade and Foreign Exchange Liberalization in the Republic of China." In *Conference on Economic Development in the Republic of China on Taiwan.* Taipei: Chung-Hua Institution for Economic Research.

Lim, Linda, and Pang Eng Fong. 1986. *Trade, Employment, and Industrialization in Singapore.* Geneva: International Labour Organisation.

Manasan, Rosario. 1990. "On the Fiscal Policy of the Philippine Government." Paper presented at the Second Annual Conference of the East Asian Economics Association, Bandung, Indonesia, August.

Nam, Sang-Woo. 1989. "Liberalization of the Korean Financial and Capital Markets." Paper presented at the United States–Korea Financial Policy Discussions, Washington, 12 December.

Nasution, Anwar. 1989. "Managing External Balances Under Global Economic Adjustment: The Case of Indonesia, 1983–1988." Paper presented at the Bangkok Conference on the Future of the Asia-Pacific Economies, organized by APDC/TDRI, Bangkok, 8–10 November.

Noland, Marcus. 1990a. "A Note on Integrating Constant Market Share and Regression Models of Export Demand." Washington: Institute for International Economics (mimeographed).

Noland, Marcus. 1990b. "Prospective Changes in Taiwan's International Trade Specialization." Washington: Institute for International Economics (mimeographed).

Noland, Marcus. 1990c. "Prospective Changes in Korea's International Trade Specialization." *Asian Economic Journal* (forthcoming).

Overholt, William H. 1990. *Hong Kong After Tiananmen Square: A Countercyclical View.* Hong Kong: Bankers Trust Securities (Pacific).

Pack, Howard, and Larry E. Westphal. 1986. "Industrial Strategy and Technological Change." *Journal of Development Economics* 22:87–128.

Pangestu, Mari. 1989. "Indonesia." Paper presented at the Seminar on Manufactured Export Expansion of Industrializing Countries in East Asia, Hong Kong, 7–9 June.

———, and Boediono. 1986. "The Structure and Causes of Manufacturing Sector Protection in Indonesia." In Christopher Findlay and Ross Garnaut, eds., *The Political Economy of Manufacturing Protection: Experiences of ASEAN and Australia.* Sydney: Allen & Unwin.

Pearson, Charles K. 1989. "The Asian Export Ladder." Paper presented at the Seminar on Manufactured Export Expansion of Industrializing Economies in East Asia, Hong Kong, 7–9 June.

Power, John H. 1971a. "The Structure of Protection in West Malaysia." In Bela Balassa, ed., *The Structure of Protection in Developing Countries.* Baltimore: Johns Hopkins University Press.

———. 1971b. "The Structure of Protection in the Philippines." In Bela Balassa, ed., *The Structure of Protection in Developing Countries.* Baltimore: Johns Hopkins University Press.

Preeg, Ernest H. 1990. "Rationale, Objectives, and Modalities." In Ernest H. Preeg, *Asia Pacific Economic Cooperation: The Challenge Ahead.* Washington: Center for Strategic and International Studies.

Psacharopoulos, George. 1973. *Returns to Education.* San Francisco: Jossey-Bass.

Pyo, Hak K. 1989. "Export-Led Growth, Domestic Distortions, and Trade Liberalization: The Korean Experience During the 1980s." Paper presented at the United States–Korea Financial Policy Discussions, Washington, 12 December.

Ray, Edward John. 1987. "The Impact of Special Interests of Preferential Tariff Concessions by the United States." *Review of Economics and Statistics* 49, no. 2:187–93.

Remolona, Eli M., Mahar Mangahas, and Filologo Pante, Jr. 1986. "Foreign Debt, Balance of Payments, and the Economic Crisis of the Philippines in 1983–1984." *World Development* 14, no. 8:993–1018.

Rhee, Yung Whee. 1989. "Managing Entry into International Markets: Lessons from the East Asian Experience." Paper presented at the Seminar on Manufactured Export Expansion of Industrializing Countries in East Asia, Hong Kong, 7–9 June.

Saxonhouse, Gary R. 1988. "Differentiated Products, Economics Scale, and Access to the Japanese Market." *Seminar Discussion Paper* no. 288. Ann Arbor: Research Seminar in International Economics, Department of Economics, University of Michigan.

Schott, Jeffrey J. 1989a. "Is the World Devolving into Regional Trading Blocs?" *The World Economy* (forthcoming).

———. 1989b. *More Free Trade Areas?* POLICY IN INTERNATIONAL ECONOMICS 27. Washington: Institute for International Economics.

Scitovsky, Tibor. 1986. "Economic Development in Taiwan and South Korea, 1965–1981." In Lawrence J. Lau, ed., *Models of Development*. San Francisco: ICS Press.

Spinanger, Dean. 1986. *Industrialization Policies and Regional Economic Development in Malaysia*. Singapore: Oxford University Press.

Staiger, Robert W. 1988. "A Specification Test of the Heckscher-Ohlin Theory." *Journal of International Economics* 25:129–41.

Tambunlertchai, Somsak. 1989. "Manufactured Exports from Thailand: Performance and Prospects." Paper presented at the Seminar on Manufactured Export Expansion of Industrializing Economies in East Asia, Hong Kong, 7–9 June.

Tan, Augustine H.H., and Chin Hock Ow. 1982. "Singapore." In Bela Balassa and associates, *Development Strategies for Semi-Industrial Economies*. Baltimore: Johns Hopkins University Press.

Tan, Norma A. 1986. "The Structure and Causes of the Manufacturing Sector Protection in the Philippines." In Christopher Findlay and Ross Garnaut, eds., *The Political Economy of Manufacturing Protection: Experiences of ASEAN and Australia*. Sydney: Allen & Unwin.

Tay, Boon Nga. 1986. "The Structure and Causes of Manufacturing Sector Protection in Singapore." In Christopher Findlay and Ross Garnaut, eds., *The Political Economy of Manufacturing Protection: Experiences of ASEAN and Australia*. Sydney: Allen & Unwin.

Trela, Irene, and John Whalley. 1988, "Do Developing Countries Lose from the MFA?" *NBER Working Paper* no. 2618. Cambridge, MA: National Bureau of Economic Research.

UNESCO. 1988. *Statistical Yearbook*. Paris: UNESCO.

US Department of the Treasury. 1989. "Report to Congress on International Economic and Exchange Rate Policy." October (mimeographed).

US Trade Representative. 1990. *Foreign Trade Barriers*. Washington: US Trade Representative.

Vincent, D.P. 1988. "Domestic Effects of Agricultural Protection in Asian Countries with Special Reference to Korea." Paper presented at the Conference on Agricultural Policies and the Non-Farm Economy, Washington, 26–27 May.

Warr, Peter G. 1986. "Export Processing Zones: The Economics of Offshore Manufacturing." *ASEAN–Australia Working Paper* no. 17. Kuala Lumpur and Canberra: ASEAN–Australia Joint Research Project.

———. 1987. "Malaysia's Industrial Enclaves: Benefits and Costs." *The Developing Economies* 25, no. 1:30–55.

Westphal, Larry E., Yung W. Rhee, and Garry Purcell. 1981. "Korean Industrial Competence: Where It Came From." *World Bank Staff Working Paper* no. 469. Washington: World Bank.

———, and Kwang Suk Kim. 1982. "Korea." In Bela Balassa and associates, *Development Strategies for Semi-Industrial Economies*. Baltimore: Johns Hopkins University Press.

World Bank. 1985. *China: Long-Term Development Issues and Options*. Baltimore: Johns Hopkins University Press.

———. 1987. *World Development Report*. New York: Oxford University Press.

———. 1989. *World Development Report*. New York: Oxford University Press.

———. 1990. *World Debt Tables 1989–1990*. Washington: World Bank.

Yoo, Jungho. 1989. "The Korean Experience with an Industrial Targeting Policy." Paper presented at the Seminar on Manufactured Export Expansion of Industrializing Economies in East Asia, Hong Kong, 7–9 June.

Young, Soogil. 1989. "Trade Policy Problems of the Republic of Korea and the Uruguay Round." *KDI Working Paper* no. 8913. Seoul: Korea Development Institute.

Index

Index

Generalized System of Preferences
62, 74, 89–90, 146, 147, 162
Geographical composition of trade
in Hong Kong 21
in Indonesia 109
in Korea 48
in Malaysia 64, 66
in Philippines 91, 92
in Singapore 25
in Taiwan 32–34
in Thailand 77
possible future diversification 174
Global economic cooperation 143–48
Goh Chok Tong 29
Government role in economy. *See also* Public enterprises
in Hong Kong 16, 22
in Indonesia 103
in Korea 40
in Taiwan 30
Guangdong 150

Hawke, Bob 142–43
Health and safety regulations, as trade barrier 44
Higher education. *See* Education and training
Hong Kong
commodity composition of trade 19
economic history 16
education and training 16
emigration from 22, 79, 118, 138, 158
exchange rates 17–18
export similarity indices 134
financial system 15, 20–22
foreign direct investment 20, 74, 97, 150
geographic composition of trade 21
laissez-faire policy in 16, 22
monetary policy 17
natural resources 16
output composition 16
services 120
tax policy 16
trade projections for 118
transfer of sovereignty to China 16, 22, 138, 151, 158
upgrading of industrial structure 16, 22, 158
Human capital. *See* Education and training

Immigration. *See* Migration
Import licensing 36, 40, 44, 90, 104–105, 112

Import substitution policy. *See* Industrial policy
Income distribution
in ASEAN–4 3
in Korea 53
in Malaysia 56, 68, 159
in NICs 3, 15
in Philippines 80
in Taiwan 30, 31, 158
in Thailand 79
Indonesia
agriculture 98, 99, 112
commodity composition of trade 108
debt problems 101
deletion program 104–05, 112
developmental path 161
economic history 98–107
education and training 112
exchange rates 108, 112
export similarity indices 135
financial system 101–02, 112
foreign direct investment 100, 104, 107, 127
geographical composition of trade 109
industrial policy 99–101, 103–04
infrastructure 109, 160
manufacturing 100, 108, 112, 161
natural resources 98–100
public enterprises 98, 100–01, 112, 160
services 107
structure of protection 106
tax policy 101, 102–03, 112
trade policy 104–07
trade projections 127
Industrial Master Plan (Malaysia) 59, 65
Industrial policy
in Hong Kong 22
in Indonesia 99–101, 103–04
in Korea 40–44
in Malaysia 56–60, 65–67
in Philippines 80, 81, 88, 95–97, 160
in Singapore 23–25, 158
in Taiwan 29–30, 159
in Thailand 69–71, 73, 79
Industrial Promotion Act (Thailand) 69
Industrial raw materials
in Hong Kong 120
in Indonesia 108, 128
in Malaysia 124
in Philippines 127

in Taiwan 122
in Thailand 76, 77, 126
Inflation. *See* Asset price inflation; Monetary policy
Infrastructure
in Hong Kong 16
in Indonesia 110–12, 160
in Malaysia 65
in Philippines 84, 93–95, 96, 160
in Thailand 70–71, 77, 160
Insurance 31, 45, 102, 107
Intellectual property protection
as bargaining chip in trade talks 146, 180
benefits to Pacific Basin countries 146
differing interests among countries 162
in Indonesia 107
in Korea 45
in Philippines 88
in Taiwan 30–31, 38
in Thailand 73, 74
regulation by GATT 178
US dispute with Thailand 147
US dispute with Korea 147–48
Interest rates. *See* Monetary policy
International Coffee Agreement 107
International Monetary Fund 11, 12, 62, 75, 82, 95, 108
Intraindustry trade 21, 136–37, 163
Intraregional investment, in ASEAN–4 161. *See also* Foreign direct investment
Intraregional trade 9–10, 141, 157
Investment Coordination Board (Indonesia) 12
Investment incentives
in Indonesia 103, 112
in Korea 45
in Malaysia 57, 59, 67
in Philippines 80, 85, 96, 160
in Singapore 23
in Taiwan 30
in Thailand 70, 79
Investment Incentives Act (Malaysia) 57
Iron and steel
in Indonesia 100, 128
in Korea 123, 159
in Malaysia 124
in Philippines 83
in Singapore 120, 158
in Thailand 74, 77
Pacific Basin trade with US 163, 168, 177

Italy 3, 135

Japan
agricultural protection in 145
as market for Pacific Basin exports 174, 175
barriers to Indonesian exports 108
barriers to Malaysian exports 62
barriers to Philippine exports 89
barriers to Thai exports 73, 145
foreign aid to region 152
foreign direct investment in region 59, 74, 96, 152
growing economic role in region 10, 153, 155
influence on Korea 47
potential dominance of East Asian bloc 143, 153
potential market share losses to Pacific Basin 173
trade with Hong Kong 20
trade with Indonesia 109
trade with Korea 48
trade with Malaysia 65
trade with Philippines 91, 92
trade with Singapore 25
trade with Taiwan 32, 36
trade with Thailand 77
Japan Export Trade Organization 41
Joint Economic Committee (US) 175

Korea
agriculture 40, 44, 46
commodity composition of trade 48
development path 136, 159, 161
economic history 39–46
education and training 47
exchange rates 40, 41, 48, 49, 51, 176
export-import link system 40
export similarity indices 134
financial system 15, 42, 44, 46, 53
foreign barriers to exports 46
foreign direct investment 45–47, 108
geographical composition of trade 48
industrial policy 40–44
labor policy 42, 52, 159
manufacturing 44, 46, 48
monetary policy 40, 42, 43
natural resources 39
output composition 46
political issues 159
services 45
tax policy 41, 42, 45, 53

Other Publications from the Institute

POLICY ANALYSES IN INTERNATIONAL ECONOMICS

BOOKS

IMF Conditionality
John Williamson, editor/*1983*
$35.00 (cloth only)   0-88132-006-4   695 pp

Trade Policy in the 1980s
William R. Cline, editor/*1983*
$35.00 (cloth)   0-88132-008-1   810 pp
$20.00 (paper)   0-88132-031-5   810 pp

Subsidies in International Trade
Gary Clyde Hufbauer and Joanna Shelton Erb/*1984*
$35.00 (cloth only)   0-88132-004-8   299 pp

International Debt: Systemic Risk and Policy Response
William R. Cline/*1984*
$30.00 (cloth only)   0-88132-015-3   336 pp

Trade Protection in the United States: 31 Case Studies
Gary Clyde Hufbauer, Diane E. Berliner, and Kimberly Ann Elliott/*1986*
$25.00   0-88132-040-4   371 pp

Toward Renewed Economic Growth in Latin America
Bela Balassa, Gerardo M. Bueno, Pedro-Pablo Kuczynski, and
Mario Henrique Simonsen/*1986*
$15.00   0-88132-045-5   205 pp

American Trade Politics: System Under Stress
I. M. Destler/*1986*
$30.00 (cloth)   0-88132-058-7   380 pp
$18.00 (paper)   0-88132-057-9   380 pp

The Future of World Trade in Textiles and Apparel
William R. Cline/*1987, rev. ed. June 1990*
$20.00   0-88132-110-9   344 pp

Capital Flight and Third World Debt
Donald R. Lessard and John Williamson, editors/*1987*
(Out of stock)   0-88132-053-6   270 pp

The Canada–United States Free Trade Agreement: The Global Impact
Jeffrey J. Schott and Murray G. Smith, editors/*1988*
$13.95   0-88132-073-0   211 pp

Managing the Dollar: From the Plaza to the Louvre
Yoichi Funabashi/*1988, 2nd ed. rev. 1989*
$19.95   0-88132-097-8   307 pp

World Agricultural Trade: Building a Consensus
William M. Miner and Dale E. Hathaway, editors/*1988*
$16.95   0-88132-071-3   226 pp

Japan in the World Economy
Bela Balassa and Marcus Noland/*1988*
$19.95   0-88132-041-2   306 pp

America in the World Economy: A Strategy for the 1990s
C. Fred Bergsten/*1988*
$29.95 (cloth)   0-88132-089-7   235 pp
$13.95 (paper)   0-88132-082-X   235 pp

United States External Adjustment and the World Economy
William R. Cline/*May 1989*
$25.00   0-88132-048-X   392 pp

Free Trade Areas and U.S. Trade Policy
Jeffrey J. Schott, editor/*May 1989*
$19.95   0-88132-094-3   400 pp

Dollar Politics: Exchange Rate Policymaking in the United States
I. M. Destler and C. Randall Henning/*September 1989*
$11.95   0-88132-079-X   192 pp

Foreign Direct Investment in the United States
Edward M. Graham and Paul R. Krugman/*December 1989*
$11.95   0-88132-074-9   161 pp

Latin American Adjustment: How Much Has Happened?
John Williamson, editor/*April 1990*
$34.95   0-88132-125-7   480 pp

**Completing the Uruguay Round: A Results-Oriented
Approach to the GATT Trade Negotiations**
Jeffrey J. Schott, editor/*September 1990*
$19.95   0-88132-130-3   256 pp

Economic Sanctions Reconsidered (in two volumes)
  History and Current Policy (also sold separately, see below)   288 pp
  Supplemental Case Histories   640 pp
Gary Clyde Hufbauer, Jeffrey J. Schott, and Kimberly Ann Elliott/
2nd ed. December 1990
$65.00 (cloth)   0-88132-015-X   928 pp
$45.00 (paper)   0-88132-105-2   928 pp

Economic Sanctions Reconsidered: History and Current Policy
Gary Clyde Hufbauer, Jeffrey J. Schott, and Kimberly Ann Elliott/
2nd ed. December 1990
$36.00 (cloth)   0-88132-136-2   288 pp
$25.00 (paper)   0-88132-140-0   288 pp

SPECIAL REPORTS

1 **Promoting World Recovery: A Statement on Global
  Economic Strategy**
  by Twenty-six Economists from Fourteen Countries/*December 1982*
  (Out of print)   0-88132-013-7   45 pp

2 **Prospects for Adjustment in Argentina, Brazil, and Mexico:
  Responding to the Debt Crisis**
  John Williamson, editor/*June 1983*
  (Out of print)   0-88132-016-1   71 pp

3 **Inflation and Indexation: Argentina, Brazil, and Israel**
  John Williamson, editor/*March 1985*
  (Out of print)   0-88132-037-4   191 pp

4 **Global Economic Imbalances**
  C. Fred Bergsten, editor/*March 1986*
  $25.00 (cloth)   0-88132-038-2   126 pp
  $10.00 (paper)   0-88132-042-0   126 pp

FORTHCOMING

TO ORDER PUBLICATIONS PLEASE WRITE OR CALL US AT:
Institute for International Economics
Publications Department
11 Dupont Circle, NW
Washington, DC 20036
1-800-229-ECON; FAX: 202-328-5432
202-328-9000